PAUL SELIGSON
CAROL LETHABY
LUIZ OTÁVIO BARROS
TOM ABRAHAM
CRIS GONTOW

2nd edition

English ID

Student's Book & Workbook Combo Edition 2A

ID Language map

	Question syllabus		Vocabulary	Grammar	Speaking & Skills
1	1.1	What's really important in life?	Life priorities	Review of present tenses & simple past	Talk about life priorities Create a personal profile Talk about working / studying from home
	1.2	Which sense do you use the most?	The senses + sense verbs & adjectives		Talk about sensations & experiences Talk about favorite things
	1.3	Do you read, hear, or watch a lot of ads?		Will / won't for predictions / unplanned decisions	Make predictions Write and act out an ad
	1.4	What shouldn't you do to stay healthy?	Common illnesses	Should / shouldn't for advice	Talk about and identify common illnesses Give advice
	1.5	Will people live on the moon by 2050?			Make predictions
		When do you ask for help?	Expressions for offering, accepting & refusing help		Offer and accept / refuse help
	Writing 1: A personal email		**ID Café 1:** Old school		
2	2.1	Do you ever read newspapers?	News media Genres of news stories		Talk about how you get your news Do a news survey
	2.2	What were you doing at 8 o'clock last night?		Past continuous	Talk about family communication Describe photos
	2.3	What's the world's most serious problem?	Global problems Natural phenomena		Talk about global / local problems Describe TV shows Talk about natural phenomena
	2.4	Was your mom living here when you were born?		Past continuous vs. simple past	Invent / test an alibi Read about a total solar eclipse Talk about dramatic interruptions
	2.5	What do you carry in your pockets?			Understand and retell a story
		Are you a good listener?	Listening & reacting phrases		Be a good listener
	Writing 2: A survey report		**ID Café 2:** Nature boy and natural woman		**Review 1** p.30
3	3.1	How often do you travel?	Traveling		Compare feelings about traveling Do a travel quiz Share travel experiences
	3.2	Have you ever been to another country?		Present perfect 1: past experiences	Talk about solutions Talk about past experiences
	3.3	Have you sung a song in English yet?	Bucket list items	Present perfect 2: completed actions (already, just, yet)	Talk about what you have already done List 10 life ambitions
	3.4	How long have you lived here?	Gap years	Present perfect 3: unfinished past (for, since)	Talk about advantages / disadvantages of taking a gap year Talk about unfinished experiences
	3.5	Do you write reviews?	Hotel descriptions		Talk about hotel reviews
		Are you a logical person?	Suffixes -ic, -ment, -al, -ion		React to unexpected information
	Writing 3: An internship application		**ID Café 3:** Under the moon		
4	4.1	Were you spoiled as a child?	Childhood Personality adjectives Do & make		Talk about the kind of child you were
	4.2	What did you use to do as a child?		Used to and simple past	Talk about childhood habits & memories
	4.3	Has your taste in music changed?	Ways of listening to music	Past simple vs. Used to	Talk about how you listen to music Write a tweet giving an opinion about music
	4.4	Do you speak English as often as possible?	Adjectives	Comparatives / superlatives / as... as...	Make comparisons Talk about first experiences
	4.5	How many pets have you had?		So / but	Talk about pets
		Have you thought about moving abroad?		Prepositions + -ing	Make recommendations
	Writing 4: A social media post		**ID Café 4:** Animal instincts		**Review 2** p.56
5	5.1	What would you like to study?	School subjects & facilities		Talk about choosing a college and career plan
	5.2	What do you have to do tonight?	Class activities	Obligation & prohibition	Talk about class activities Talk about rules in your life
	5.3	Are you a good student?	Good study habits	Too / enough / too much / too many	Give tips about school Talk about reasons for quitting school / a job
	5.4	What will you do when you pass this course?		Zero & first conditional	Talk about how to make friends Make suggestions for changes
	5.5	How do you usually get in touch?	Ways of communicating Family generations	Pronouns & referencing	Compare generations Understand references
		Do you often take risks?	Warnings & promises phrases		Give warnings & make promises
	Writing 5: A personal statement		**ID Café 5:** Man and cyberman!		**Mid-term review** p.70

Grammar p. 138   Irregular verbs p. 158   Sounds and usual spellings p. 160   Audioscript p. 162

ID Language map

	Question syllabus	Vocabulary	Grammar	Speaking & Skills
1				
1.1	What's really important in life?	Life priorities	Review of present tenses & simple past	Talk about life priorities
1.2	Which sense do you use the most?	The senses + sense verbs & adjectives		Talk about sensations & experiences
1.3	Do you read, hear, or watch a lot of ads?		*Will / won't* for predictions / unplanned decisions	Make predictions
1.4	What shouldn't you do to stay healthy?	Common illnesses	*Should / shouldn't* for advice	Give advice
1.5	When do you ask for help?	Expressions for offering, accepting & refusing help		Offer and accept / refuse help
2				
2.1	Do you ever read newspapers?	News media / Genres of news stories		Talk about how you get your news / Summarize a news survey
2.2	What were you doing at 8 o'clock last night?		Past continuous / State vs. action verbs	Talk about events
2.3	What's the world's most serious problem?	Global problems / Natural phenomena		Talk about the weather & natural phenomena
2.4	Was your mom living here when you were born?		Past continuous vs. simple past	Talk about dramatic interruptions
2.5	What do you carry in your pockets?			Understand or retell a story
3				
3.1	How often do you travel?	Traveling		Share travel experiences
3.2	Have you ever been to another country?		Present perfect 1: past experiences	Talk about past experiences
3.3	Have you sung a song in English yet?		Present perfect 2: completed actions (*already, just, yet*)	Take part in a research project
3.4	How long have you lived here?	Points & periods in time	Present perfect 3: unfinished past (*for, since*)	Talk about unfinished events
3.5	Are you a logical person?	Suffixes *-ic, -ment, -al, -ion*		React to unexpected information
4				
4.1	Were you spoiled as a child?	Personality adjectives		Talk about the kind of child you were
4.2	What did you use to do as a child?		*Used to* and simple past	Talk about childhood habits & memories
4.3	Has your taste in music changed?	Ways of listening to music	Past simple vs. *Used to*	Talk about how you listen to music
4.4	Do you speak English as often as possible?	Adjectives	Comparatives / superlatives / *as... as...*	Make comparisons
4.5	How many pets have you had?		*So / but*	Talk about pets
5				
5.1	What would you like to study?	School subjects & facilities		Talk about school subjects / Talk about your school & plans
5.2	What do you have to do tonight?	Class activities	Obligation & prohibition	Talk about class activities / Talk about rules
5.3	Are you a good student?	Good study habits	*Too / enough / too much / too many*	Give tips about school
5.4	What will you do when you pass this course?		Zero & first conditional	Give advice about traveling
5.5	How do you usually get in touch?	Ways of communicating	Pronouns & referencing	Warnings & promises phrases

Audioscript p. 54   Answer Key p. 60   Phrase Bank p. 66   Word List p. 70

English ID

Welcome to English ID!

Finally, an English course you can understand!

Famous **song lines** illustrate language from lessons.

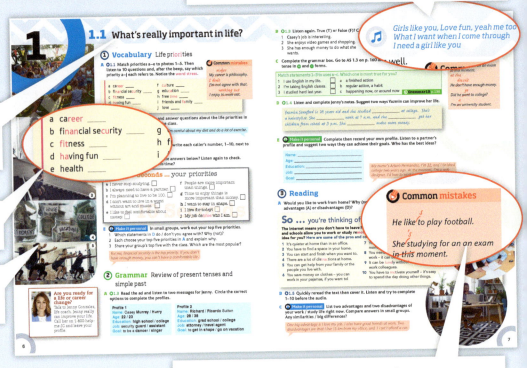

Lesson titles are questions to help you engage with the content.

Word stress in pink on new words.

Contextualized Picture Dictionary to present and review vocabulary.

Focus on **Common mistakes** accelerates accuracy.

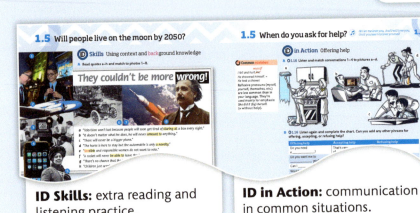

ID Skills: extra reading and listening practice.

ID in Action: communication in common situations.

Authentic videos present topics in real contexts.

ID Café: sitcom videos to consolidate language.

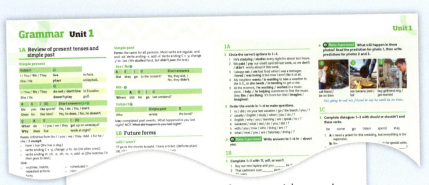

A complete **Grammar** reference with exercises.

Reviews systematically recycle language.

Welcome

Stimulating **Grammar** practice.

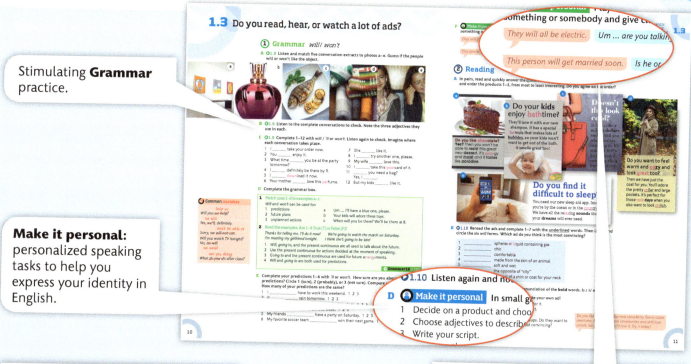

Make it personal: personalized speaking tasks to help you express your identity in English.

Speech bubbles: models for speaking.

Audio script activities to consolidate pronunciation.

Pictures to present and practice **Pronunciation**.

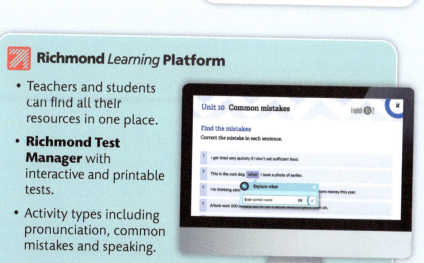

- Teachers and students can find all their resources in one place.
- **Richmond Test Manager** with interactive and printable tests.
- Activity types including pronunciation, common mistakes and speaking.

Workbook to practice and consolidate lessons.

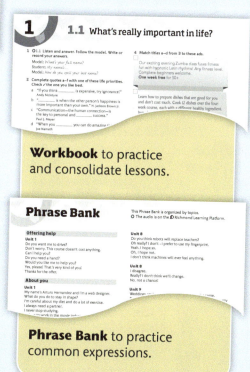

Phrase Bank to practice common expressions.

Learn to express your identity in English!

1.1 What's really important in life?

1 Vocabulary Life priorities

A ▶1.1 Match priorities a–e to photos 1–5. Then listen to 10 questions and, after the beep, say which priority a–j each refers to. Notice the word stress.

a	career ____	f	culture ____
b	financial security ____	g	education ____
c	fitness ____	h	free time ____
d	having fun ____	i	friends and family ____
e	health ____	j	love ____

> **Common mistakes**
> *major*
> My ~~career~~ is philosophy.
> *I don't*
> ~~I'm not~~ agree with that.
> *working out*
> I enjoy ~~to work out~~.

B Get to know a partner. Ask and answer questions about the life priorities in **A**. Report two discoveries to the class.

> What do you do to stay in shape?
>
> I'm careful about my diet and do a lot of exercise.

C ▶1.2 Listen to the radio show and write each caller's number, 1–10, next to their top priority in **A**.

D ▶1.2 Which caller 1–10 gave the answers below? Listen again to check. What else did you pick up this time?

Life in 10 Seconds ... your priorities

a I never stop studying. ☐
b I always need to have a partner. ☐
c I'm planning to live to be 100. ☐
d I don't want to live in a world without art and music. ☐
e I like to feel comfortable about money. ☐
f People are more important than things. ☐
g Time to enjoy things is more important than money. ☐
h I want to stay in shape. ☐
i I live for today! ☐
j My job defines who I am. ☐

E 🗣 **Make it personal** In small groups, work out your top five priorities.
1 Which statements in **D** do / don't you agree with? Why (not)?
2 Each choose your top five priorities in **A** and explain why.
3 Share your group's top five with the class. Which are the most popular?

> For me, financial security is the top priority. If you don't have enough money, you can't have a comfortable life.

2 Grammar Review of present tenses and simple past

A ▶1.3 Read the ad and listen to two messages for Jenny. Circle the correct options to complete the profiles.

Are you ready for a life or career change?
Talk to Jenny Gonzalez, life coach. Jenny really can improve your life. Call her on 1-800-help-me-JG and leave your profile.

Profile 1
Name: Casey **Murray / Hurry**
Age: **22 / 23**
Education: **high school / college**
Job: security **guard / assistant**
Goal: to be a **dancer / singer**

Profile 2
Name: **Richard / Ricardo** Sutton
Age: **28 / 38**
Education: **grad school / college**
Job: **attorney / travel agent**
Goal: to **get in shape / go on vacation**

B ▶1.3 **Listen again. True (T) or False (F)? Correct the false ones.**
1 Casey's job is interesting.
2 She enjoys video games and shopping.
3 She has enough money to do what she wants.
4 Ricardo likes his job a lot.
5 He speaks three foreign languages well.
6 He's going to night school at the moment.

♪ *Girls like you, Love fun, yeah me too*
What I want when I come through
I need a girl like you

1.1

C **Complete the grammar box. Go to AS 1.3 on p. 162 and find one example of each tense in ⊕ and ⊖ forms.**

Match statements 1–3 to uses a–c. Which one is most true for you?
1 I use English in my life. ☐   a a finished action
2 I'm taking English classes. ☐   b regular action, a habit
3 I studied hard last year. ☐   c happening now, or around now   → **Grammar 1A** p. 138

Common mistakes

He like**s** to play football.

She**'s** studying for an an exam ~~in this~~ **at the** moment.

He ~~don't~~ **doesn't** have enough money.

Did he ~~went~~ **go** to college?

I'm ~~an~~ **a** university student.

D ▶1.4 **Listen and complete Jenny's notes. Suggest two ways Yazmin can improve her life.**

Yazmin Stanford is 29 years old and she studied _____ at college. She's a hairstylist. She _____ work at 7 a.m. and she _____ get her children from school at 3 p.m. She _____ make more money.

E 🎤 **Make it personal**   Complete then record your own profile. Listen to a partner's profile and suggest two ways they can achieve their goals. Who has the best ideas?

Name: _____
Age: _____
Education: _____
Job: _____
Goal: _____

My name's Arturo Hernandez, I'm 22, and I finished college two years ago. At the moment, I'm a web designer. I'd love to work in the movie industry.

③ Reading

A Would you like to work from home? Why (not)? Then read the article. Are 1–10 advantages (A) or disadvantages (D)?

So ... you're thinking of working from home?

The Internet means you don't have to leave home to work anymore and many companies and schools allow you to work or study remotely from your own home. But, is it a good idea for you? **Here are some of the pros and cons you need to consider:**

1 It's quieter at home than in an office.
2 You have to find a space in your home.
3 You can start and finish when you want to.
4 There are a lot of distractions at home.
5 You can get help from your family or the people you live with.
6 You save money on clothes – you can work in your pajamas, if you want to!
7 You don't have to spend time and money on travel.
8 You need to separate your home and work – it can be hard to do this.
9 It can be lonely without classmates or work colleagues.
10 You have to motivate yourself – it's easy to spend the day doing other things.

B ▶1.5 Quickly reread the text then cover it. Listen and try to complete 1–10 before the audio.

C 🎤 **Make it personal**   List two advantages and two disadvantages of your work / study life right now. Compare answers in small groups. Any similarities / big differences?

One big advantage is I love my job. I also have good friends at work. Two disadvantages are that I live 15 km from my office, and I can't afford a car.

1.2 Which sense do you use the most?

1 Listening

A ▶1.6 Listen to five conversations and number the photos 1–5.

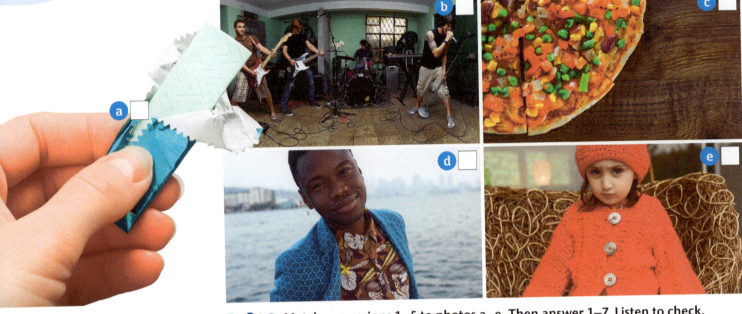

B ▶1.6 Match expressions 1–5 to photos a–e. Then answer 1–7. Listen to check.

1 It feels rough. /rʌf/ ☐ 3 It tastes awesome. ☐ 5 They smell awful. ☐
2 They sound great. ☐ 4 It looks cool. ☐

1 How often do the band practice?
2 Does the boy think the band are going to be famous?
3 Did the man make a quick decision to buy the jacket?
4 Is the jacket his favorite color?
5 What flavor is the gum?
6 Do the couple plan to stay at the restaurant?
7 Why doesn't the girl like wearing the sweater? Why does she need to wear it?

C 🔘 **Make it personal** Do the photos in **A** remind you of anything or anyone?

> Number 1 reminds me of a band my brother was in. They were awful!

> The girl in photo 5 looks a bit like my cousin.

⚠️ **Common mistakes**

remind me of
Those pizzas ~~remember me to~~ my dad's cooking!

2 Vocabulary and pronunciation The senses

5D SENSORY CINEMA – A NEW DIMENSION!

First we had 3D, then it was 4D. Next up, 5D cinema, coming to a movie theater near you soon!
Find out for yourself what it *REALLY* means to totally experience a movie using all five of your senses!

COMING SOON!

8

1.2

♪ *I feel alone in your arms, I feel you breaking my heart, Say my name, say my name, If you love me, let me hear you*

A Look at the ad and …
1 match the senses to photos 1–5.

> hearing   sight   smell   taste   touch

2 match these verbs to the senses. Which is your favorite verb?

> eat   feel   hear   listen (to)   look (at)   see
> smell   sound   stink   taste   touch   watch

You eat with your mouth so that goes with taste.

3 order the senses from the most to the least important for you.

The one I use the least is …

> **Common mistakes**
>
> What are you doing?
> I'm ~~looking at~~ TV.
>   watching
>
> ~~Look at~~
> ~~Watch~~ that plane. Can you see it?
>
> *See* refers to ability and is unintentional, *look (at)* is intentional, and *watch* is intensive.

B ▶1.7 Listen to 10 conversations and notice the connections between consonant and vowel sounds in the answers. Listen again while reading AS 1.7 on p. 162.

C ▶1.7 Test your memory! Listen and try to answer the questions before the audio. How many did you get right?

D In pairs. Take turns asking and answering questions using these verbs and adjectives. Remember to use linking.

> sound   look   smell   amazing   awesome   awful
> feel   taste   think   cheap   expensive old

What do you think about chocolate?
It tastes awesome!

E Match the senses to the adjective groups. In pairs, define or give an example for each. The underlined pairs are opposites. Which group can be used with any sense?

It feels   delicious sweet smoky fresh / rotten
It smells   awful / great   bad / good   awesome / terrible
It sounds   bland / spicy   sweet / sour   salty delicious
It tastes   soft / rough
It looks   loud / quiet

Bland means "without taste." For example, soup without salt or pepper.   *A kitten feels soft.*

F Study **Common mistakes** and choose the best sense verb from **A** to complete 1–5.
1 It's very noisy here. We can't _____ you very well.
2 Where are we? It's too dark to _____ anything.
3 Hey! _____ that poster over there! It's really funny!
4 Do you want to _____ the radio? There's a good show coming on now.
5 Why don't you _____ the match with me? It's really exciting!

G 🎤 **Make it personal** Complete the chart. Compare with a partner and ask about their chart.

My favorite	The best thing I
sound *is children laughing.*	heard yesterday
taste	ate yesterday
smell	smelled yesterday
item of clothing	saw yesterday

My favorite sound is my mom singing.   *Really! Does she have a good voice?*

The best thing I heard yesterday was a new song by Cardi B.   *Oh yeah? What's the name of the song?*

9

1.3 Do you read, hear, or watch a lot of ads?

1 Grammar will / won't

A ▶1.8 Listen and match five conversation extracts to photos a–e. Guess if the people will or won't like the object.

B ▶1.9 Listen to the complete conversations to check. Note the three adjectives they use in each.

C ▶1.9 Complete 1–12 with *will* / *'ll* or *won't*. Listen again to check. Imagine where each conversation takes place.

1 I _____ take your order now.
2 You _____ enjoy it.
3 What time _____ you be at the party tomorrow?
4 I _____ definitely be there by 9.
5 I _____ download it now.
6 Your mother _____ love this perfume.
7 She _____ like it.
8 I _____ try another one, please.
9 My wife _____ love this.
10 I _____ take this postcard of it.
11 _____ you need a bag?
    Yes, I _____.
12 But my kids _____ like it.

D Complete the grammar box.

> **1** Match uses 1–3 to examples a–c.
>
> *Will* and *won't* can be used for:
> 1 predictions   a Um … I'll have a blue one, please.
> 2 future plans   b Your kids will adore these toys.
> 3 unplanned actions   c When will you be there? We'll be there at 8.
>
> **2** Read the examples. Are 1–4 True (T) or False (F)?
>
> *Thanks for telling me. I'll do it now!   We're going to watch the match on Saturday.*
> *I'm meeting my girlfriend tonight.   I think she's going to be late!*
>
> 1 *Will*, *going to*, and the present continuous are all used to talk about the future.
> 2 Use the present continuous for actions decided at the moment of speaking.
> 3 *Going to* and the present continuous are used for future arrangements.
> 4 *Will* and *going to* are both used for predictions.
>
> ➔ **Grammar 1B** p.138

> **Common mistakes**
>
> ~~help us~~
> Will you ~~we help~~?
> ~~we will~~
> Yes, ~~we'll~~, definitely.
> ~~won't be able to~~
> Sorry, we ~~will not can~~.
> Will you watch TV tonight?
> No, ~~no will~~.
> ~~we won't~~
> ~~are you doing~~
> What ~~do you do~~ after class?

E Complete your predictions 1–6 with *'ll* or *won't*. How sure are you about your predictions? Circle 1 (sure), 2 (probably), or 3 (not sure). Compare with a partner. How many of your predictions are the same?

1 I _____ have to work this weekend. 1 2 3
2 It _____ rain tomorrow. 1 2 3
3 There _____ be homework for this class. 1 2 3
4 I _____ eat chicken this week. 1 2 3
5 My friends _____ have a party on Saturday. 1 2 3
6 My favorite soccer team _____ win their next game. 1 2 3

F **Make it personal** Play *Crystal ball!* **A:** Predict the future of something or somebody and give clues. **B:** Guess what or who it is.

🎵 *When the night has come, And the land is dark, And the moon is the only light we'll see, No I won't be afraid, no I won't be afraid, Just as long as you stand, stand by me.*

1.3

They will all be electric.   Um ... are you talking about stoves?   No. There won't be any more gas stations.   Oh, OK. Cars?   Yes!

This person will get married soon.   Is he or she in this class?

② Reading

A In pairs, read and quickly answer the questions in the product ads. Then read the ads and order the products 1–5, from most to least interesting. Do you agree on the order?

a **Do you like chocolate?** Yes? Then you won't be able to **resist** this great new **dessert**. It's **spon**gy and **moist** and it **tastes** like **paradise**.

b **Do your kids enjoy bathtime?** They'll love it with our new shampoo. It has a special **for**mula that makes lots of **bubbles**, so your kids won't want to get out of the bath. It **smells** great too!

c **Doesn't this look cool?** It looks like a million **dollars** and so will you when you are carrying it. It's made of 100% **leather** and it comes in black, brown, or red.

d  **Do you want to feel warm and cozy and look great too?** Then we have just the coat for you. You'll adore the pretty **collar** and large pockets. It's perfect for those **cold days** when you also want to look **styl**ish.

e **Do you find it difficult to sleep?** You need our new sleep aid app. Imagine you're by the ocean or in the **coun**tryside. We have all the re**lax**ing **sounds** that your **dreams** will ever need.

B ▶1.10 Reread the ads and complete 1–7 with the underlined words. Then listen and circle the six *will* forms. Which ad do you think is the most convincing?

1 _____ spheres of liquid containing gas
2 _____ chic
3 _____ comfortable
4 _____ made from the skin of an animal
5 _____ soft and wet
6 _____ the opposite of "city"
7 _____ the part of a shirt or coat for your neck

C ▶1.10 Listen again and notice the pronunciation of the **bold** words. Is *s* /s/ or /z/?

D **Make it personal** In small groups, make your own ad!
1 Decide on a product and choose a photo for it.
2 Choose adjectives to describe your product.
3 Write your script.
4 Rehearse, then read your ad to other groups. Do they want to buy your product? Which ad is the most convincing?

Do you like ice cream? Our new strawberry flavor tastes awesome. Made with fresh strawberries and delicious cream, we guarantee you'll love it. Try it today!

11

1.4 What shouldn't you do to stay healthy?

1 Vocabulary Common illnesses

A ▶1.11 Listen and say why there's nobody at the party.

B ▶1.11 Match illnesses a–g to photos 1–7. Listen again to check pronunciation.

a a cold ☐ /oʊ/
b a cough ☐ /ɔ/
c a fever ☐ /iː/
d the flu ☐ /u/
e a headache ☐ /ɛ/ /eɪ/
f a stomach ache ☐ /ʌ/ /ə/ /eɪ/
g a toothache ☐ /u/ /eɪ/

Common mistakes
My head hurts me.
I have headaitch (hedeɪk).
a ache

C ▶1.11 Try to match the people to illnesses a–g in **B**. Listen again to check.
Fran ____ Lenny ____ Gaby ____ Helen ____ Marcos ____ Jenny ____ Brad ____

D Match the expressions with a similar meaning.
1 My stomach hurts.
2 He has backache.
3 She has a toothache.
4 His head hurts.

a His back hurts.
b Her tooth hurts.
c He has a headache.
d I have a stomach ache.

E 👤 **Make it personal** In pairs, play **Ouch!**
A: Mime a health problem and say, "Ouch!"
B: Say what the problem is.

Your ears hurt and you're very tired? I know, you have earache!

2 Grammar should / shouldn't

A ▶1.12 Listen to four conversations and write what the problems are.
1 _____   3 _____
2 _____   4 _____

B ▶1.12 Complete the suggestions with *should* or *shouldn't*. Listen again to check. Notice the *o* and *l* are silent.
1 You _____ take a **pain**killer. You _____ go to the party.
2 You _____ stay in bed and rest. You _____ eat anything.
3 You _____ see a dentist as soon as possible. You _____ eat or drink anything hot or cold.
4 You _____ go out. You _____ drink a lot of warm fluids and you _____ stay warm.

C Complete the grammar box with *should* or *shouldn't*.

> Use *should / shouldn't* to give and ask for advice.
> ➕ They _____ be more careful.
> ➖ Your son _____ watch so much TV. What should I do to stop him?
> ❓ Short answers
> _____ I eat anything?
> Yes, you _____.
> No, you _____.
> → Grammar 1C p. 138

D What's a good idea and a bad idea for each problem in photos 1–7? Take turns making suggestions to a partner, using the ideas below, plus your own. Who has the best suggestions?

drink cold fluids / lots of fluids   eat chicken soup / chocolate / spicy food   talk to a teacher   visit friends   work out   go to bed / class / work / a party / the beach / the movies   stay in bed / relax / rest   see a dentist / a doctor   take a painkiller / some medicine

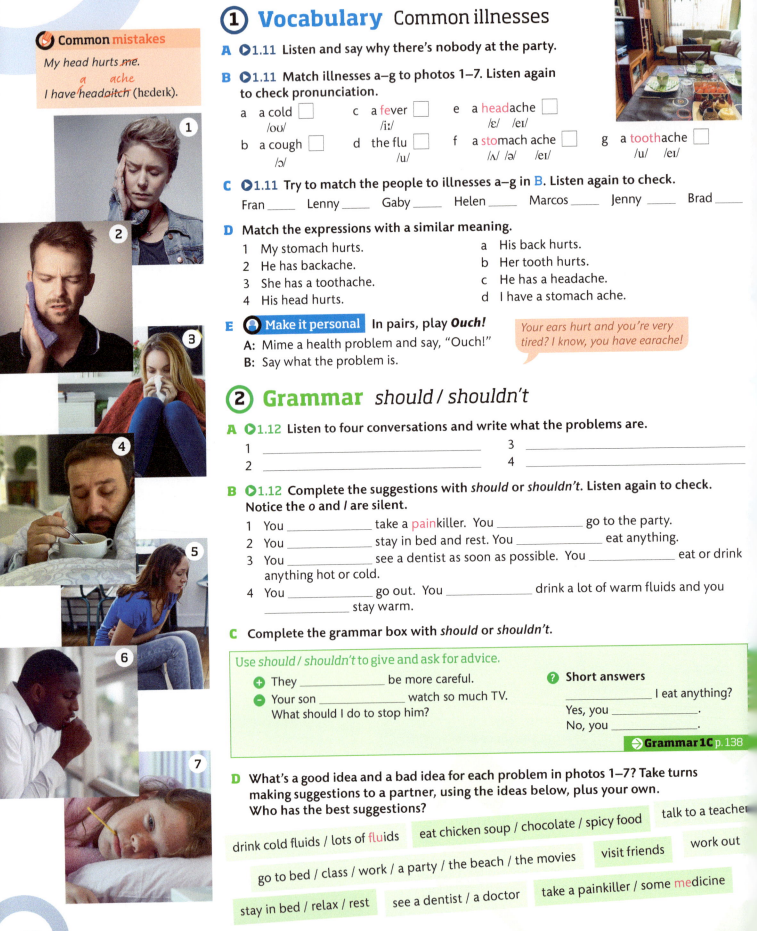

1.4

E 🗣 **Make it personal** In pairs, role-play these situations.
1. **A:** You need to learn English but work 12 hours a day and often miss classes.
   B: You're A's teacher. Make some suggestions.
2. **B:** You're a hypochondriac and often see the doctor with imaginary illnesses. Tell the doctor how you feel.
   A: You're the doctor. Give your patient some advice.

> *I missed class last week and I have a test tomorrow. I'm really worried.*

🎵 *Should I stay or should I go now? If I go, there will be trouble, And if I stay it will be double, So you gotta let me know, Should I stay or should I go?*

⏱ **Common mistakes**

~~an~~ some
I have ~~an~~ advice for you.
You should ~~to~~ stay in bed.
When you ~~will~~ take an aspirin, you'll feel better.
I'll
Good idea. ~~I'm going~~ to do that.

3 Reading

A Read these "Letters to Lori". Match her replies 1–3 to letters a–d. One letter has no reply.

Letters to Lori

a Dear **Lori**,
I'm 22 years old and I'm in my second year of college. My problem is that I want to leave. I don't want to be a student. I'm a very inde**pen**dent person and I love to travel. I need to be free and see the world. What should I do?
Free Spi**r**it ☐

b Dear **Lori**,
My son is 19 and he has a great girlfriend and a baby son who is a year old. He works hard and is a good father to my grandchild, but he doesn't spend enough time with him and his girlfriend. I'm **wo**rried that his girlfriend will leave him and she'll take the child and then I won't see them again. How can I make my son spend more time with his family?
Worried Grandma ☐

c Dear **Lori**,
My father-in-law lives next door to us. He comes in and out of our house as he likes and borrows things when we're not here. We have no **pri**vacy. I always fight with my husband about my father-in-law. My husband won't talk to his father about this problem. How can I make him understand that this is not his house?
Unhappy Wife ☐

d Dear **Lori**,
I have a **se**rious problem. I can't find a girlfriend. I am very **pick**y and I have a long list of things that I want. No one is good enough for me. What can I do? Where can I find a partner?
Lonely Boy ☐

1 You shouldn't try to find a girlfriend by using a **check**list. You should date different people and get to know them. At the moment, you're re**je**cting people before you know anything about them.

2 You can't force your son to spend more time with his family. He has to decide that for himself. You should continue to visit and sup**port** his girlfriend and your grandchild. That way, if your son and his girlfriend decide to separate, you will still see your grandchild.

3 You should try to find a career that will give you the oppor**tu**nity to travel. For example, if you are a teacher of English, you can live in other places. You shouldn't leave college right now, but you should choose a pro**fe**ssion that is right for you and your independent spirit.

B ▶ **1.13** Listen and reread. In pairs, after each letter and answer, say if you agree with Lori's advice. Think of one more piece of advice for each person.

C 🗣 **Make it personal** Now be Lori!
1. In groups, brainstorm advice for the problem in **A** with no reply. Then, in pairs, write a short reply. Present your reply to the group and decide which is the best one.

> *Why don't you tell him you'll move house if he doesn't stop?*   *He shouldn't have a key to your house.*

2. ▶ **1.14** Listen to Lori's reply to the problem. Is the advice similar to or different than yours? What do you agree or disagree with?

> *Her answer isn't as good as ours.*

1.5 Will people live on the moon by 2050?

Skills Using context and background knowledge

A Read quotes a–h and match to photos 1–8.

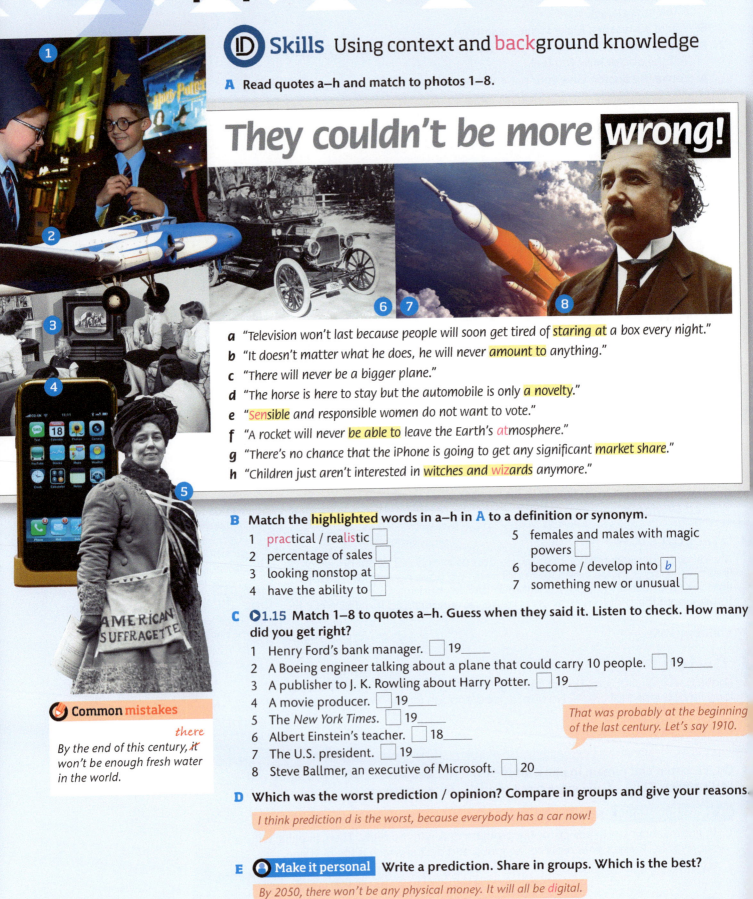

They couldn't be more wrong!

a "Television won't last because people will soon get tired of staring at a box every night."
b "It doesn't matter what he does, he will never amount to anything."
c "There will never be a bigger plane."
d "The horse is here to stay but the automobile is only a novelty."
e "Sensible and responsible women do not want to vote."
f "A rocket will never be able to leave the Earth's atmosphere."
g "There's no chance that the iPhone is going to get any significant market share."
h "Children just aren't interested in witches and wizards anymore."

B Match the highlighted words in a–h in **A** to a definition or synonym.

1 practical / realistic ☐
2 percentage of sales ☐
3 looking nonstop at ☐
4 have the ability to ☐
5 females and males with magic powers ☐
6 become / develop into [b]
7 something new or unusual ☐

C ▶ 1.15 Match 1–8 to quotes a–h. Guess when they said it. Listen to check. How many did you get right?

1 Henry Ford's bank manager. ☐ 19____
2 A Boeing engineer talking about a plane that could carry 10 people. ☐ 19____
3 A publisher to J. K. Rowling about Harry Potter. ☐ 19____
4 A movie producer. ☐ 19____
5 The *New York Times*. ☐ 19____
6 Albert Einstein's teacher. ☐ 18____
7 The U.S. president. ☐ 19____
8 Steve Ballmer, an executive of Microsoft. ☐ 20____

> That was probably at the beginning of the last century. Let's say 1910.

Common mistakes

By the end of this century, ~~it~~ *there* won't be enough fresh water in the world.

D Which was the worst prediction / opinion? Compare in groups and give your reasons.

> I think prediction d is the worst, because everybody has a car now!

E 🧑 **Make it personal** Write a prediction. Share in groups. Which is the best?

> By 2050, there won't be any physical money. It will all be digital.

14

1.5 When do you ask for help?

♪ *Girl let me love you, And I will love you, Until you learn to love yourself*

ID in Action Offering help

Common mistakes

I fell and hurt ~~me~~. → *myself*
He showered himself. = He took a shower.
Reflexive pronouns (*myself, yourself, themselves*, etc.) are less common than in your language. They're used mainly for emphasis:
She did it (by) herself. (= without help).

A ▶1.16 Listen and match conversations 1–4 to pictures a–d.

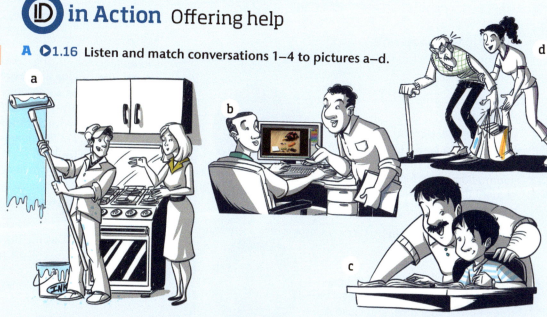

B ▶1.16 Listen again and complete the chart. Can you add any other phrases for offering, accepting, or refusing help?

Offering help	Accepting help	Refusing help
Do you need a _____?	That's very _____ of you.	Thanks for the _____.
Do you want me to _____ you?	Yes, _____!	Thanks, but I have to do it _____.
Can I _____ you?		
Would you _____ me to help?		

C Role-play pictures 1–3. In pairs, take turns offering help and accepting / refusing.

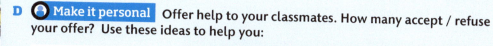
Do you need a hand?   Yes, please. I don't know what to do!

D **Make it personal** Offer help to your classmates. How many accept / refuse your offer? Use these ideas to help you:

turn on / off	the fan / the A/C
open / close	the window / door
borrow / lend (me / you)	a pen / some money / my phone
carry	your bag / shopping
buy	a sandwich / a cookie
get	a coffee / some water
do	your homework / your chores

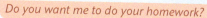
Do you want me to do your homework?
  Thanks for the offer, but I can do it myself!

1

2

3

Common mistakes

Can you ~~borrow~~ me some money? → *lend*
Do you want to ~~lend~~ my coat? You look cold! → *borrow*
Do you need ~~of~~ a ride to the party?

15

Writing 1   A personal email

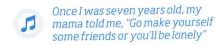 *Once I was seven years old, my mama told me, "Go make yourself some friends or you'll be lonely"*

A Read Laura's message and Nathan's reply. True (T) or False (F)?
1. Laura's been to New York and knows it well.
2. Nathan spends too much time partying.
3. Nathan's answer is full and friendly.

Hi Nathan,

I'm from Córdoba in Argentina and I'm coming to New York to study in September. Can you give me some information about the city and being a student there?

Thanks, Laura

Hi Laura,

a) I was a stranger here too – I come from a small town 200 km away. I've been here a year now, and I love it.

b) New York is an amazing place. **Personally, I think** it's one of the most interesting, exciting cities in the world. The problem is, I'm so busy with college work that I don't get much time to enjoy it. **I mean,** I have classes every day and lots of homework. I really enjoy my course, though.

c) **Anyway,** this weekend I plan to do some sightseeing. There are great museums, beautiful parks, and famous landmarks everywhere you look. **To be honest**, this is one of the best things about the city. **Basically**, it's full of history and culture.

d) **Speaking of** culture, if you like music, there are live music venues everywhere. **It seems to me** that you can find just about any kind of music here any night of the week – from classical to Latin to hip-hop. **In fact,** I'm going to a concert tonight with some friends.

e) **By the way,** there are lots of Argentinian students at the university. I met two cool guys from your city at a soccer game last week. Small world, huh?

f) OK, I need to go and start planning my next essay. Take care,

Nathan

B Match paragraphs a–f to questions 1–6.
1. What can you do in New York?
2. Have you ever met anyone from Argentina?
3. Have you lived in New York for a long time?
4. What kind of live music can you listen to?
5. Are you enjoying your course?
6. Do you have any plans for the weekend?

C Read **Write it right!** Match the six other **bold** linking expressions in the email to categories a–c.

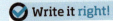 Write it right!

In less formal writing, like emails and social media posts, use linking expressions to:
a introduce an opinion
   Personally, I think *Billie Ellish is great.*
b support with additional information
   In fact, *I'm listening to her right now.*
c change topic
   Anyway, *hope to hear your news soon.*

D Complete the message with linking expressions.

I'm a student in Beijing, but I don't always enjoy the city. _____¹ it's a really difficult place to live and study. _____², it's one of the most polluted cities on the planet, it's noisy, and it's really crowded, so getting around takes a long time. _____³, if you come here, you should take language classes in Mandarin. It's a difficult language to learn, but I think you'll enjoy it. _____⁴ if you're going to spend time in another country, you should try to learn the language. _____⁵, it can help you communicate more easily, make new friends, and understand the culture better. _____⁶ making friends, I recently met some Canadian students who are here on an exchange program. _____⁷, they are some of the nicest people I've ever met!

E Imagine Laura has emailed you about coming to your city. Make notes about:
• three aspects of your city you could tell her about
• three aspects of being a student there.

F 🎧 **Make it personal** Write your reply to Laura in 150–200 words.

Before	Use your notes in **E**. Look back at Nathan's post in **A** and underline any words or phrases you want to use in your own email.
While	Follow the structure of the email in **A**. Include six paragraphs and use linking expressions to introduce an opinion, add information or support an opinion, and change the topic.
After	Exchange replies with another student. Are your suggestions / opinions similar?

1 Old school

1 Before watching

A Check the items you prefer.

Old school	Modern
printed books	downloaded books
newspapers and magazines	news websites
text messages	tweets, WhatsApp
letters	emails
birthday cards	ecards
LPs or CDs & MP3s or MP4s	streaming, downloads

B 🗣 Make it personal In pairs, compare and explain your lists. Who's more "old school"?

> I don't really see the point of ecards.

C Watch the ID Café intro once. In pairs, remember and describe each person and what they were doing. If you studied English ID 1, what do you know about them?

| Rory | Daniel | Paolo | Andrea | Lucy |
| August | Genevieve | Zoey | | |

> First up was Rory. He's sporty, for sure, and he was …

D Use the photo and exercises above to guess what the people are saying, thinking, and planning.

> Maybe Genevieve is trying to interrupt Lucy and Daniel's date for some reason?

2 While watching

A Watch up to 0:56. Check the words each time you hear them. Compare in pairs. Listen again to check. What else did you pick up?

| birthday | cousins | hang out | partied | party |
| perfect | place | together | twins | |

B Watch up to 1:58 and check the correct name in the chart. Which of them do you think will be "old school"?

Lucy	Daniel	
		has made invitations
		is critical of them
		suggests a better alternative
		is defensive because they were hard to make
		apologizes for not looking closely
		justifies evites in many ways
		enjoys traditional books and mailing
		likes to get cards at special times

C Watch again. What five advantages does Daniel give for evites? What does he decide to do?

D Watch from 2:00–2:44. Which of the characters in 1C …
1 does martial arts?
2 really likes Zoey?
3 requested Lucy on Facebook?
4 is from Quebec?
5 should meet Genevieve?
6 remembers to invite Rory?
7 adds more names to the list?
8 takes the invitations home?

E How do you think the episode ends? Watch again to check. What justification does Daniel give?

3 After watching

A Complete 1–5 with *will / won't* or *be + going to*.
1 Where _____ we _____ have this party for August and Andrea's birthday?
2 Auggie and Andrea _____ love it!
3 If you guys need any help, my boss _____ let you rent the place out.
4 They're better and faster. We _____ send evites.
5 … evites are faster, cheaper, and we can easily see how many people _____ attend. And plus, we're not using paper, so we _____ make an impact on the planet.

B In pairs, check the things that are important for a party. Then order the actions logically, 1–8. What else is important?

- [ ] choose a date
- [ ] choose food and drinks
- [ ] create a party playlist
- [ ] decide on a theme
- [ ] decorate the party room
- [ ] make a guest list
- [ ] rent a place / venue
- [ ] send out invitations

> First, I guess you need to …

> Maybe we should decide how much money we have for the party!

C What does "old school" mean to you? In pairs, plan an "old school" party, then compare with another pair. Which party sounds better?

> OK, where should we have the party?

17

2.1 Do you ever read newspapers?

1 Vocabulary News media

A Match the phrases to photos 1–6. How many digital screens can you see?

in a **news**paper ☐   on **so**cial **me**dia ☐
on a **mo**bile de**vi**ce ☐   on the **ra**dio ☐
on a news **web**site or app ☐   on TV ☐

B ▶2.1 Listen and match the interviewees' answers 1–6 to the photos.

C ▶2.1 Listen again and match their answers to reasons a–f. Do you know anyone like these people?
a can discuss the news at family mealtimes ☐
b it's better for the environment ☐
c it's the easiest ☐
d prefers this experience of reading ☐
e is on the Internet all the time ☐
f gets the news and exercises at the same time ☐

> A friend of mine refuses to read newspapers. He doesn't believe anything in them.

Common mistakes

That's an important new. *(piece of / s)*
You lose time reading. *(waste)*
I saw it in a news app. *(on)*
Use *on* with electronic devices / digital media, but *in* with traditional paper items.

D 🧑 **Make it personal** In groups. How do you get your news? How often? Explain your answers. Do you think newspapers have a future? Then summarize the most common trends in your group.

> I'm like the man in number 1. I look quickly at the headlines until I see something interesting.

> I hardly ever read the news, it's always so depressing. But I always check the sports results on my phone.

> Most of us get our news online now.

18

Tell me why are we wasting time, on all your wasted crying, when you should be with me instead?

2.1

② Listening

A ▶2.2 Listen and match news stories 1–7 to the genres. There's one extra genre.
- ☐ entertainment / celebrity gossip
- ☐ local news
- ☐ national news
- ☐ sports
- ☐ traffic
- ☐ weather
- ☐ world news
- ☐ business news

B ▶2.2 Listen again and circle the correct answers. What else did you hear?
1. It will be **a lot** / **a little** colder **today** / **tomorrow**.
2. **Miracle** / **Medical** Men stars **Ben** / **Bill** Gardner.
3. There's a lot of **traffic** / **pollution** on the **highways** / **downtown**.
4. **Texas** / **Arizona** is in the final of the **National** / **World** Series.
5. There were **only 8** / **more than 50** leaders at the **summit** / **meeting**.
6. **People** / **Students** are protesting about **taxes** / **high prices**.
7. Maria **Braun** / **Brown chased** / **spoke to** reporters.

C In groups, write sentences for seven different news genres. Take turns reading them to another group. They identify the genre and say if the story is real or invented.

> *A cat walked onto the court during the Brazil–Spain volleyball match yesterday.*

> *OK, that's a sports story and it isn't real!*

D 🎤 **Make it personal** In groups, do the Class News Survey. Who follows day-to-day news most closely?

> *For me, the most important story was when Mexico beat Argentina 3–1 at soccer.*

> *Yeah, it was an exciting game, but I think the President's visit to China was more important.*

💬 Common mistakes

I never pay attention to celebrity gossip*s*.

Last night's news w~~ere~~ *was* shocking.

News and gossip are uncountable.

Class News Survey
1. What were the two most important news stories this week?
2. Which two ways do you usually get your news?
3. How often do you check the news headlines?
4. Do you pay more attention to local, national, or international news?
5. What news genres are you most / least interested in?
6. Do you ever post comments about news stories?
7. Do you ever check news is true before you share it? How?
8. Have you heard a fake news story recently? What was it?
9. Did you ever appear on TV or in the papers? If so, why?

2.2 What were you doing at 8 o'clock last night?

1 Listening

A ▶2.3 Listen to Allie and her dad. How many calls did he make last night? Did he sound happy or unhappy? Why?

B ▶2.3 True (T) or False (F)? Listen to check.
1 Allie couldn't hear the phone when her dad called because she was watching TV.
2 Her dad also called Mike on the phone.
3 Mike often makes burgers.
4 The best way to contact the twins is to call them on the phone.
5 Allie's dad had some important news for the family.

C 🔵 Make it personal   How is your family similar to or different than the family in **A**?

> My mom's like that, she calls me at least three times a week!

2 Grammar   Past continuous

A ▶2.3 Listen again and circle the correct options.
1 What **did you do** / **were you doing** when I called last night?
2 I **watched** / **was watching** a fantastic nature show about the jungle.
3 He **made** / **was making** dinner at 8 o'clock.
4 They **played** / **were playing** video games.

B Look at 1–4 in **A**. Then complete the grammar box.

> **Common mistakes**
>
> *working*
> I was ~~work~~ when the Internet went down and I ~~was losing~~ all my work.   *lost*
>
> *Were*
> ~~Was~~ you sleeping when she called?
>   *taking*
> No, I wasn't. I was ~~take a~~ shower. / Yes, I ~~were~~.
>   *was*

1 Circle the correct options.
   Past continuous is formed with was / were + **infinitive** / **-ing**.
   Word order and short answers are **the same as** / **different than** the present continuous.

2 Match 1–3 to a–c. Use:
   1 past continuous for   a an event that started and finished in the past
   2 present continuous for b an event in progress at a specific time in the past
   3 simple past for   c an event that is happening right now or a future arrangement.

➡ **Grammar 2A** p.140

20

C Put 1–3 in order to make questions. In pairs, ask and answer.
1 doing / were / what / you / night / at / 7 p.m. / last / ?
2 about / night / at / 9 p.m. / last / you / eating / were / dinner / ?
3 Sunday / 11 p.m. / you / were / sleeping / night / at / on / ?

 Thought we were going strong, Thought we were holding on, Aren't we? You and me got a whole lot of history, We could be the greatest team that the world has ever seen

2.2

D Read and circle the best options. Give a reason for your answer.
1 I **was really enjoying** / **really enjoyed** / **really liked** the movie last night when my dad changed the TV channel.
2 Yesterday at 5 p.m. her parents **texted** / **was texting** her.
3 **Were you having** / **Did you have** / **Were you going to have** a car when you were a student?
4 **Did you have** / **Were you having** / **Didn't you have** dinner when I called yesterday?
5 Now, **I'm thinking** / **I thought** / **I was thinking** this is a good idea.
6 How **did that soup tasting** / **did that soup taste** / **was that soup tasting**?

E Who's the best eye witness? Study this picture for 45 seconds, then close your book. Remember and note as much as you can about what the eight people were doing.

In groups, compare what you wrote. Who had the most accurate information?

Ken was driving the red car.   *I thought he was driving the blue car.*

No, he wasn't. He was driving the red one and he was texting at the same time.

Make it personal In pairs. Show and describe a photo for one minute, explaining what you / the people in it were doing, where you were, why, when, etc. Then hide it. Your partner remembers and describes the photo.

You were having dinner with your girlfriend and you were wearing a new shirt that she gave you.

Correct! What color was the shirt?

2.3 What's the world's most serious problem?

1 Vocabulary   Global problems

A ▶2.4 Match the words in column 1 to photos a–d. Try to pronounce all eight words. Listen to the radio show, check, and number them 1–8 in the order you hear them.

Common mistakes

~~pollution~~
Air ~~contamination~~ is a big problem for cities.

- [ ] disease /dɪziːz/
- [ ] pollution
- [ ] poverty
- [ ] unemployment
- [ ] animal extinction
- [ ] climate /klaɪmət/ change
- [ ] crime /kraɪm/
- [ ] corruption /kərʌpʃn/

B How do the problems in **A** affect these things?

oceans   lakes and rivers   wildlife   cities
rainforests   deserts   jungles   people

> I think pollution affects oceans, lakes, rivers, and cities.

> I agree. It can kill fish and contaminate the food we eat.

C 🔵 **Make it personal** What do you think are the most serious problems in your country? Order the problems in **A** from 1 (most serious) to 8 (least serious). In groups, compare your lists. How similar are they?

> I think crime is the most serious problem here.

> For me, it's unemployment. Unemployment leads to poverty and crime.

2 Reading

A ▶2.5 Read the TV guide and match the shows to channels 1–6. Listen to check.

CHANNEL	8 p.m.–9 p.m.	EID TV GUIDE
	The Wilsons Carrie is upset because her grandmother Betty won't give her her secret chocolate cake recipe. Penelope shows Brendon that it's possible to have fun even when you don't have much money.	
	Jungle Stories Jungles are rich habitats that support amazingly diverse plants and animals. This episode looks at the inhabitants of the tropical rainforests of Indonesia.	
	What on Earth Is Happening? Most scientists agree: Earth's temperature is increasing. This show investigates climate change and asks if human activity is accelerating the process. Are we responsible for the extreme weather events happening around the world?	
	Kitchen Stars Four young chefs compete to create the best plate of food using surprise ingredients. The two best chefs advance to the semi-finals. And is romance in the air too?	
	Alvarez and Novak: Washed Away The cool Californian surfing detectives investigate some missing jewelry, but soon discover a fraud involving millions of missing dollars.	
	MOVIE: Captain Marvel Carol Danvers becomes Captain Marvel, a galactic superhero who uses her powers to end a war between two extraterrestrial civilizations.	

B ▶2.6 Listen and match conversations 1–6 to the show in **A** they were watching.

C In pairs, choose and compare the shows you would most and least like to watch. Explain why.

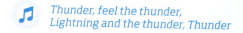 Thunder, feel the thunder, Lightning and the thunder, Thunder

2.3

I'd go for the movie because I love action movies!

Ugh, really?! A movie about superheroes?! No, I prefer real life so I'd watch the show about the jungle.

D 🔵 Make it personal   In groups, take turns describing what was happening in a show or movie you watched recently. The rest of the group guess its name.

A family was visiting Disneyworld.   *Were you watching Modern Family?*   *No, I wasn't.*

Were you watching Fresh off the Boat?   *Yes, I was!*

③ Listening

A ▶ 2.7 Match the first three weather words plus any others you recognize to photos 1–9. Use the pink stress and vowel phonetics to guess their pronunciation. Then listen to the TV show to check. Were your guesses close?

☐ an eclipse /ɪklɪps/   ☐ a drought /draʊt/   ☐ a wildfire
☐ a hurricane /hərəkeɪn/   ☐ an earthquake /ərθkweɪk/   ☐ a rainbow
☐ a tsunami /tsunɑmi:/   ☐ a flood /flʌd/   ☐ a thunderstorm

B ▶ 2.7 Listen again and match places 1–9 to what's happening a–i.

1 Bangladesh   a high waves
2 London   b daytime darkness
3 Argentina   c sun and rain together
4 Florida   d power outages
5 South Africa   e no rain
6 Chile   f strong winds
7 Indonesia   g destruction of buildings
8 Mexico   h too much rain
9 Greece   i an uncontrolled fire

🔥 **Common mistakes**

afraid / scared / terrified
I was ~~having fear~~.

frightening / scary / terrifying
That was ~~scaring~~.

C 🔵 Make it personal   In pairs. Which phenomenon in **A** is the scariest? Why? Compare with other pairs. Can the class agree on the scariest phenomenon?

For me, a hurricane is the scariest.   *Me too. I was in a hurricane in Cuba and it was terrifying.*

23

2.4 Was your mom living here when you were born?

1 Grammar Past continuous vs. simple past

A ▶ 2.8 Listen to a conversation about a thunderstorm. Why does the woman say she has to go?
1 Because the lights went out and she couldn't see.
2 Because her phone had no battery charge left.
3 Because she needed to help her son with his homework.

B ▶ 2.8 Listen again and circle the words you hear.
1 What **were you doing / did you do** when the outage **happened / was happening**?
2 I **was cooking / cooked** dinner when suddenly the lights **went out / were going out**!
3 The lights **went out / were going out** while he **was watching / watched** TV.
4 So what **were you doing / did you do** when the lights **went out / were going out**?
5 I **was finding / found** a flashlight and some candles.

C Answer a–e in the grammar box about the sentences in **B**. Then complete f with the correct tenses.

> ⚠ **Common mistakes**
>
>   *ate*
> When I was a kid I was eating a lot of candy.
>
>   *was running*
> Jay ran in the park when he slipped on a banana skin.

a In 2 and 3, which two actions were in progress? What verb form do they use?
b What action interrupted them? What verb form is used for that action?
c Which two words in 1–4 connect the two clauses?
d In 4, does *when* mean "after" or "at the same time"?
e Is 5 an action in progress or a result?
f So, for actions in progress use _____, and for actions that interrupt use _____. For resulting actions use _____.

➡ **Grammar 2B** p. 140

D ▶ 2.9 Use these words to summarize the story in **A** in two sentences. Listen to check.

| call | cook | go out | find | flashlight | happen |
| husband | lights | outage | she | then | |

E ▶ 2.10 Check the best options to complete the picture story. Listen to check.

☐ Jane was chatting online when her phone rang.
☐ Jane's phone was ringing when she chatted online.

☐ Her mom was coming in when she talked on the phone.
☐ Her mom came in when she was talking on the phone.

☐ When she was hanging up, her mom read her emails.
☐ When she hung up, her mom was reading her emails.

☐ Her parents were talking when Jane went downstairs.
☐ Her parents talked when Jane was going downstairs.

F In pairs, cover the story and take turns retelling it. Do you think Jane's mom was wrong to read Jane's emails? Why (not)?

> *I think she was right to read her daughter's emails. Jane is young and her mother needs to protect her.*

24

G Make it personal Play *Alibi!*

1 In pairs, make an alibi for last night between 8 and 10 p.m.
   What / doing / eating / drinking / watching / listening to / playing?
   Who / with? / talking to?
   / go out? Where? How long? What time / leave / arrive home?
2 Test the alibi. Another pair ask you questions individually to check that your stories are exactly the same.

I was blind, now I can see, You made a believer out of me, I'm movin' on up now, Getting out of the darkness, My light shines on

2.4

> What were you doing last night between 8 and 10 p.m.? We were watching a movie.

> What time did the movie start? 8.15 p.m. What time did it end?

2 Reading

A ▶ 2.11 Cover the article and listen. After each web post 1–8, say if the person had a positive or negative experience.

What were you doing when the world went dark?

Solar eclipses are not uncommon – they occur every two years or so somewhere on the planet – but everyone who sees one remembers the experience. **Here are some of our favorite posts about the 2017 total eclipse in the U.S.**

1 I was standing in a sports field when suddenly I **screamed**, "It got dark!" I knew this was going to happen, but I don't know why it still surprised me. *Louise*, Oregon

2 I was watching quietly with my family when it went dark. I felt small and I felt connected to the **universe**. I understand what all those scientists were trying to say now. I saw **tot**ality for only about one second, because of the cloud, but it was enough. *Jason*, Illinois

3 We drove 10 hours to a place that was in the path of **totality**, but we couldn't buy any eclipse glasses because they were sold out. We had nothing to eat and nothing to drink and it was over very quickly. One of the most **overrated** experiences of my life! *Martha*, California

4 We walked two blocks from home to a public park. People were sitting in chairs on the **grass**. They were wearing eclipse glasses and looking up at the sky. Everyone was outside and everyone was waiting. *Brooke*, Wyoming

5 As it started to get darker, I was feeling weird and **uneasy**. When totality happened those feelings left me and I was filled with **joy**. Some people were shouting but the only noise that came out of me was the word "Wow!" The event wasn't **shocking**, it was calming and inspiring. *Taylor*, Idaho

6 As the time for totality was getting nearer, the clouds got thicker and the rain came down. It was dark and raining – what a disappointment after all the expectation! *Tariq*, Nebraska

7 Darkness fell over Nashville and **cicadas** started **screech**ing, while birds everywhere returned to their nests all at the same time. *Marina*, Tennessee

8 My boyfriend and I climbed to the top of Table Rock Mountain and we were watching **eagles** when the eclipse began. Everyone was silent and lost in thought, and then Venus suddenly appeared like a jewel. It was su**blime**. *Rosie*, South Carolina

B Read the article and and say who:
1 had different feelings during the eclipse. ☐
2 talks about insects. ☐
3 saw a planet during the eclipse. ☐
4 saw the eclipse from near their home. ☐
5 was surprised at the darkness. ☐
6 didn't see the eclipse because of the weather. ☐
7 understood why people talk about eclipses so much. ☐
8 had a long journey to watch the eclipse. ☐

In pairs, take turns describing or miming a **highlighted** or pink-stressed word for your partner to say.

Make it personal

1 Which posts in **A** remind you of experiences you have had?
2 What were you doing when something dra**ma**tic or interesting happened? How did you react? Who had the most interesting reaction?

Common mistakes

~~knew~~ knew
I ~~was knowing~~ this was going to happen.

~~saw~~ saw
I ~~was seeing~~ totality for a second.

~~had~~ had
We ~~were having~~ nothing to eat or drink.

State verbs aren't usually used in the continuous. See Grammar 2A p.140.

> It's like the world but bigger.   It's the opposite of easy.
> Universe.   Uneasy.

> Number 3 reminds me of one New Year's Eve. We waited hours for the fireworks, but then it started raining really heavily at 11.30!

25

2.5 What do you carry in your pockets?

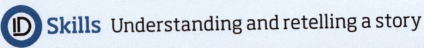

Skills Understanding and retelling a story

A Read the story on the "Strange Things Happen" website and choose the best title.

| Cooking can be dangerous | Woman hurt by beach rocks | Kids find phosphorous at home |

Strange Things Happen!

UNBELIEVABLE! Did you read this story about the woman who had rocks in her cargo shorts when suddenly something weird happened?

So, the woman was carrying the orange stones in her shorts, because her children found them on the beach and gave them to her. (What nice kids! 😃) The poor woman was standing in the kitchen about an hour after they got home when her shorts caught fire! Yes!! Her shorts CAUGHT FIRE!! Imagine her husband's surprise too – the poor guy was reading the paper or something and suddenly he saw that his wife was on fire!! Well, he thought fast and he took her outside and started hosing her down with water from the garden hose. And that's when the firefighters and paramedics arrived – as he was spraying his wife with water. So, of course, the surprised paramedics treated her and took her off to the hospital. They said it was the first time they ever saw something like that. The rocks were still smoking when they arrived at the hospital! Those were very flammable rocks!

Anyway ... so what on earth happened? Well, the authorities are investigating, but they think that there was phosphorous on the rocks (if you look at the photo you can see that they're orange – that's phosphorous). Apparently, when phosphorus is exposed to air, it burns at extremely high temperatures. And the woman? Well, she got severe burns on her right leg and her right arm and her husband got burns on his arm too, but they survived.

The moral of the story? Don't put things your kids give you in your pockets! 😂

B ▶ 2.12 Listen, reread, and, in pairs, whenever the teacher pauses the audio, imitate the last five words you heard.

C True (T) or False (F)?
1 The rocks were in the woman's pocket. ☐
2 She found the rocks on the beach. ☐
3 The woman was sitting down when the rocks caught fire. ☐
4 Her husband put water on the fire. ☐
5 The paramedics often see burning rocks. ☐
6 Phosphorous caused the fire. ☐
7 Both of them got badly burned arms and legs. ☐

D 🔵 **Make it personal** Imagine you are a character from the story. Write a blog about what happened from your perspective. Then, in groups, read each other's stories and choose the best one.

> You're not going to believe this! Yesterday, we were relaxing at the fire station when someone called to say there was a woman on fire!

2.5 Are you a good listener?

 You can't start a fire, You can't start a fire without a spark, This gun's for hire, even if we're just dancing in the dark

ID in Action Being a good listener

A ▶2.13 Listen to the conversation and order the pictures 1–4.

B ▶2.13 Listen again and check the expressions you hear. Can you think of any more?

Show you're listening	React to something positive	React to something negative
Uh-huh?	Wow! Really?	Oh no!
Yes?	How interesting!	No way!
And then what happened?	That's good.	That's awful!
	That's great!	That's terrible!

How about "Is that right?"

Common mistakes

What happened ~~with~~ *to* you?
He ~~let fall~~ *dropped* the food.
He ~~fall~~ *fell* down.

C In pairs, take turns telling the story in your own words. Your partner reacts using the expressions in **B**.

So the boy was riding his bike to school. *Yes?* *And he got a flat tire.* *Oh no!*

D Role-play. In pairs, take turns telling the picture story, choosing different characters. What's the same and what's different in your versions?

Last night I was having dinner with my boyfriend in a restaurant in town. *Yeah? Then what happened?*

E **Make it personal** Think of a story that happened to you recently. In groups of three, take turns:
- A: telling your story.
- B: listening carefully and reacting to the story.
- C: observing and noting the expressions B uses to react to A's story. Does B sound interested? Give them feedback.

So, I was going to work on the bus on Tuesday when suddenly the bus stopped. *Really? What happened?*

Well, we got off the bus and I waited for another bus. *Uh-huh.*

OK, you said "Really?" and "Uh-huh" but you didn't make eye contact. You didn't look very interested!

Writing 2 A survey report

*Everybody's changing and I don't feel right,
Everybody's changing and I still feel the same,
Everybody's changing and I don't feel the same*

A Read the report and match it to graph 1 or 2.

Survey Report — by Marc Hernandez

a. We conducted an online survey of people in four Latin American countries to find out where they usually get their news. Here is a summary of the results for Chile.

b. Most people said they get their news online or on television. Just under 90 percent get news online, and three-quarters get news from TV. Approximately 70% get their news from social media – the most popular platforms are Facebook, WhatsApp, and YouTube. Some people still get their news from print newspapers and magazines, but this is only around 40% (or two-fifths). A small number of people, 9%, said they pay for online news.

c. The results show that most people get their news from four main sources, and that traditional sources such as newspapers and magazines are now much less popular than TV or online. I found it surprising that just over half of all interviewees said they trust the news, which means that around 50% of people don't believe what they read or hear!

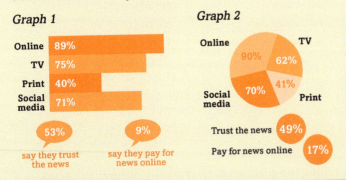

Graph 1
- Online 89%
- TV 75%
- Print 40%
- Social media 71%
- 53% say they trust the news
- 9% say they pay for news online

Graph 2
- Online 90%
- TV 62%
- Print 41%
- Social media 70%
- Trust the news 49%
- Pay for news online 17%

B Match paragraphs a–c to 1–3.
a introduction ☐   b results ☐   c conclusion ☐

1 The writer's reaction to the results.
2 The topic of the survey and information about where it refers to.
3 Survey details, starting with the largest number.

C Read **Write it right!**, then find and underline the 10 number expressions in the report. Express them another way.

✓ Write it right!

- In formal text, write numbers one to nine as words. Write larger numbers in figures.
- Write fractions in words or figures, but be consistent.
  10% = one tenth (1/10); 50% = a half (1/2); 25% = a quarter (1/4); 1/3 = a third; 2/3 = two-thirds.
- To talk about approximate numbers, use *approximately, around, just over / under*, or these expressions:

  0 ———————————————— 100%
  no one | some people | most people | everyone
  a small number of people   many people

D Complete this report about the other graph in **A** with numbers or expressions from **Write it right!**

We interviewed people in Mexico to find out where they usually get their news. Here is a summary of the results.

We found that _____¹ people get their news online and from social media. _____² of people said they get their news online, and _____³ 75% get their news from social media – the most popular platforms are Facebook, WhatsApp, and YouTube. Just _____⁴ 60% of people get their news from TV. _____⁵ still get their news from print newspapers and magazines, but this is only _____⁶. A small number of people, _____⁷, said they pay for online news.

The results show that _____⁸ get their news from four main sources. I found it surprising that just under _____⁹ of all interviewees said they trust the news, which suggests that just _____¹⁰ half don't believe what they read or hear!

E Choose a question, 1–5. Think of five possible categories to form a more detailed survey question.
1 What kind of news is the most interesting for you?
   sports, international, local, celebrity gossip, business
2 What do you do most online?
3 Which social media platforms do you use most often? What for?
4 What do you like to read most in your first language?
5 What do you read most in English?

F Conduct the survey with your class and record the results. Look at the example.

What kind of news is the most interesting for you?	
sports	●●●●
international news	●●●●●
local news	●●●
celebrity gossip	●●●●●●
business	●●

G 🎧 **Make it personal** Write a report of your survey in 100–120 words. Include a graph to show the results.

Before	Look back at the reports in **A** and **D**. Decide how to display your results in a graph. What are your main conclusions?
While	Write a report on your survey in three paragraphs, following the structure in **B**. Include: 1) an introduction describing what your survey was about; 2) the results of your survey; 3) a personal conclusion from your survey.
After	Share your report with someone who chose the same question. Are your results and conclusions similar?

2 Nature boy and natural woman

1 Before watching

A Match words 1–5 to meanings a–e.

1 an audition
2 coverage
3 a host
4 a nightmare
5 to wonder

a the presenter of a (TV) show
b a bad dream
c a short test performance
d ask yourself
e the media reporting of an event

B 🔵 **Make it personal** What's Daniel doing in the photo? In pairs, answer 1–3.

1 Are you good with a camera?
2 How good are you on camera? Would you make a good host?
3 How many (online) interviews have you done? Do you interview well? Have you ever done an audition?

> I love taking photos and videos. I think the result is normally pretty good!

> I had an audition for a part in a play once, but I was terrible!

2 While watching

A Watch until 0:53. Complete Daniel's mistakes with these words. Do you often make mistakes when recording yourself?

| coverage | my | news shows | the | we |

1 He says _____ instead of _____.
2 He pauses in the middle of the phrase _____ and _____.
3 He gives up after saying, "Here _____."

> Yes, I get very nervous. I hate hearing myself, especially in English!

B Watch until 2:20. True (T) or False (F)? Guess how the episode ends.

1 Lucy and Genevieve are planning a party.
2 Genevieve called Daniel "natural boy" because of his eco-obsessions.
3 The girls were discussing party invitations when Daniel called.
4 Genevieve leaves to give Lucy some privacy.
5 Lucy was thinking about travel-themed decorations.
6 Daniel's audition video is going well.
7 Lucy was waiting for him to ask for help.
8 Lucy's a film director.

C Watch the rest of the episode. Did you guess correctly? Then order what Daniel says his show will be about, 1–6. There are two extra.

a animals
b birds
c close-ups of green celebrities
d down inside the Earth
e Earth's daily activities
f marine life
g nature news
h news from around the globe

3 After watching

A In pairs, explain the lesson title.

> It's called this because ...

B Correct three mistakes in each sentence.

Daniel
1 Lucy was making mistakes when she was recording herself.
2 Daniel was thinking he could edit it himself and make it look really cool.
3 Lucy was very nervous until Daniel helped her through it.

C Order Daniel and Lucy's dialogue, 1–6, and complete with ⊕ or ⊖ of simple past or past continuous, according to the video.

☐ I _____ (try) to record myself and it _____ (be) a nightmare. I _____ (wonder) ... _____ (can) you help me out?
☐ Hey, you got a minute?
☐ And I _____ (wonder) when you were gonna ask me. Don't worry, it'll be great!
☐ Maybe.
☐ Can I ask you something?
☐ Sure.

D Put the words in order to make sentences from the video. Who said them?

1 he / they / I / me / wanted / green / out / paper / convinced / to / ones / send / but / weren't / that
I wanted _____
2 that / I / thinking / be / a / too / much / might / little / to / ask / was
I was _____
3 ever / wonder / slept / while / what / you / doing / was / our / planet
Ever wonder _____

E 🔵 **Make it personal** Role-play! Use the dialogue in 3C to help you. **A:** You're Daniel. Ask B for help. Then role-play introducing your own TV show. **B:** Agree to help A. Then film and direct A's TV show.

29

R1 Grammar and vocabulary

A **Picture dictionary.** Cover the words on these pages and use the pictures to remember:

page	
6	5 life priorities
8	5 senses and 2 adjectives for each one
12	7 common illnesses
18	6 ways to get news
21	5 actions that were happening in the picture
22	4 global problems
23	9 natural phenomena
24	Jane's story
158	11 pairs of picture words for the 11 vowel sounds

B 🎧 **Make it personal** Choose two of photos 1–6. In pairs, take turns using sense verbs to describe each of them, until your partner guesses which it is. Use X instead of the pronoun.

> X smell bad but taste amazing!

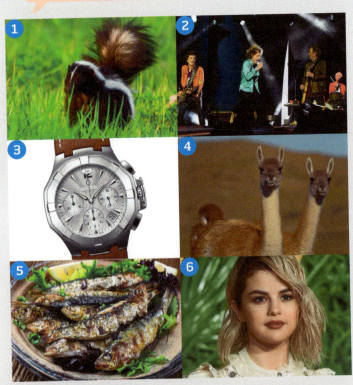

C 🎧 **Make it personal** Use prompts 1–6 to make questions. In pairs, ask and answer, and ask at least two follow-up questions. What's the most interesting thing you found out about your partner?

1 have / get up early?
2 want / be famous?
3 where / last vacation?
4 what / after work or school?
5 how / feeling today?
6 need / study before a test?

> Do you have to get up early?
>
> It depends on the day. I get up …

D You're Lori. Read 1–6 and write a piece of advice using *should* for each. In pairs, compare and choose the best advice in each situation.

1 I have a test tomorrow morning, and I'm really worried about it!
2 My house is full of water from the flood!
3 I have a toothache, but I'm terrified of dentists!
4 My 4-year-old son has a fever and can't sleep.
5 My kids are 13 and 17. They want to go to a party, but they have school tomorrow.
6 We don't have any money and we have to pay for our electricity, our car, and our vacation. Help!

E 🎧 **Make it personal** Record five things you think your partner will / won't do before next class. Then check.

> OK. My first prediction was "He'll eat pizza." Did you eat pizza?
>
> Yes, in fact I did! I had an awesome pizza last night.

F ▶R1.1 🎧 **Make it personal** Put the words in 1–4 in order and add an auxiliary verb to make questions. Listen, check, and repeat. Then, in pairs, ask and answer.

1 doing / what / you / last night / 6 p.m. / at / / ?
2 evening / yesterday / you / do / what / / ?
3 work / in / who / you / the / last activity / with / / ?
4 you / doing / what / class / before / the / started / / ?

G In pairs, compare the two problems in 1–5. Which is more serious and why? Any disagreements?

1 animal extinction or pollution?
2 unemployment or crime?
3 climate change or poverty?
4 corruption or diseases?
5 droughts or earthquakes?

> I think animal extinction is more serious than pollution because …

H Correct the mistakes. Check your answers in units 1 and 2.

🔸 **Common mistakes**

1 We enjoy play the video games. (2 mistakes)
2 I go to the movies yesterday. (1 mistake)
3 When you will start working, you'll get up more early. (2 mistakes)
4 Will you to help we with our homework? (2 mistakes)
5 I will writing that on my notebook. (2 mistakes)
6 Here is an advice and a news for you. (2 mistakes)
7 What was you doing at 8 p.m. the last night? (2 mistakes)
8 Was you scared during the thunderstorm? (1 mistake)
9 When he was young he was crying all the time! (1 mistake)
10 I played soccer when I fell and broke the leg. (2 mistakes)

Skills practice

🎵 *Blackbird singing in the dead of night, Take these broken wings and learn to fly, All your life, You were only waiting for this moment to arise*

R1

A 👤 **Make it personal** In pairs, play **Crystal Ball!**
A: Predict the future of something or somebody.
B: Guess what or who A is talking about.

> Everyone will have them.   Are you talking about cars?
> No, they will do chores in the house.
> Children! Only joking. Robots!   You got it! Your turn.

B Read the email. Are 1–7 True (T) or False (F)? Correct the false ones.
1 His head was aching before he went to the store.
2 It was raining all day.
3 He took his bike into the mall.
4 He was wet when he went into the store.
5 His bike was there when he left the mall.
6 He knows where his keys are.
7 He opened a window to get into his apartment.

D ▶R1.2 Listen to a message from Larry's sister. What five pieces of advice does she give him? Listen again to check. Is any of her advice the same as yours?

E In pairs. **A:** You're Larry. Tell B your story. Can you remember all the details? **B:** Listen and react to A's story.

> You won't believe what happened yesterday!   What?

F In groups, take turns miming a problem. The others race to offer advice. Use these ideas to help.

| heavy bags | hot | hungry | no money |
| really tired | sick | too much work | |

> You shouldn't go clubbing this week!

H ▶R1.3 👤 **Make it personal** Question time!
1 Listen to the 12 lesson titles in units 1 and 2.
2 In pairs, practice asking and answering. Use the book map on p. 2–3. Ask at least two follow-up questions. Try to answer in different ways. Can you have a short conversation about the questions?

> What's really important in life?
> For me, it's having fun! You have to enjoy life.
> What do you do to have fun?

Hi!
What a terrible day! First, I had a really bad headache, but I had to go to the store to get some food. So, I was riding to the mall when the rain started. There was a huge thunderstorm and I was on my bike, so I got really wet! Then I left my bike outside the mall and went in. When I came out of the mall my bike wasn't there! Gone! Can you believe it??? After that I had to walk home, wet and cold. Then when I got home I couldn't find my keys! Guess what I did. I climbed in an open window at the back! But a neighbor saw me, thought I was a thief, and called the police. Now I have to take my ID to the police station, I have no keys, no bike, and a terrible cold from the rain! What should I do?
Larry :-(

C In pairs, imagine Larry is your friend. Think of three pieces of advice you could give him.

> You should get a car!   Yeah, and take care of your keys!

3.1 How often do you travel?

1 Vocabulary Traveling

A ▶3.1 Listen to Vic talking about his vacation and number pictures a–g in the order you hear them, 1–7.

B In pairs, use the phrases and expressions below to compare your feelings about traveling. Any big differences?

| I | love / like / hate | to travel / traveling | alone. |
| | enjoy / don't mind / can't stand | traveling | with family / friends. |

- traveling long distances by car / plane / train / bus / boat
- going to exotic places
- taking short day trips
- doing nothing / rushing around
- hitchhiking

I don't mind traveling long distances by car. I find it relaxing.

That's because you don't drive! I hate driving.

32

C Cover the second column of the quiz. Match the **bold** words to the photos in **A**. Check in pairs and predict how sentences 1–8 end.

♪ *I'm on my way, Driving at ninety down those country lanes, Singing to "Tiny Dancer", And I miss the way you make me feel, and it's real*

3.1

What kind of traveler are you? Take our quiz and find out.

BEFORE THE JOURNEY

1. You've saved a lot of money and **booked** an expensive hotel online. The kind you've always dreamed of. When you get there … | … you discover the place is not what you saw on the site. It's not even finished! What do you do?

2. It's 4 p.m. You've tried all you could, but you couldn't get to the station on time and **missed** your train. Now you have to … | … wait five hours for the next one. All the stores at the train station are closed. What do you do?

3. It's December 23rd. You're at a **crowded** and cold bus station, **stand**ing in line. The ticket agent says … | … there are no more tickets available. You won't be home on December 24th. What do you do?

4. It's time to go to the airport. You've **packed** all your bags, turned off the lights, and called a taxi. On the way to the airport … | … the taxi breaks down and stops in the middle of the street. What do you do?

DURING THE JOURNEY

5. You've **board**ed an old and crowded plane. All you want to do is get some sleep. You hope there's no one sitting next to you, but … | … you see a mother and a very young kid. What do you say?

6. You're on the plane. The flight attendant has dropped a cup of coffee on your laptop. You turn it on … | … but it isn't working. You don't know if the problem is permanent. What do you do?

AFTER THE JOURNEY

7. You've arrived at the hotel and checked in. You're ex**haust**ed after your journey. The three **e**levators … | … are out of order and your room is on the 10th floor. What do you do?

8. You've just come back from a shopping trip to Miami. You're stopped at **cus**toms. In your **suit**case … | … there are a lot of things you forgot to declare. What do you do?

D 💬 **Make it personal** In pairs, uncover the second column and check your predictions. How many endings were similar to yours? Then answer the questions.

> *In a situation like this, I stay calm and don't shout. I ask for my money back.*

⏰ **Common mistakes**

pack
I have to ~~make~~ my bags.

missed
I got up late and ~~lost~~ my plane.

We need to ~~do the~~ check in before dropping our bags.

② Listening

A ▶ 3.2 Listen to the complete quiz and choose a, b, or c for each question.

B Calculate your score, then read what it means. Do you agree?

What kind of traveler are you? Score **a** = 3, **b** = 2, **c** = 1

8–11 Calm and in control	**12–19** Balanced	**20–24** Stressed and impatient
Your friends probably think you're a great travel companion. You don't get stressed when things go wrong and you always see the positive side of any bad situation.	You know how to have a good time and don't usually let small incidents interfere with your vacation, but, depending on the situation, you can get angry or impatient.	It's probably hard to travel with you. You get really annoyed if things go wrong and don't enjoy your vacation as much as you could.

> *Well, it says I'm stressed, which is true, but I don't think I'm impatient.*

C 💬 **Make it personal** In pairs, use the pictures in **1A** to remember and tell your own funny / stressful / surprising travel experiences. Are they "good traveler" or "bad traveler" stories?

> *Photo b reminds me of my grandma's birthday party. I missed the bus and then the train was canceled. I had to take a cab. It was really expensive!*

> *OK, that's a "bad traveler" story!*

33

3.2 Have you ever been to another country?

1 Listening

A ▶3.3 Which city does the photo show? What do you know about it? Listen to part one of Paula and Harry's conversation and complete 1–4.
1. Paula has seen the photos of _____.
2. Cathy lives in _____.
3. She wants Harry to _____.
4. Paula went there on _____.

B ▶3.4 Why do you think Harry is hesitant to go? Listen to part two to check. Were you right?

> Well, maybe's he's nervous about meeting her face to face.

C ▶3.5 Listen to part three. True (T) or False (F)?
1. Cathy makes a lot of money.
2. She knows about Harry's phobia.
3. Harry goes to therapy twice a week.

D 🗣 **Make it personal** In pairs, answer 1–3. Any similar opinions / stories?
1. What do you think is the best solution to their problem?
2. Do you think long-distance relationships can be successful in the long term?
3. Do you know anyone who has a phobia? What is it?

> I think he should be honest with Cathy.

> Some friends of mine have been together for three years, and they live in different countries!

> My son is afraid of spiders.

🔥 Common mistakes

Avicii ~~has~~ died in 2018.
    has
Ed Sheeran sold five million albums this year so far.
    did
When ~~has~~ Ariana Grande last played in Asia?

2 Grammar Present perfect 1: past experiences

A ▶3.6 Match 1–5 to Paula and Harry's responses a–e. Listen to check.

1. I've **been** to Australia twice.
2. Have you **seen** photos of her?
3. Have you ever **traveled** by plane?
4. Have you ever **tried** therapy?
5. She's **seen** photos of me too.

a. Once. My mom took me to Disneyland when I was five.
b. Yep, you showed them to me last week.
c. And she still liked you after you showed them to her?
d. Oh yeah? Did you go on business?
e. Twice. It didn't work.

B Complete the grammar box.

> 1. Study the sentences in **A**. Read and circle Yes (Y) or No (N).
>   - Sentences 1–5 in **A** are about past experiences. Y / N
>   - We don't know / care when the things happened. Y / N
>   - The **bold** verbs are in the simple past. Y / N
>   - The present perfect = *have* / *has* + past participle. Y / N
>   - Some past participles end *-ed* and have the same form as the simple past. Y / N
>   - Some past participles are irregular and have a different form. Y / N
> 2. In the responses, which tense is used to ask for / give more details?
> 3. Is a similar tense used for the sentences in **A** in your language?

➡ **Grammar 3A** p.142

34

C Read **Common mistakes**. In pairs, how many true sentences about Harry's story can you make in two minutes? Pronounce the s in 's and hasn't /z/ not /s/.

Oh, simple thing, where have you gone? I'm getting old, and I need something to rely on, I'm getting tired and I need somewhere to begin

3.2

Paula
Harry
Cathy

be
see
travel
try

Australia
plane
Disneyland
therapy
–'s photos

before
once
twice

Common mistakes

've   been to
I ~~never was in~~ Moscow.
            been
I've ~~gone~~ to a U2 show.
Use *been* for completed visits (there and back), *gone* if someone hasn't returned.

Harry's been to Disneyland once. That's one.

D Make questions to ask Paula about her trip. Each / means a missing word. Stress the **bold** words.
1 when / you **go** there?   *When did you go there?*
2 how long / / **stay** there?
3 what **places** / / visit?
4 how / / **weather**?
5 / you stay / / **hotel**?
6 / your **partner** / with you?
7 how much **work** / / do?
8 / / like / **go** again?

E Match 1–6 in the survey report to photos a–f. Complete with these verbs in the present perfect.

be (x 2)   meet   see   travel   try

Class Survey Report

1 Two or more people <u>have been</u> to the United States.

2 Four or more students _____ by plane.

3 No one _____ an A-list celebrity face to face.

4 At least two students _____ all the *Avengers* movies.

5 Everyone in the group _____ Japanese food.

6 Most of the students _____ to a live, professional soccer game.

a   b   c   d   e   f

F **Make it personal**   Class survey! In pairs, use the verbs in E to ask and answer *Have you …?* questions about different subjects. Ask at least one follow-up question each time. Report your answers to the class.

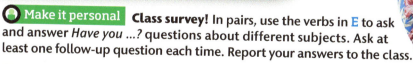

Let's see … Have you ever seen the Amazon River?   Yeah, once.

Really? When did you see it?   I flew over it in 2018.   Wow! Where were you flying to?

35

3.3 Have you sung a song in English yet?

1 Reading

A In groups, look at the title of the article. Decide which tip, 1–4, is the most important when traveling with a friend. If you disagree, try to convince your group.
1 Be pre**pa**red to com**pro**mise.
2 Dis**cuss** money.
3 Do things se**pa**rately sometimes.
4 Plan carefully.

I think it's really important to compromise. *Of course, but for me that's not ...*

B ▶3.7 Read the article and match tips 1–4 in **A** to paragraphs a–c. There's one extra tip. Then listen, reread and, after each paragraph, repeat the pink-stressed words. What's your reaction to the text?

You are so irritating. *Why did I travel with you?*

How to travel together without killing each other!

Traveling with people you don't know in**ti**mately can be fun ... or a nightmare. Your perso**na**lity differences can get mul**ti**plied by 10. So here are three things to con**si**der before you go:

a **Be honest about your bu**dget.** If you can only spend $60 a night for accommo**da**tion, say it before you go. Also, plan how you intend to share all the other ex**pen**ses: transpor**ta**tion, food, and enter**tain**ment. And think about this: is it OK for you to travel with someone who has more money than you? Would you mind paying a bit extra to help a friend who has less?

b **Sometimes you'll need to make quick decisions on the road** and maybe disa**gree** on what you want to do. If your personalities and in**te**rests are different, you'll have to plan a bit and be fle**xi**ble with each other. If one of you is a heavy smo**ker** and the other hates smoke, it's important to find a so**lu**tion that sa**tis**fies both sides. So, consider this: can you make con**ces**sions when you travel with others? Would you ever travel with someone who has a few i**rri**tating habits?

c **Spending too much time with each other can be very irritating.** Plan to take some breaks from each other from time to time, es**pe**cially on a longer trip. Then you can meet for dinner and share fun sto**ries**. So, before traveling ask your**self**: are you comfortable spending the en**tire** day with a friend when you travel? Do you need to spend some time a**lone** when traveling?

⚠ Common mistakes

It depends ~~of~~ *on* your budget.

~~To travel~~ *Traveling* without ~~have~~ *having* money is difficult.

Before ~~leave, anticipate~~ *leaving, anticipating* problems is essential.

Use *-ing* forms when the subject is a verb + preposition.

C 👥 **Make it personal** In pairs, ask and answer the last two questions in each paragraph. Are you compatible travelers?

Is it OK for you to travel with someone who has more money than you?

I guess so, but it depends on how much, I think.

2 Listening

A ▶3.8 Lisa and Meg are spending a few days in London. What problems are they having? Listen and match days 1–3 to the travel tips in **1A**.
Day 1 ☐ Day 2 ☐ Day 3 ☐

B ▶3.8 Listen again and write Lisa (L) or Meg (M) for 1–4. Who ...
1 really dislikes the hotel?
2 went shopping yesterday?
3 probably likes art?
4 's reading *101 Things To Do Before You Die*?

C 👥 **Make it personal** Who would be worse to travel with – Lisa or Meg? Why?

Lisa wants to stay in expensive rooms so that ruins the holiday.

3 Grammar Present perfect 2: completed actions

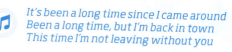

*It's been a long time since I came around
Been a long time, but I'm back in town
This time I'm not leaving without you*

3.3

A Match 1–5 to their present result.
1 This place has changed.
2 Have you stayed here before?
3 We've only just arrived!
4 We haven't paid yet.
5 I've already told you.

☐ They don't have our money.
☐ We haven't checked in yet.
☐ You know that.
☒ 1 It's different now.
☐ It's my second visit.

> **Common mistakes**
> *hasn't called*
> She ~~haven't call~~ me yet.
> *have already*
> We ~~already have~~ worked together.
> I ~~have~~ studied a lot yesterday evening.

B Study sentences 1–5 in **A** and **Common mistakes**. Then complete the grammar box.

> Cross out the incorrect options in rules a–d.
> a The experience and / or present result of the action is **more / less** important than the time it happened.
> b *Just* (very recently) and *already* (before now) are used in **positive / negative** sentences.
> c *Yet* (up to now) can be used in questions and **positive / negative** sentences.
> d **Use / Don't use** the present perfect for specific past times (*a week ago, when I arrived*).
>
> → **Grammar 3B** p. 142

C ▶ 3.9 Complete 1–7 with the verbs in the correct tense. Listen to check. In pairs, say which rule a–d each sentence illustrates.
1 Julie _____ (**be**) there and she says it's fantastic.
2 I _____ (**not be**) to the West End yet.
3 You _____ (**spend**) a lot of money yesterday.
4 The weather _____ (**change**). It's really cloudy now.
5 I'm reading *101 Things To Do Before You Die*. _____ (**you / read**) it?
6 I _____ (**start**) it when we got on the plane.
7 I _____ (**already / read**) the first 20 ideas.

D Test a partner. Take turns choosing a photo on p. 32 and describing what's just happened. Your partner identifies it.

> *He's just booked the hotel.*   *Picture g, right?*

E ▶ 3.10 Read the list. Guess which seven activities Lisa and / or Meg have done. Listen to check, and notice the irregular past participles of the **bold** verbs. Describe what Lisa and Meg have / haven't done using *already, just,* and *yet*. Listen again to check.

> *Well, they're visiting London, so they've already done that.*
>
> *Yeah, of course. And …*

101 things to do before you die

☐ **be** a DJ at a party
☐ **do** volunteer work
☐ donate blood
☐ **fall** in love
☐ go abroad
☐ **have** a child
☐ learn to dance

☐ **make** a birthday cake
☐ plant a tree
☐ **ride** an animal
☐ **swim** with dolphins
☐ try an extreme sport
☐ visit London
☐ **write** a story

Make it personal List 10 things you really want to do. In groups, compare lists, ask, and answer. Who wants to do the most unusual thing? Who has done the most things? Have you made any plans to achieve your ambitions?

> *I really want to go to Europe.*   *I've been abroad, but only once.*   *Oh really? Where did you go?*

37

3.4 How long have you lived here?

1 Reading

A Would you like to spend a year somewhere different before you start college or work? Where would you go and what would you do? Consider these ideas.

- a learn a new language
- b work as a volunteer
- c work in a restaurant / store / hospital
- d work with children
- e travel to different places
- f learn new skills

I'd go to Italy and learn Italian.   *Would you work there or travel around?*

B Read the article. Was each person's experience Positive (P) or Negative (N)?

Taking a Gap Year
A waste of time or the time of your life?

Parents, teens, and educators all talk about the benefits of taking a gap year before college. It's become so popular that even the British royal family have done it! Prince William, for example, volunteered in Chile, and Prince Harry worked on a ranch in Australia and helped to build a clinic in Lesotho, Africa. We spoke to six people and asked, "Is a gap year a good idea?" Read their stories and get some inspiration but also some warnings.

Derek I'm very shy. Really, you have no idea how shy I am. So guess how I'm spending my gap year? Teaching English as a foreign language in Cambodia. Yep – to groups of 30 students. And you know what? I love my students and I think they love me back. I've only known them since June[1], but it feels like we've always been friends[2]. I don't get paid, but I get free board and accommodation and that's really all I need.

Sandra My gap year has been amazing so far! I'm traveling alone around South America practicing my Spanish and meeting incredible people. So far I've been to Chile, Argentina, Uruguay, Paraguay, and Bolivia[3] and I plan to go to Peru, Ecuador, and Colombia before I go home. I've learned so much! I've met a lot of people and I've had some great experiences as well as a couple of bad bad ones.[4] By the time I get home, I'll be ready to start college next fall.

Ross Well, I lived in Cairo for a year with my aunt and uncle[5] and the experience taught me more valuable lessons than my last 10 years at school. I learned to be much more open to other cultures, values, and religions – things you don't learn in class. And I learned to be fluent in Arabic which was my goal![6]

Rita In 2015 I lived and worked as an au pair in Barcelona for nine months[7]. All I wanted was to get some cash, and then start a new life when I got back home. But I fell in love with the twins that I looked after, and the rest is history. So, thanks to my gap year, I decided I didn't want to be a lawyer, but a primary school teacher. Mom and Dad were a bit surprised, but in the end they just accepted my decision.

Tina I've been in Scotland for six months[8] and it's been a nightmare. I got a part-time job at a big grocery store and have worked there for only three weeks[9], but I hate it. In the winter it gets dark at 4 p.m. and I think this is affecting my mental health. I'm getting really depressed and all I do is cry night and day. I really want to get on a plane and go back home soon. Luckily, my cousin has just come to visit, so I hope to have some fun with her.

C ▶ 3.11 Quickly reread and match 1–6 to the correct person. Then listen and, after each paragraph, repeat the pink-stressed words.

Who:
1 wants to go home as soon as possible?
2 changed her mind about her future?
3 stayed with family during the gap year?
4 doesn't have to pay for their apartment?
5 is visiting more than one country?
6 mentions language learning?

D **Make it personal** The time of their lives? In groups, take turns saying if you or someone you know has had one of experiences a–f in **A**. Answer questions about it. Any similarities? Were any experiences a waste of time?

My sister's worked as a volunteer in Africa.   *Wow! What did she do?*

She helped to build a school.

2 Grammar Present perfect 3: unfinished past   3.4

♪ *I have run, I have crawled, I have scaled these city walls, These city walls, Only to be with you. But I still haven't found, What I'm looking for.*

A Who's still on their gap year in **1B**? Write *present* or *past* next to each underlined phrase.

B ▶ 3.12 Listen to two interviews with Rita and Tina. Find two incorrect details in their paragraphs in **1B** based on the interviews.

C Complete the grammar box. Is the present perfect similar in your language?

a Read **Common mistakes** and the four example sentences, and look at the graphics. Then circle the correct options in rules 1–3.

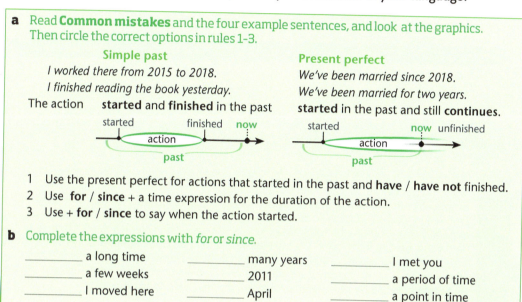

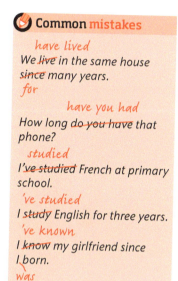

1 Use the present perfect for actions that started in the past and **have / have not** finished.
2 Use **for / since** + a time expression for the duration of the action.
3 Use + **for / since** to say when the action started.

b Complete the expressions with *for* or *since*.

_____ a long time   _____ many years   _____ I met you
_____ a few weeks   _____ 2011   _____ a period of time
_____ I moved here   _____ April   _____ a point in time

→ Grammar 3C p. 142

D ▶ 3.12 In pairs, use the prompts to write questions and sentences about Tina and Rita's gap year. Listen again to check.

1 How long / you / be / UK?
2 I / be / UK / September.
3 How long / you / work there?
4 I / see / her / long time.
5 How long / you / live / Barcelona?
6 I / live / there / seven months.
7 I / work / au pair / four months.
8 Mom and Dad / in**sist** / long time.

E Meet Sam Same. He doesn't like change. Use pictures 1–6 to talk about him. Imagine his other habits.

Sam's probably had the same food every day for 30 years.

same house / 1990

same hairstyle / many years

foreign language / he was 20

same TV / 15 years

his girlfriend / 1995

same kind of music / many years

Make it personal Have you changed a lot? In pairs, ask and answer *How long ...?* questions to find out. Change pairs and ask and answer about your previous partner. Did you learn anything new?

How long have you had the same hairstyle?   *Oh, since I was 15. I like my hair the way it is.*   *How long has Joe had the same hairstyle?*   *Since he was 15.*

39

3.5 Do you write reviews?

🆔 Skills Using evidence for your answers

Common mistakes
disappointment
It was a big ~~deception~~.

A Put these words in the correct category. Add the opposites of the underlined words.

cheap	a coffee maker	dirty	econ**om**ical	fi**l**thy	**friendly**
good value	helpful	a kitche**nette**	near the beach	near the center	
polite	a pool	quiet	reasonable	spotless	wifi

price	cl**ean**liness	a**men**ities	location	service

B Read these reviews and give an overall rating for each hotel.

◉◉◉◉◉ excellent
◉◉◉◉○ very good
◉◉◉○○ average
◉◉○○○ poor
◉○○○○ terrible

We stayed at the Central Hotel for one night and I have to say I don't think it's good value for money, which was a big disappointment. The rooms are very basic and there's no coffee maker in the room and the wifi signal is too weak to use. The biggest problem for us was that the pool was empty, so we couldn't swim. The room was generally clean, but the bathroom was filthy – like they didn't clean it at all! There was hair in the tub and in the sink. On the plus side, the hotel is very central and you can walk everywhere, which is fantastic. Check-in and check-out were very easy and the staff were re**spon**sive to our needs, but the hotel really needs reno**v**ation **u**rgently! And more entertainment – the only thing in our room was an old television.

Rating _____

We stayed at Golden Sands in October and the weather was amazing – warm, but not too hot. We had a dramatic ocean view room with a super comfortable bed. The service was the best we've ever had on vacation – staff and m**an**agement were phe**nom**enal. The food and drinks were excellent and the prices were very reasonable for a big resort like this. The hotel was not expensive at all for the service and amenities, and its location in front of the beach was s**uperb**. Everything in the room worked perfectly, from the wifi to the hairdryer. The only problem was that the room was a little small for a family of four, but that's kind of logical when you book one room for four people! Next time we'll get two rooms.

Rating _____

C ▶ 3.13 Listen, reread, and underline the parts in each review that relate to each category in **A**.

D In pairs, use the parts you underlined in **C** to decide on a star rating for each category in each hotel. Compare with another pair. How similar are your ratings?

	price	cleanliness	amenities	location	service
Central Hotel					
Golden Sands					

We've given this only two stars for price.

Once we stayed in a fantastic hotel on the beach. It wasn't cheap ...

E 👤 Make it personal

1 Have you ever stayed in a hotel like either of these? Were you paying?
2 In accommodation reviews, what is the most important category for you? Order the categories 1–5 (most to least important) and find someone with the same list.

Price is number 1 for me. I always look for the cheapest places.

Really? Sometimes the cheapest place is really awful and far away from the center

3.5 Are you a logical person?

🎵 *Look what you made me do, I'm with somebody new, Ooh, baby, baby, I'm dancing with a stranger*

ID in Action Reacting to unexpected information

A Read the paragraph and find 14 Latin words in it.

About 50 percent of all English words are Latin in origin. So if you're a native speaker of Spanish, Portuguese, French, etc., you can understand and express many ideas using these words, even if your English is still limited. The reviews you just read on p. 40, for example, contain approximately 50 Latin-based words.

B Scan the hotel reviews again and find three examples of each suffix.

-ic	-ment	-al	-ion
dramatic			

C Study the words in B and complete rules 1–3.

1 The suffixes _____ and _____ are typical of nouns.
2 The suffixes _____ and _____ are typical of adjectives.
3 Suffixes _____ usually stressed.

D Complete 1–6 with the correct form of the words. Write one more question using a word from the chart in B. In pairs, ask and answer the questions. Would you ask a stranger these questions?

Fun questions to ask a STRANGER!

1 Is there a lot of electrical *equipment* in your bedroom? (**equip**)
2 Do you think TV is still good _____? (**entertain**)
3 Has anyone ever considered you an _____? (**intellect**)
4 Is it possible to have too much _____? (**inform**)
5 Were you _____ as a child? (**music**)
6 Are you a _____ person? (**romance**)

> First one. Is there a lot of electrical equipment in your bedroom?

> Oh, yeah, lots. A TV, a reading light, my laptop, my phone ... what else? Oh, and my alarm clock.

Common mistakes
~~expect to~~
I didn't ~~wait~~ you/say that.
~~un~~
That was ~~an~~ inexpected news.

E ▶3.14 Listen to two conversations. Which question in D is each one about?

F ▶3.14 Listen again and complete 1 and 2 with two words in each gap.

1 Barry learned how to play _____ when he _____ and _____ very first song when he was nine. It was called "_____ and the Stars."
2 Linda dislikes TV. She says there are one _____ good shows, and they're mostly late _____ or on cable. She doesn't let _____ watch TV, but she lets _____ time on the Internet.

G ▶3.14 Complete 1–5. Listen again to check. In pairs, practice different ways of reacting to surprising information.

Meaning	What you actually say	Or just ...
I don't understand. / Please explain.	1 What do you _____ nothing?	What?
I'm surprised to hear this.	2 You've never _____ me that.	Wow! Really? You're kidding me!
Please confirm what you said.	3 Wait a _____. Did I hear you say that ...?	What?
That is not logical.	4 But that makes no _____.	No way!
I have a different opinion.	5 I don't _____.	Oh, come on!

> Wow! You have much less equipment in your bedroom.

H 🔵 **Make it personal** Change partners. Repeat activity D. Use sentences from G. Try to do it a little faster. Are your new partner's answers similar?

41

Writing 3 An internship application

🎵 *Just give me a reason, Just a little bit's enough, Just a second we're not broken just bent, And we can learn to love again*

A Read internship ads a–c and Marcia's email. Answer 1–3.
1. Which internship is she applying for?
2. Does she have the necessary experience and qualifications?
3. Complete the email with the correct country.

a  **Kenya**
Sports science graduate wanted for a six-month athletics training program. This is an opportunity to develop a career in top-level coaching. *Must have a relevant degree and be fluent in English. Ability to drive essential.*

b **Mexico**
Our marine conservation project has a vacancy for a suitably qualified intern. Get valuable career experience while contributing to important marine conservation work. *Must be able to scuba dive and have a good command of Spanish.*

c **Jamaica**
Join our news team in the Caribbean, filming reports on local issues for our online video channel. *Experience is not necessary as training will be given, but you must speak English and be a good communicator.*

Dear Ms. Walton,

I would like to apply for the internship in _____ listed on the internship page of your website.

As you will see from my résumé (attached), I have recently graduated from Miami University with a degree in environmental science. I am a qualified scuba diver. I am also fluent in Spanish and English, and have a good command of Portuguese.

I am currently employed by the local environment agency, where I have worked for the past six months. I am responsible for testing water quality on local beaches, and helping to keep our beaches clean.

I am looking for a new opportunity to develop my experience of marine conservation. I have always been interested in everything related to the oceans, and I am sure I can make a positive contribution to your program.

Thank you for considering my application. I am available for interview at any time. If you have any questions, please feel free to call me on (1) 8989-7888. I look forward to hearing from you.

Sincerely,
Marcia Fernandez Ruiz

B Order the topics in the email, 1–5.
- [ ] education and qualifications
- [ ] work experience
- [ ] availability for interview
- [ ] position interested in
- [ ] reasons for applying

C Study the email and **Write it right!**, then complete tips 1–7 with *Do* or *Don't*.
In formal emails and letters:
1. _____ use an informal, conversational style.
2. _____ address the reader by his / her first name.
3. _____ include your contact information.
4. _____ thank the reader.
5. _____ end with your first name only.
6. _____ refer to your résumé.
7. _____ use contractions (*It's, I'm*, etc.).

✅ **Write it right!**

There are specific ways to open and close a formal email or letter.
Opening: *Dear Mr. Lee (Mrs. / Ms. + last name); Dear Sir / Madam*
Closing: *Sincerely, Kind regards, Best wishes*

D Complete 1–8 with the correct preposition. Scan the email to check.
1. Apply _____ a position or job.
2. Graduate _____ (name of university) _____ a degree _____ (subject).
3. Be responsible _____ something at work.
4. Be fluent _____ / Have a good command _____ (a language).
5. Have experience _____ something.
6. Be interested _____ something.
7. Make a positive contribution _____ something.
8. Be available _____ an interview.

E 🔴 **Make it personal** Write an email applying for an internship in 150–200 words.

Before	Choose an internship in **A** or imagine one you'd like to apply for. Brainstorm why you would be the right person for the job.
While	Write an application following the order in **B**. Include five paragraphs and follow the tips in **C**. Compare each paragraph carefully with the one in Marcia's email.
After	Exchange emails with another student. Decide if you will give each other the internship.

3 Under the moon

Café

1 Before watching

A In pairs, check what's important for school / work projects.

☐ be creative
☐ have a good memory
☐ have experience
☐ have inspiration
☐ know how to write well
☐ have good research skills
☐ have a strong Internet connection

> I think it's important to …

B 🔵 **Make it personal** In pairs. Have you ever had to do a big project?

> I worked on a big project for my art class.   What was it about?

C Guess how Andrea feels and why.
☐ homesick ☐ not inspired ☐ sleepy ☐ tired

> Maybe she's been up all night?

2 While watching

A Watch up to 2:40 to check. Complete 1–6 with the correct numbers. What else did you pick up?
1 Andrea's had _____ cups of coffee.
2 She has _____ more designs to complete.
3 She has to design _____ rooms in total.
4 The twins lived in Argentina when they finished _____ grade / just before their _____ birthday.
5 They lived in France _____ or _____ years ago.
6 They lived in Mexico from _____ to _____ grade.

B Watch again and complete 1–6.
1 Her designs have to be about places _____.
2 The last time the twins were in Argentina was when _____.
3 According to them, Andrea is _____ and August is _____.
4 French kids made fun of August's _____.
5 After leaving France, they moved back to _____.
6 The inspiration for her difficult design came from _____.

C Read 1–8 then watch the rest. Check August (Au), Genevieve (G), or Andrea (A).

		Au	G	An
1	comes from Montreal and misses it			
2	doesn't really have one home			
3	has got a lot of inspiration from travel			
4	recognizes where the design is from			
5	sent a postcard from Australia			
6	imagined she lived on the moon			
7	inspired a song to be written			
8	asks a question about the moon			

D Who says 1–10, Andrea, August, or Genevieve? Watch again to check.
1 Hey, you could tell?
2 Those were good times!
3 You are way more talented than I thought.
4 Hey! That was, like, a strange kind of compliment.
5 You know what I mean.
6 What does it remind you of?
7 They were just picking on you.
8 You have a good memory.
9 I get homesick sometimes.
10 We don't really have one home.

3 After watching

A Complete 1–6 with the correct form of these verbs.

be	do	have	live	see	think

1 You've _____ four cups already.
2 Let me see what you've _____ so far.
3 We haven't _____ back in years.
4 These are some of the best rooms I've _____.
5 It has to be a place you imagine you've _____ in.
6 I haven't _____ about that in a long time.

B Complete 1–7 with *has / have* or *'s / 've*.
1 _____ you worked out today?
2 I _____ got two more to do.
3 You _____ always been the pretty, fun, popular twin, and I _____ been the nerd.
4 This _____ been difficult for Andrea.
5 How long _____ it been since we lived there?
6 Andrea _____ always wondered about Genevieve's song title.
7 Well, we know man _____ walked on the moon …

C 🔵 **Make it personal** Have you ever been homesick? If so, what did you miss most?

> When I went to college, I missed my grandmother's cooking.

43

4 4.1 Were you spoiled as a child?

1 Vocabulary Childhood

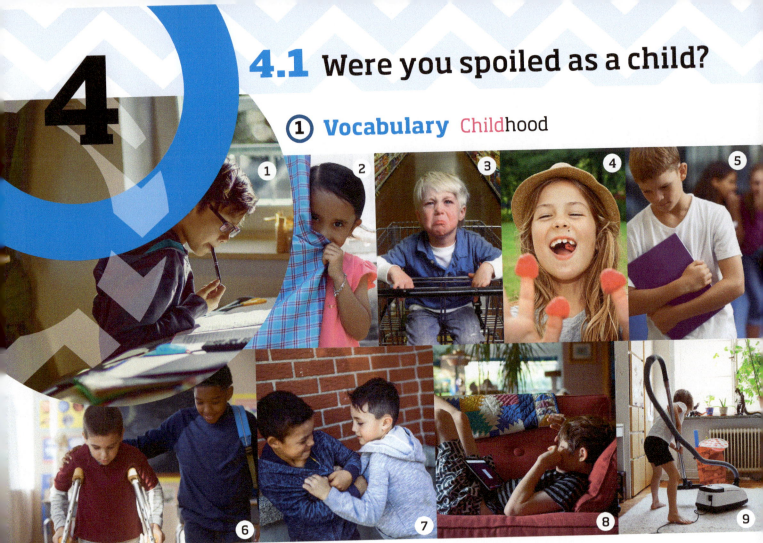

A ▶4.1 Read and listen to the website and match photos 1–9 to the **bold** words.

What kind of child were you?

Which group best describes you as a kid? Based on years of intensive study, psychologist Donald Elliot has created five categories to describe children aged 4–10. Here's a summary of his study.

	These kids are …		So they …
Group 1 Party kids	funny	→	like to **laugh** and entertain people.
	active and creative	→	do many activities at the same time and never get tired.
	sociable	→	make lots of friends – their own age or older – very easily.
Group 2 "Please love me" kids	kind	→	are always helping people in trouble.
	hardworking	→	like to do well in school to make their parents happy.
	sensitive	→	cry if other kids **make fun of** them.
Group 3 "But why?" kids	shy	→	like to be alone sometimes.
	curious	→	like to know how machines work, for example.
	independent	→	like to explore the world on their own.
Group 4 Explosive kids	honest	→	don't hesitate to tell people what they think of them.
	spoiled	→	won't stop until they get what they want.
	aggressive	→	**fight** more often than most other kids.
Group 5 Mini adults	obedient	→	wash their hands and take showers without a fight.
	critical	→	hate **lazy** people and always expect perfection.
	responsible	→	take the initiative to **do chores** around the house.

B ▶4.2 Listen to the children and say the correct bold word(s) after the beep.

C ▶4.2 Listen and reread. Which kind of child would say a–g? Write the group number, 1–5.

♪ *My father said, Don't you worry, don't you worry child, See heaven's got a plan for you Don't you worry, don't you worry now, yeah*

4.1

a "I want the new iPad right now, Daddy, not next week." ☐
b "Mmm ... what happens if I put my watch in the microwave?" ☐
c "Go to bed? Mom, but it's only 11 p.m. I want to play video games. Please!" ☐
d "What? I only got 95 percent on that easy test? What was I thinking?" ☐
e "Grandpa, you look sad. What's wrong?" ☐
f "Mommy, can I help you wash the dishes? Please?" ☐
g "Yes, you're my aunt, I know, but I still don't like your voice." ☐

D ▶4.3 Complete the word stress chart with adjectives from the second column in **A**. Listen to check. Then circle the correct option to complete the rule.

Adjectives					
●	●●	●●●	●●●●	●●●●	
kind	funny	sociable	creative	obedient	

Suffixes like *-able*, *-ible*, *-ive*, *-ent*, *-al*, *-ous* are **sometimes / never** stressed.

E 🔵 **Make it personal** What kind of child were you? In pairs, use the adjectives in **A** to find two similarities and two differences.

First one, funny ... Yeah, that was me.

Not me. I was very serious, and didn't laugh a lot.

② Listening

A ▶4.4 Listen to two conversations. Which group from **1A** does each child belong to?
Michael ☐   Susan ☐

B ▶4.4 Listen again. Are 1–6 True (T) or False (F)? Correct the false ones.
1 Some of Michael's friends have wireless headphones.
2 His mother thinks wireless headphones are too expensive.
3 He probably helped his mother with the housework recently.
4 Susan wants to get an A on her test.
5 She likes to eat at McDonald's.
6 Her parents are young.

C ▶4.5 Complete opinions 1–4 with *do* or *make*. Listen to check. Do you agree?
1 If you _____ a promise to a kid, you can never, ever break it.
2 It's important to make children _____ the dishes, _____ the bed and help around the house.
3 Children who _____ a lot of of homework every day don't necessarily _____ well in exams.
4 Young parents usually _____ more mistakes with their children.

⚠️ **Common mistakes**

make
I still ~~commit~~ mistakes when I speak.

I can't talk to you now, I have to ~~make~~ my homework.
do

Mike, can you ~~make~~ me a favor?
do

make
I never ~~do~~ my bed in the morning.

Use *do* for work, jobs, or tasks and *make* for creating.

D Complete the text with *make* or *do*. Then find and add seven more *make* / *do* phrases from this lesson to the chart.

Romance languages only have one verb for *make* and _____. Sadly, there are no concrete rules for when to use _____ or *do* in English. So _____ this exercise and _____ a big effort to remember the phrases.

Make			Do		
money	an effort	a decision	the laundry	a project	a favor

🔵 **Make it personal** Complete 1–5 with *do* or *make* phrases. In small groups, compare and choose the one that is true for most people in your group.

When I was young,
1 I had to _____ every day / week. I hated that!
2 my parents never asked me to _____.
3 I went to a good / bad school. For example, _____.
4 I was / wasn't spoiled. For example, _____.
5 I found it difficult to _____.

When I was young, I had to wash the car every week. I hated that!

My dad washed our car. But I had to do the dishes every day, and I hated that!

45

4.2 What did you use to do as a child?

1 Reading

A What embarrassing things do children do? Use pictures 1–4 to guess what the stories are about. Then read the online forum and match the pictures to stories a–d.

How embarrassing is that!?

Tell us your stories and let our members decide how embarrassing they are!

a When I was in third grade or something, I used to sit in the back row, near the fish tank. When I was hungry, I ate the fish food flakes. Oh, boy, I loved fish food. No one knew about my secret eating habits, except my best friend, Sue. One day, she told everyone. I was so embarrassed and humiliated I had to move to another school. I think the fish food did me good though because a few years later, I became a swimming champion. Pretty ironic, isn't it? **Orbit606** posted at 2:30

b When I was around six, I had a phase where I only wanted to be called "Adele." You see, I knew an older girl called Adele and I liked her, so on my sixth birthday I decided to adopt her name. Mom almost went crazy! She used to wake me up calling my real name and I said, "Go away, I'm Adele, you know that!" This Adele phase lasted like an entire year. Then, after my seventh birthday, I got tired of Adele, so I chose a different name: Lisa. Guess what TV show I used to watch? **Ex789** posted at 8:00

c When I was about two, one of my favorite things to do was open Alfredo's mouth and pull his tongue out. Did he like that? Well, every time he saw me, he ran to my mother's bedroom and stayed there for hours, so I guess the answer is no. But, poor Alfredo, we used to love him! Oh, by the way, Alfredo was our Labrador Retriever. **Weirdo9** posted at 10:15

d When I was a child, I didn't like school, so I made lots of excuses to stay home. One morning, when I was about seven or eight, I woke up and told my parents I couldn't move my left leg. They took me to the hospital immediately and I spent the entire day in the emergency room. Obviously, the doctors didn't find anything wrong with me. After a few hours, my leg "magically" started to work again. I still don't know if my parents believed that story. **Smith7** posted at 12:49

B ▶ 4.6 Listen, reread, and rate the stories, 1, 2, or 3. In groups, compare opinions.
1 Normal for a kid   2 A bit embarrassing   3 Seriously embarrassing!

C 🧑 **Make it personal** In pairs, share stories about embarrassing things that you or someone you know did as a child. Which is the most embarrassing?

When he was four, my brother once ate all the dog's food from her bowl!

That's seriously embarrassing!

2 Listening

A ▶ 4.7 Listen to part one of a conversation about one of the stories in 1A. Who's talking?

B ▶ 4.7 Listen again. True (T) or False (F)? Correct the false ones.
1 Julia still hates her school days.
2 Her brother enjoys school.
3 She was always sick when she was a teenager.
4 She used to eat bird food every day.

C ▶ 4.8 Read options 1–3 and guess how her dad is going to react. Listen to part two to check.
1 Happy she wasn't sick.   2 Pleased she confessed.   3 Angry she lied and wasted time

D 🧑 **Make it personal** In pairs, role-play Julia's parents talking about her. Decide what to do next. Who has the best solution?

I can't believe she did this to us!   *I think we should take away her phone for a week.*

She needs her phone. And it was a long time ago …

♪ *We don't talk anymore, Like we used to do,*
We don't laugh anymore, What was all of it for?
Oh, we don't talk anymore, Like we used to do

4.2

③ Grammar   *Used to* and simple past

A Check if 1–6 happened one time (OT) or over a period of time (PT).

	OT	PT
1 Did you use to like school?		
2 You used to be sick all the time, Julia.		
3 I didn't use to do it all the time.		
4 One day you ate bird food, remember?		
5 But, Julia, we took you to the hospital!		
6 I never lied about the serious stuff.		

Common mistakes

~~I'm use~~ *usually* to download music.
You ~~use to~~ *used to* call me on my cell phone.
Did you ~~used~~ *use* to have a CD player?
Who did you ~~used~~ *use* to play computer games with?

B Study 1–6 in **A** and **Common mistakes** and complete the grammar box.

> **1** Complete a and b with simple past (SP), *used to* (U), or both (B).
>   a To describe repeated past habits, facts, and states, you can use _____ .
>   b To describe actions that happened once, you can only use _____ .
> **2** Circle the correct options to complete the rule.
>   *Where did you use to study English before?*
>   *Just on my own. I didn't use to go to classes.*
>   Form questions and negatives using the auxiliary **did(n't) / do(n't)** + **use to / used to**.
>
> ➡ **Grammar 4A** p. 144

C Study 1–6 and, if possible, rephrase the underlined words using *used to*.
 1 When I was hungry, I <u>ate</u> the fish food flakes. I <u>loved</u> fish food.
 2 One day, she <u>told</u> everyone.
 3 On my sixth birthday, I <u>decided</u> to adopt her name. Then I <u>got</u> tired of Adele, so I <u>chose</u> a different name.
 4 <u>One of my favorite things to do was open</u> Alfredo's mouth and pull his tongue out. <u>Did he like that</u>? Well, every time he saw me, he <u>ran</u> to my mother's bedroom.
 5 When I was a teenager, I <u>didn't like</u> school.
 6 I <u>couldn't</u> move my left leg. They <u>took</u> me to the hospital immediately.

D In pairs, using only pictures 1–4 in **1A**, take turns retelling the stories.

> *When this horrible child was two, he used to pull the dog's tongue.*

E In pairs, look back at the photos on p. 44 and ask and answer questions with *used to*. How many things do you have in common?

> *Did you use to make fun of other kids?*   *Oh yeah. I used to call my brother Bart Simpson.*

F **Make it personal**   **Childhood memories!** Read the speech bubbles, then in pairs:
 A: Draw a memory about something you used to do when you were young.
 B: Try to guess **A**'s memory while she / he's drawing.
 A: Respond with *Yes* or *No* until **B** guesses correctly. Mime or give clues if **B** can't guess. Change roles.

> *Mmm … maybe you used to listen to music walking to school.*   *No!*
>
> *OK, but did you use to listen to music when you exercised?*   *Yes. Here's a clue – we used to have a pet.*
>
> *Did you use to listen to music when you walked the dog?*   *Yes!*

47

4.3 Has your taste in music changed?

1 Listening

A In pairs, answer survey questions 1–6. Are your answers similar?

I never listen to CDs. I usually stream music, but I download things that I love.

Neither of us listens to CDs. We both prefer downloading music.

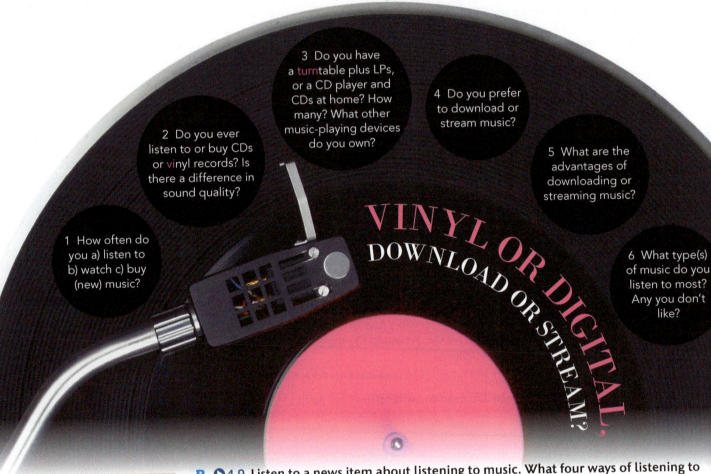

VINYL OR DIGITAL. DOWNLOAD OR STREAM?

1 How often do you a) listen to b) watch c) buy (new) music?
2 Do you ever listen to or buy CDs or **vinyl** records? Is there a difference in sound quality?
3 Do you have a **turn**table plus LPs, or a CD player and CDs at home? How many? What other music-playing devices do you own?
4 Do you prefer to download or stream music?
5 What are the advantages of downloading or streaming music?
6 What type(s) of music do you listen to most? Any you don't like?

Common mistakes

I don't have the same taste like my parents.
as

B ▶ 4.9 Listen to a news item about listening to music. What four ways of listening to music are mentioned?

C ▶ 4.9 Circle the correct options in 1–6. Listen again to check.
1 The program associates vinyl records with the '50s / '60s–'70s / '80s.
2 Young people today think records are **boring / cool / weird**.
3 Jack Lowenstein prefers to listen to **CDs / MP3s / records**.
4 Sarah Griffith is buying more **punk / rock / pop** records.
5 In the early 2000s, most people used to **buy CDs / buy vinyl / download**.
6 The most important revolution in music is **stream**ing / vinyl LPs / digital **for**mats.

D 🎤 **Make it personal** Take turns role-playing an interview with your parents or an older family member. Are the types of music they're into and their habits very different from yours? Why (not)?

A: You're the interviewee. Choose to be someone you know well.
B: Ask questions 1–6 in **A**, and follow-up questions.

I usually stream music, but my parents have CDs or they download. They like rap and dance music, but I like contemporary pop.

48

2 Reading

A ▶ 4.10 Read tweets 1–8 and choose the correct **hash**tag for each. Listen to check.

a #love2download   b #streaming4ever   c #cantbeatCDs   d #vinylisthebest

1 Peter Ince @Pince • 3m
Vinyl is back. I can see why – LPs are more au**then**tic – you can hear everything – even the mistakes! Digital songs don't sound as good as LPs.

2 Claire Sayer @SayClare • 15m
My parents have thousands of CDs. They're more expensive and not as cool as new music! As soon as it comes out I love to have the newest music on my phone.

3 Sam Same @Ssame • 17m
I used to like to sit in front of the turntable for hours and watch the LP go around – it's more relaxing than just listening. I love old music and I love to hear how it was played originally. And the covers are works of art!

4 NicoleMcArthur @DrNic • 36m
The quality is better, without a doubt! And no need to pay for a streaming service when you can download the music.

5 Candy @Candy1256 • 41m
Digital music is the best – the sound is crisp and clear – with a good quality **ste**reo you can't beat a **com**pact disc – and they're prettier than LPs!

6 Luke Johnson @JustLuke12 • 50m
Why would you want to buy music when you can just "rent" it? I stream any music I want at any time using a cheap streaming service – it's much more practical and eco**log**ical in every way.

7 James Marshall @jamesmarshall • 53m
I love collecting music – how can you collect something that you are just borrowing? Give me something I can hold in my hand – in a digital format that I can put on my shelf and play whenever I want to.

8 Syreeta Singh @SySings • 57m
Downloading music is as ridiculous as buying CDs and records. I just want to hear the music I want when I'm in the mood and when it's new. The best way to do that is to use an online service.

♪ *Have your friends collect your records and then change your number, I guess that I don't need that though, Now you're just somebody that I used to know* 4.3

B Reread, then match a–h to 1–8 in **A**. Cross (✗) those you disagree with.
a doesn't want to pay for a streaming service
b doesn't want to own or collect music
c likes to collect music
d likes to hear musicians make mistakes
e thinks CDs have the best quality
f says that streaming is better for the environment
g thinks watching LPs improves the experience of listening
h thinks CDs cost a lot of money

In groups of three, talk about opinions a–h in **B**. Which ones do you disagree with? Which one is closest to your opinion?

I don't agree that LPs sound better than digital songs.

🎤 **Make it personal** Write a tweet giving your opinion. Share it with the class. Choose the best hashtag for each one.

In my opinion, CDs are the highest quality music.   *The best hashtag for that is " #cantbeatCDs."*

49

4.4 Do you speak English as often as possible?

1 Grammar Comparatives and superlatives, as ... as

A ▶ 4.11 Listen and write six phrases from the tweets on p. 49. Compare in pairs. Which are comparatives and which are superlatives? How do you pronounce the -est ending? Listen again to check.

B Complete the grammar box. Which group, A–D, is most similar in your language?

1 Complete the chart.

Type	Adjective	Comparative	Superlative
A	big	_____	the biggest
	fast	faster	_____
B	ugly	_____	_____ ugl_____
	crazy	crazier	_____ craz_____
C	expensive	_____	the _____ expensive
	practical	more practical	_____
D	good	_____	_____ best
	bad	worse	_____

(not) as ... as ...

2 Choose the best meaning for a and b.
   a Downloading music is **as ridiculous as** buying CDs and records.
      Only downloading is ridiculous. / Only buying is ridiculous. / Both are ridiculous.
   b Digital songs **don't** sound **as good as** old LPs.
      Digital songs sound better. / Digital songs sound worse.

→ Grammar 4B p.144

Common mistakes

~~Cats are smaller than dogs.~~
~~A cat is more small than a dog.~~
              highest
Everest is the ~~most high~~
mountain ~~of~~ the world.
          in
            as
I'm not as big ~~like~~ my brother.

C Classify adjectives 1–14 by their type, A–D, in **A**. Then test a partner.

1 cheap	5 exciting	9 pretty	13 thin
2 complicated	6 funny	10 rich	14 light
3 convenient	7 heavy	11 sleepy	
4 easy	8 nice	12 small	

D In pairs. How many different ways can you compare 1–3? You have one minute for each.

1 a tablet / a laptop   2 your country / the U.S.   3 your language / English / Chinese

OK, let's think. A tablet is not as big as laptop.   *A laptop is more useful than a tablet. That's two.*

But I think a tablet is as useful as a laptop, so that's three.

The guy on the left looks funnier than the one on the right.

E Do you recognize the actors? Use the adjectives to compare the actors and the cars.

funny
tall
good-looking
successful
young

good
modern
fast
expensive
damaged

F ▶ 4.12 Listen to 10 examples. How many are the same as yours in **E**?

♪ Makes me that much stronger, Makes me work a little bit harder, It makes me that much wiser, So thanks for making me a Fighter

4.4

G 🎤 **Make it personal** Play *Who? What? Where?*
1 Write answers for a–d on separate pieces of paper.
   a two cities or places in your country?
   b two electrical items?
   c three celebrities?
   d three common objects?
2 In groups of three, put all your answers on the table.
3 Take turns comparing two or more of the items without saying the answers. Who can guess correctly which items are being compared the fastest?

It's smaller, but I think it's more interesting than this other one.   *Temuco and Santiago?*

Not Temuco. It's nearer to the coast.   *Valparaíso and Santiago?*

Correct!

② Listening

A ▶ 4.13 Listen to Jason interviewing his grandmother. Then match 1–6 to a–f to make phrases. Listen again to check.

1 get	a dating / learning English / eating healthier food
2 start	b your first pet / job / phone
3 learn to	c the Internet / apps / VR goggles
4 go on	d driving lessons / evening classes / exams
5 take	e a trip alone / a boat / a date
6 use	f ride a bike / swim / get dressed by yourself

B ▶ 4.13 True (T) or False (F)? Listen to check. What else did you pick up?
1 Grandma was more social as a child.
2 Benji was a little duck.
3 Her father was more patient than her mother.
4 She used to go dancing frequently.
5 She got better at Spanish during her trip to Mexico.
6 She was 15 when she took her driving test.
7 She used the Internet before she started her master's.

C ▶ 4.14 Ask Jason's questions using the verbs in **A**. Listen to check. Notice which words are stressed and the pronunciation of "did you".

D 🎤 **Make it personal** Do you remember the first time? In pairs, interview your partner using the ideas in **A**. How similar / different are your experiences? Any surprises?

When did you get your first pet?

When I was about six. We got a parrot called Lola.

I wanted to get a pet, but I couldn't because my dad is allergic.

⏵ **Common mistakes**

How ~~many years did you have~~ old were you when you first rode on a motorbike?

51

4.5 How many pets have you had?

🆔 Skills Understanding an anecdote

A Read the story as fast as you can and match pictures 1–6 to paragraphs a–f. Then identify the **bold** words / phrases in the pictures.

Weird Sophie

a ☐ The only pet I've ever had was a neurotic cat named Sophie. When Sophie was still a **kitten**, she accidentally drank half a bottle of detergent. Mom and I were worried, of course, so we took her to the **vet** immediately. Sophie didn't die, but she started to behave very strangely after that.

b ☐ For a long time, I was reluctant to let Sophie leave the house, (1)_____ I knew I couldn't keep her inside forever. One day, when she was an adult, I finally decided that it was time for her to be brave and explore the outside world, (2)_____ I opened the front door.

c ☐ Sophie took a few steps and then completely lost her mind. She had never felt grass, (3)_____ she didn't know what to do. She started to jump up and down like crazy and wouldn't stop. Sophie only ran back to the house when she heard Toby's **bark**. Toby was only a small, four–month old **puppy**, (4)_____ Sophie was terrified of him. Yes, my cat was afraid of a baby poodle.

d ☐ Sophie used to sleep in the sink from time to time, (5)_____ , for some mysterious reason, she never noticed when the water was running. One night, I was getting ready to go to bed and went to the other room to answer the phone. When I came back a few minutes later, Sophie was sub**merged** in the sink, **hyp**notized. Cats are supposed to be afraid of water, right? Not Sophie.

e ☐ She also loved to sleep in the washing machine, especially if there were dirty towels inside. One day, Mom didn't know she was there, (6)_____ she almost closed the door and turned on the machine. That was Sophie's second near-death experience.

f ☐ As time progressed, Sophie started to believe that she was a guard dog. She used to follow strangers around the house and **make weird noises**. Trouble is, she couldn't always differentiate between strangers and her owner, (7)_____ she used to **bite** and scratch everyone – including me. Sophie died at the age of 21. Can you believe it? I wonder how she's doing in Cat Heaven. She was a weird, weird cat, (8)_____ she was the only true friend I had during my entire adolescence.

The kitten is the baby cat in picture 4.

B ▶ 4.15 Study the use of *so* and *but* in paragraph 1 and complete the rules. Then complete paragraphs 2–6 with *so* or *but*. Listen, check, and repeat the pink-stressed words.

Use _____ for consequences.
Use _____ for contrast.

C In pairs. Cover the text and uncover a line at a time. Guess the next word(s), uncover, and check. How many did you get right?

D 🎤 **Make it personal** In groups, share stories about pets you and your friends have had. Choose your favorite. Use these ideas:

kind of pet?   he or she?   name?   color?   intelligent?   friendly?
noisy?   aggressive?   weird?   "almost human?"   favorite moment?

⚠️ **Common mistakes**
He died at the ~~12 years~~. *age of 12*

We had a cat when I was a kid. I remember it used to eat grass.   *Was it a he or a she?*   *A she. She was called Cupcake*

52

4.5 Have you thought about moving abroad?

in Action Making recommendations

A ▶ 4.16 Roy and Brenda are at an animal shelter, looking for a pet. Listen and answer 1–3.
1. Who's more reluctant to adopt a pet? Why?
2. What pet does the owner of the shelter recommend initially?
3. What pet does the man want for his daughter?

B ▶ 4.17 Listen to the rest. True (T) or False (F)? Do you empathize more with him or her?
1. Brenda probably prefers cats to dogs.
2. Poodles bark more than Labradors.
3. Roy and Brenda like the idea of having a house rabbit.

C ▶ 4.16 & 4.17 Complete 1–4 with *get* or *getting*. Listen again to check and circle the correct option to complete the rule.
1. You should definitely _____ her a pet.
2. Have you considered _____ a cat?
3. Why don't you _____ a dog that's easy to train?
4. Have you thought about _____ a house rabbit?

Use *to + infinitive* / *verb + -ing* after prepositions and certain verbs (*enjoy, consider, keep, mind, finish*).

D ▶ 4.18 Listen and notice the stressed words. Listen again and repeat. Then, complete the rules with *usually* and *rarely*.

Words that carry the message, like nouns, adjectives, and verbs, are _____ stressed.
Grammar words, like articles, prepositions, and auxiliary verbs, are _____ stressed.

E Complete the email with the correct form of the words and circle *make* or *do*.

> To: **Martin**
> Subject: Re: Hello from London
> Today at 09:05
> All Mail
>
> Hi Martin
>
> Sorry to hear you _____ _____ (**feel**) a bit lonely in London! Not really surprising in such a big city. It can be difficult to **make** / **do** friends in a new city. You need to **make** / **do** something positive fast. You should think about _____ (**contact**) Valentin or Sally. Valentin lives _____ (**close**) to you than Sally, but Sally's _____ (**sociable**) than Valentin. Or _____ you _____ (**think**) about _____ (**join**) a club or evening class? Why _____ you _____ (**learn**) French? 😊 You should think about _____ (**visit**) me in Paris! That would definitely **make** / **do** you feel much _____ (**good**). You might even _____ (**move**) here instead!
> Call me soon. I miss your voice. Lots of love Sophie xx

F 🔵 **Make it personal** Recommendations! In pairs, role-play situations 1 and 2. Choose one to perform for another pair.

Why don't you …

Situation 1:
A: You need a new computer to download / watch movies and write short college papers.
B: Compare options (desktops, laptops, tablets …) and make a recommendation.

Situation 2:
B: You're under a lot of stress and you need to get away for a few days, alone.
A: Compare options (the beach / mountains, a spa / retreat …) and recommend somewhere.

Common mistakes

Have you thought about ~~to move~~ to another place?
moving

Jake should think about ~~to quit~~ his job.
quitting

I don't enjoy ~~to take~~ care of animals.
taking

And I don't mind bleeding, Any old time you keep me waiting, Oh, oh-oh I got a love that keeps me waiting, I'm a lonely boy, I'm a lonely boy

Writing 4 A social media post

 All we know is that we don't know, How it's gonna be, Please brother let it be, Life on the other hand, Won't make us understand, We're all part of the masterplan

A Read the two social media posts and answer 1–3.
1 What's Lucy's request?
2 What's Maya's recommendation? Do you agree?
3 Think of four positive and four negative aspects of working as a server.

B In which paragraphs a–e does Maya:
1 compare two different options? _____
2 suggest an option and discuss its pros and cons based on her own experience? _____
3 suggest a type of job and say why _____
4 make a recommendation? _____
5 talk about the pros and cons of a second option? _____

C Read **Write it right!**, then match the **bold** expressions in Maya's post to uses 1–5.
1 suggest an option
2 introduce a positive (pro)
3 introduce a negative (con)
4 add information
5 make a recommendation

> ✓ **Write it right!**
>
> Use linking expressions to compare options.
> **Introduce a pro:** *The good thing about … is, One advantage is*
> **Introduce a con:** *On the other hand, However*
> **Add another point:** *Another thing is, What's more*

D Complete the post with suitable expressions.

> ¹_____ a bar called Valiani. I used to work there. ²_____ Valiani is always busy, so you'll never get bored and the manager is nice. ³_____, the customers are really friendly and give good tips. ⁴_____, it's hard work and it can be tiring. ⁵_____, the hours are very long. ⁶_____ give them a call?

E Choose two restaurants or cafés you know in your city. List two pros and one con for working in each.

F 🎧 **Make it personal** Write a post in about 150 words replying to Lucy about working as a server in your city.

Before	Use your notes in **E**. Look back at the post in **A** and underline any words or phrases you want to use in your own post.
While	Follow the paragraph structure of the post in **B**. Include five paragraphs and use appropriate linking expressions.
After	Exchange posts with another student. Do you agree with their recommendations?

Hi Maya,
I'm moving to San José in the fall for my gap year to improve my English and volunteer at a charity for home**less** people. I need some part-time work to support myself there, but I don't know what kind of job would fit around my volunteer work. Can you help me with some ideas?
Thanks,
Lucy

Hi Lucy,

a **Have you thought about working** as a server in a restaurant? There are lots of restaurants and bars in the center of the city and they're always looking for new staff. They can usually offer flexible hours, so it's not difficult to fit the work around your studies.

b **One option is** a restaurant called La Cantina. I used to work there in the evenings and at weekends. **The good thing about** La Cantina is it's nearly always full and the work is fast-paced, so you never get bored. The customers are mostly young professionals and they usually give good tips. **Another thing is,** you get free food! **On the other hand,** when you're very busy, it can be stressful and tiring, especially if customers are rude.

c **An alternative is** Café Rio. It's more of a café bar that serves food. **One advantage is,** it's quieter, with a more relaxed atmosphere, so it's not as stressful as working at La Cantina. **What's more,** if you work late the manager gets you a taxi home. **However,** if you're not busy it can sometimes be boring, and the tips are not as good.

d Anyway, you need to decide what you really want from the job. Personally, I think La Cantina is a more en**joy**able place to work, but if you just want to earn money and have an easy time, Café Rio is probably the better option.

e **Why don't you** contact both of them and see what they say?
Good luck!
Maya

54

4 Animal instincts

 **Café**

1 Before watching

A 🔘 **Make it personal** In pairs, define *instinct*. Write an example sentence to illustrate its meaning. Which is the class favorite?

B Rate each job by level of stress, danger, and difficulty, 1–5. Compare and choose the most and least for each category.

Jobs	Stressful	Dangerous	Difficult
an animal trainer			
a cowboy			
an environmental scientist			
a pet shop owner			
a veterinarian			
a zookeeper			

C 🔘 **Make it personal** When you were a child, did you ever want to work with animals? Why (not)?

> When I was little, I used to want to be a …

> Really? That's cool. I wanted to be …

D Using A–C as clues, guess some of the phrases August and Daniel will say.

2 While watching

A In pairs, try to pronounce these words. Then watch to check. Did you guess correctly?

to consider   a gecko   a golden retriever
a labrador   a ranch   surprised   totally
a zebra

B In pairs, try to answer 1–7. Watch again to check.
1 Which five other animals do they mention?
2 Who gets lonely?
3 Whose dog was bigger than him?
4 Who loves big dogs?
5 Which animal was a) Hector b) Gordon c) Morris d) Bruno?
6 Who insists on one condition for getting another pet?
7 Who used to have lots of land before moving to Missouri?
8 Why do you think they choose to go to a shelter and not a pet store?

C Which animal(s) …
1 uses a litter box in their house?
2 lived a) in a big glass tank b) a long life c) outside? (4 answers)
3 was smart and fast but got sold?
4 was the best of its kind – ever?

3 After watching

A 🔘 **Make it personal** In pairs, remember all you can about Daniel and August: their pets, where they lived, and their old jobs. Are you like either of them? If so, how?

> Like Daniel, I used to own a rabbit.

B Check the correct situation for 1–9.

Jobs	Breaking the news	Reacting to news
1 Oh, it's so cool.		
2 That sounds amazing.		
3 You won't believe …		
4 Alright, check this out!		
5 Bummer!		
6 Tell me this is a joke.		
7 Does / Would that bother you?		
8 I'm totally OK with that.		
9 As long as (you clean the litterbox).		

C 🔘 **Make it personal** In pairs, compare pets you or someone you know used to have. What's the best / worst aspect of each one? Would you consider getting a pet now? If so, where from? Any surprises?

> I used to have a big dog but we moved to a smaller apartment. We had to find him a new home.

> What a shame! Did you think about replacing him?

55

R2 Grammar and vocabulary

A **Picture dictionary.** Cover the words on these pages and use the pictures to remember:

page	
32	7 travel words / expressions
39	6 sentences about Sam Same
40	10 adjectives to describe the hotels
44	9 words to describe children and childhood
50	5 comparisons about the actors / cars
52	Sophie's story
158	5 pairs of picture words for the 5 diphthongs

B Look at the chart in **2D** on p. 45. In pairs, take turns miming four *do / make* expressions for your partner to guess.

Are you making your bed?

C Read the product reviews of a new tablet and circle the correct tenses. Have you had any similar experiences with technology?

★★★★★ **Pure Perfection!**
I**'ve had / had** my iTab for two weeks and I absolutely love it. It's fast, practical, and not very expensive. Some people say the screen freezes, but that **hasn't happened / doesn't happen** to me yet. ⌄More

★★★☆☆ **It's just OK.**
I **have bought / bought** my iTab in April and it's an OK product – nothing out of this world. It has **never frozen / never freeze** or anything, but the battery doesn't last long and it's just too slow. ⌄More

★☆☆☆☆ **Worst tablet ever!**
My life **has been / was hell** since I bought this stupid machine. The iTab is the worst product I have **ever bought / ever buy**. Guess what, mine **has exploded / exploded** this morning! Can you believe it? The warranty has **already expired / already expires**, so now I don't know what to do. ⌄More

I've had my laptop for a year and it's been fantastic!

D 🔵 **Make it personal** Think of your favorite device. Complete 1–7 with the verbs. In pairs, ask and answer. Can you guess the device?

1. How long _____ this product _____ on the market? (**be**)
2. How long _____ you _____ it? (**have**)
3. Where _____ you _____ it? (**buy**)
4. _____ you _____ it yesterday? (**use**)
5. What _____ you _____ it for? (**use**)
6. _____ it ever _____ working? (**stop**)
7. _____ the product warranty _____ yet? (**expire**)

E 🔵 **Make it personal** In pairs, compare 1–6 using some of these adjectives or your own. Give reasons. How many can you agree on?

bad	difficult	easy	expensive	famous
good	healthy	modern	nice	
popular	practical	repetitive	talented	

1. English / Chinese / my first language
2. laptops / tablets / smart watches
3. Japanese / Italian / Mexican food

4. Jennifer Lawrence / Seth Rogan / Chris Pratt
5. Samsung / Apple / Huawei
6. rap / pop / rock

I think English is easier than Chinese.

Yeah, you're right. I think Chinese is the most difficult language to learn. And Spanish is the easiest for me!

F Correct the mistakes. Check your answers in units 3 and 4.

⚠️ **Common mistakes**

1. Maybe I'll stay home. It depends of the traffics. (2 mistakes)
2. My sister have never been to Australia. (1 mistake)
3. My son doesn't call me yet. (2 mistakes)
4. I study English during three years. (2 mistakes)
5. How long do they live in Brazil? (1 mistake)
6. David Bowie has died on 2016. (2 mistakes)
7. I learned how to drive when I had 18 years. (2 mistakes)
8. Did you watch a lot of TV when you was younger? (1 mistake)
9. I use to go to the beach on weekends. (1 mistake)
10. Tablets are more small than laptops. (1 mistake)

56

Skills practice

*'Cos baby, now we've got bad blood,
You know it used to be mad love,
So take a look what you've done*

R2

A ▶R2.1 Listen to six sentences from units 3 and 4. What does each person mean? Circle the correct options in 1–6.
1. I **know** / **am in** Australia.
2. We checked in **a few minutes** / **a long time** ago.
3. The weather is **the same** / **different**.
4. I **am** / **was** an au pair.
5. Digital songs sound **better** / **worse** than old LPs.
6. She **follows** / **followed** strangers around the house.

B ▶R2.1 Read AS R2.1 on p. 167. Listen again and repeat each sentence. Pay attention to the <u>connections</u>.

C ▶R2.2 Read the survey question, then listen and number the sentences, 1–4. There's one extra sentence.

Which sentence best describes your childhood?

> Dad, I wasn't kicking him!

> I'm going to wash your mouth out with soap!

> It wasn't my fault!

> Hey, I was watching that!

> Good night, God bless.

Write two sentences that best describe your childhood. Share them in pairs and try to guess the details.

Hmm ... let's see. I think you used to be a very shy child and ...

E ▶R2.3 Read the travel article and cross out two sentences that shouldn't be there. Listen to check and repeat the **bold** words.

4 Travel Tips
to help you eliminate travel stress

A good vacation is a break from real life, but sometimes vacations can be extremely stressful. Here are some hot ways to help **keep you cool** when traveling:

1. Re**du**cing stress starts before you leave home. Try to book direct flights so that you can e**s**cape those awful connections. By doing that, you can **avoid** long **lay**overs, missed connections, or the worst problem: canceled flights.
2. Traveling can be stressful on any day, but Mondays and Fridays are a nightmare, especially between 7 and 9 a.m. and 4 and 7 p.m. Friday is actually my favorite day of the week. So do yourself a favor and don't travel then. Period.
3. Bad things are going to happen when you travel, so don't try to control everything. If you're angry, try to **lose** your anger in a calm way. Drink a cup of tea, practice deep breathing, or, if you can, try to find some humor in the situation.
4. Give yourself **plenty of** time for things right from the start: taking a **cab** to the airport, checking in at the airport, boarding your flight, renting a car, and finally checking in at your hotel. Remember you can book online. Remember: the less you **rush**, the less stressful your vacation will be.

F Match the bold words in E to meanings 1–6.
1. stay calm
2. lots of
3. do things quickly
4. eliminate
5. stops between two flights
6. taxi

G **Mini role-play. A:** It's Christmas Eve. You're having lots of problems at the bus station. You're afraid you won't make it to your parents' house. **B:** You're A's mom / dad. Ask for details and try to help.
Use at least two of these phrases:
What do you mean ... ?
Wait a second. Did I hear you say that ...?
You should definitely ... Have you thought about ...?

H ▶R2.4 🎧 **Make it personal** Question time!
1. Listen to the 12 lesson titles in units 3 and 4.
2. In pairs, practice asking and answering. Use the book map on p. 2–3. Ask at least two follow-up questions. Try to answer in different ways. Can you have a short conversation about all the questions?

How often do you travel?

When I take a vacation, one or two times a year.

Do you enjoy traveling alone?

5.1 What would you like to study?

1 Vocabulary and pronunciation
School subjects

A ▶5.1 Read pronunciation rule 1, and try to pronounce the nine school subjects. Listen to the first part of the ad for Marlbury College to check. Then match the subjects to icons a–i.

---

1. The suffix *-ology* means "the study of," e.g. *technology*, *ecology*. The stress is on the third syllable from the end (●●●●).

   biology   geography
   history   psychology /saɪˈkɒlədʒi/
   philosophy   languages
   sociology   chemistry /ˈkɛməstri/
   politics

2. Another common suffix is *-ics*: *ethics*, *statistics*. The stress is on the second syllable from the end (●●●●).

   economics   physics
   business /ˈbɪznəs/
   math(ematics)   engineering
   computer systems

3. Romance language speakers sometimes find these school subjects hard to pronounce:

   art /ɑrt/
   (rhymes with *heart*, *smart*)
   law /lɔ/
   (rhymes with *draw*, *saw*)
   literature /ˈlɪtərətʃər/
   (rhymes with *signature*, *adventure*)

What's this school subject in English?

B ▶5.2 Read rules 2 and 3, and try to pronounce the nine school subjects. Listen to part 2 of the ad to check. Then match the subjects to icons j–r.

C Test a partner using the icons.

D Put the subjects into the categories in the chart. Compare in groups. Do you all agree? Which subject(s) could be in more than one category?

Arts	Sciences	Social sciences	Others

E ▶5.3 Listen to final part of the the ad and check the items you hear. Which item doesn't the college have?

Numbers, letters, learn to spell
Nouns, and books, and show and tell
Playtime, we will throw the ball
Back to class, through the hall

5.1

an attractive campus	babysitting facilities	bachelor's degrees (BA, BS)
evening classes	free public lectures	good teachers and administrators
master's degrees (MS, MA)	modern facilities	online classes
vocational education		

> **Common mistakes**
> I have a bachelor's degree in history.
> Our professor gave an excellent conference on human rights.
>   lecture

F ▶5.3 Listen again and circle the best answers. What else did you hear?
1. You can get a catalog **by phone / online / in person**.
2. There **'s only one / are two / are many** professional qualification(s).
3. You **have to / don't need to / should** go to a classroom.
4. **All / Some / A lot of** classes are in the evening.
5. **The best classes / All the classes / Some classes** are free if you're not a student.

G 🔵 **Make it personal** Imagine you're choosing a major at Marlbury College. Which factors in **E** are most important and not important for you? In pairs, explain why.

> The two most important for me are good teachers and modern facilities, because I want the best education. Evening classes aren't important for me.

> Evening classes and babysitting facilities are most important to me! I have a young son and I work during the day.

② Listening

A ▶5.4 ▶ In pairs, listen to / watch this student. **A:** answer question 1. **B:** answer question 2. Share your answers, change roles, watch, and share again.
1. What did you learn about her and her personal life?
2. What did you learn about her university life and career plans?

B ▶5.4 ▶ Listen / Watch again and order Zena's words, 1–9.

20 ☐	England ☐	Olympic Village ☐
Brighton ☐	London ☐	Queen Mary University ☐
British ☐	Marshall ☐	south coast ☐

C ▶5.4 ▶ Listen again. Are 1–8 True (T) or False (F)? Correct the false ones.
1. Zena chose European Literature because she loves reading and writing.
2. She goes home to get her washing done and sleep.
3. It's one of two London universities with a campus.
4. It's very cosmopolitan and people are friendly.
5. Her boyfriend's French and he's called Didier.
6. She sometimes finds her major a bit boring.
7. The teachers can be strict, and are often difficult.
8. After university, she'd like to do one of three jobs.

> **Common mistakes**
>   on
> Lima is in the coast.

D 🔵 **Make it personal** Life choices.
1. In pairs, find out:
   • why your partner chose her or his school / university / current job;
   • the positive and negative aspects;
   • any future plans.
2. Make a simple video like Zena's to introduce yourself, your school or workplace, and any career plans.

> Why did you choose to study at this school?

> Because it's close to home and it has a great reputation. And you?

59

5.2 What do you have to do tonight?

1 Vocabulary Class activities

A ▶5.5 Match classroom activities 1–10 to examples a–j. Listen to 10 extracts to check.

1. an exam
2. an exercise
3. a group work activity
4. online practice / research
5. a journal entry
6. a pair work activity
7. student presentations
8. a project
9. a test
10. a summary

a In your journal, write or record an audio about how you felt about class today. What were the things you understood? Write a question that you have for next class.

b In a group of four, discuss the movie extract that we watched and find two things that you liked about it and two things you didn't like.

c You have two minutes to write the past tense of these verbs. Then hand your answers to me.

d You have ONE HOUR. Answer three out of five questions. You should spend about 20 minutes on each question.

e Use PowerPoint to present your family to the class.

f Write a one-paragraph summary of the last chapter of the book.

g Talk about your plans for the weekend. Ask your partner what she or he is going to do. Then answer your partner's questions.

h Complete these sentences with an appropriate word from the list below. Then listen to check.

i Search online for a song line that you like featuring the words "used to." Bring a recording of it to the next class.

j Houses: We'll look at the construction of houses in different parts of the world and we'll consider the materials used and why.

B Which of the activities in A do you have in:
1. your English classes?
2. any other classes you take?

In English class, we have pair work and group work activities. But we don't have these in my economics class.

C 👤 **Make it personal** Which activities in A do / did you:
1. find useful? 2. hate? 3. love?

I hated taking exams in college. It was so boring.

2 Which homework activities do you find most useful for learning English?

I enjoy looking for examples of grammar in songs.

I enjoy watching clips from movies, first with subtitles, then withou[t]

60

2 Grammar Obligation and prohibition

🎵 *Will we ever learn? We've been here before, It's just what we know, Stop your crying, baby, It's a sign of the times, We gotta get away*

5.2

A ▶5.6 **Listen to two students and answer 1–3.**
1. How many obligations do they discuss?
2. What are they?
3. Who's the better student, Mark or Candy?

B ▶5.6 **Listen again and complete Mark's notes for a friend.**

> Ms. Cosby's class:
> You've _____ come to every class.
> You _____ write a paper for _____.
> You _____ arrive late.
> You _____ take notes. It's all _____.

C Complete the grammar box with the verbs from B.

Obligation
Use _____ or _____ for obligations.
I've got to or *I gotta* is more informal.

Prohibition
Use _____ for prohibition. (This means it is not permitted.)

No obligation
Use _____ when you can do something if you want, but it's not essential.

→ **Grammar 5A** p. 146

Common mistakes
doesn't have
He ~~hasn't~~ to work today.
do
You can't ~~doing~~ that here!
We gotta ~~to~~ go now.

D ▶5.7 **Circle the correct options in the dialogue. Listen to check.**

Mark: What are you doing tonight?
Candy: **I've got to / I got to** study, because I have a test tomorrow.
Mark: Another one! That's too bad! Do you **have got / have** to study on Saturday too?
Candy: Uh, I **can't / don't have** to study on Saturday, but I want to, because I really need to get good grades this time. Why?
Mark: Well, I wanted to invite you to a party on Saturday. Should be a good one!
Candy: Oh! Well, my mom gets worried so I **have to / can't** stay out later than 12, but I could go for a while. But **you'll have to / won't have to** ask my mom, and persuade her.
Mark: OK, pass me over. Hello, Mrs. McCormack. This is Mark.
Mrs. M.: Hello, Mark. Busy studying?
Mark: Yes, you know me! Er, can Candy come to a party with me on Saturday?
Mrs. M.: Sure, but she **doesn't have to / has to** be home by 12, please. I really worry if she stays out too late.
Mark: Not a problem, Mrs. McCormack. I **have to / can't** drive my dad's car after 11, so I have to be home by then, anyway.

🟢 **Make it personal** What are "the rules" where you live?
1. List five things you have to do and five things you (or others you live with) can't do.
2. Compare in groups. Which "rules" are the most restrictive? Who has the easiest and most difficult time?

> *I have to tell my mom when I'm going to be late, and I can't borrow the car if she needs it.*

> *Well, I've got to pay all the bills and do all the shopping. I can't leave my kids alone at home.*

> *My son can't use his PS4 during the week, only at weekends. He hates it!*

5.3 Are you a good student?

1 Reading

A Read the college handout and match summaries 1–8 to the eight students.
1 Ask a classmate to summarize if you can't go to a class.
2 You need to study regularly and frequently.
3 You can't prepare for an exam in one night.
4 You shouldn't be timid or quiet if things are hard to understand.
5 It's important to be punctual and look interested.
6 You should be interested in what you study.
7 Make sure you're familiar with all the course program.
8 Teachers like students who prepare for class and get involved.

> **Common mistakes**
> attend / come to
> I can't ~~assist to~~ class tomorrow.
> miss
> I'm going to ~~lose~~ the next class.

Streetway College
How to pass a college class – here's what our students say

"Take classes because you want to, not because you have to. You have to attend a lot of classes, so it's much better if you like the subject!" *Katia Browning*

"Be on time and pay attention – that's really important! Your teacher will notice if you're always late or day-dreaming." *Jerome Manzanillo*

"Ask questions when something isn't clear. Your instructor is there to help, so don't be shy about asking questions in class." *Charles Murphy*

"You don't have to participate if you don't want to, but your teacher will notice you if you do volunteer or ask questions, and you're prepared. Research the next lesson – or at least take a look at it – before class starts." *Natalie Krazinski*

"You have to read the syllabus. This is the most important document you'll receive from your professor." *George Smith*

"You have to find time every day to study. A little and often is the best way. You don't have to study at the same time every day, but you can't leave it until half an hour before class." *Muhammed Burton*

"If you miss a class, the easiest way to find out what you missed and catch up is to talk to someone who's also in that class." *Konstantina Spanos*

"If you know you have to do an assignment, start working on it early. If you know you have a test, prepare for it early. You can't learn everything the night before an exam." *Charlotte Spalding*

B ▶ 5.8 Listen to and reread the handout, and circle the four most important tips for you. In pairs, compare. Can you agree which two are the most important?

> I can't choose between these two.
> Which ones?

C 🗣 **Make it personal** List five tips for a new student at your English school. Read them out. Score a point for each original tip. How many points did you score?

> Don't worry about making mistakes. Fluency is more important than mistakes and you have to make mistakes to learn!

> Listen to some English every day.

62

2 Grammar *too / enough, too much / too many*

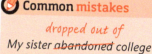

🎵 *I'm not too shy to show I love you, I got no regrets. I love you much too much to hide you, this love ain't finished yet. So, baby, whenever you're ready, When you're ready come and get it, Na na na na*

5.3

A ▶5.9 Why do people drop out of school? Listen and match ex-students' answers 1–4 to photos a–d.

⚠️ **Common mistakes**
dropped out of
My sister ~~abandoned~~ college at ~~the~~ 17 ~~years~~.

 a ☐  b ☐  c ☐ 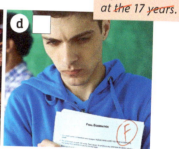 d ☐

B ▶5.9 In pairs, listen again for three phrases in each answer using *too* and *enough*. Pause after each answer to write the phrases.

C Study the nine phrases in **B** in AS 5.9 on p. 168 and complete the rules with *before, after, many, more, much*.

1. *Enough* means "sufficient" and goes _____ an adjective but _____ a noun.

   too + adjective = _____ than necessary: *This room's too hot.*
2. Use *too* + _____ for U nouns.
3. Use *too* + _____ for C nouns.

→ **Grammar 5B** p. 146

⚠️ **Common mistakes**
a lot of
I have ~~too many~~ friends.
enough
I'm not ~~enough~~ tall to reach the clock.

The first one is definitely work – unfortunately we don't get a salary for going to school!

D Complete the article with *too* or *enough*. Do the reasons refer to school (S), work (W), or both (B)?

Why do people quit?

The top 10 reasons why people drop out of school or quit their jobs.

a Their salaries aren't high *enough*.
b They don't have good communication or a strong _____ relationship with the boss.
c They don't have _____ money to continue what they're doing.
d Their workload is _____ heavy.
e They want better benefits like health insurance.
f They feel _____ isolated and homesick.
g They don't have _____ self-discipline.
h They have _____ many personal problems.
i They're not happy with the workplace.
j They're not interested _____ in what they're doing.

▶5.10 Listen to the conversation and order the reasons in D 1–5 for quitting a job (W) and 1–5 for dropping out of school (S).

🔵 **Make it personal** In groups of three, compare people you know who quit a job or dropped out of school. Was it for one of the reasons in D? Do your stories have happy endings?

A friend of mine dropped out of school last year because he really missed his family. He used to drive 200 kilometers every weekend to see them, so he never had enough time to study.

So did he go to a different school or get a job?

He got a great job near home!

63

5.4 What will you do when you pass this course?

1 Grammar Zero and first conditional

A ▶5.11 Listen to two conversations and complete emails 1 and 2.

1 To: **All managers**   Today at 10:23

Research shows that if employees _____ unhappy with their pay, they _____ the job well, or they find another job.
Note: We need to raise salaries. If we _____ more, our best employees _____.

2 To: **Heads of Department**   Today at 14:55

A recent study shows that if students _____ a lot of classes, they _____ of school.
Note: We need to check on our students who miss a lot of classes. If they _____ a lot of classes, they _____ of college.

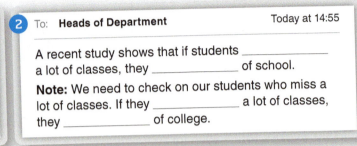

Common mistakes
If I ~~will~~ go on vacation, I'll buy you a souvenir.

B Read about conditional tenses, then complete the rules in the grammar box.

If is one of the most common words in English because it's used to express conditions.
  Zero = *If you don't have photo ID, you can't fly.*
  First = *If we leave now, we'll arrive on time.*
Zero conditionals are generalizations. The speaker thinks it's a fact.
First conditionals refer to a specific future event that is probable or certain.
Both conditionals are formed and used in the same way as in Romance languauges.

Zero conditional
If you play sports, you meet athletic people.
If clause = _____ tense, result clause = _____ tense.

First conditional
If you play soccer tomorrow, you won't meet my best friend.
If clause = _____ tense, result clause = _____ tense.

You can invert the clauses without changing the meaning. When the *if* clause comes first, use a comma and rising intonation to indicate that there is more to come.

➡ **Grammar 5C** p.146

If you can't laugh at yourself, no problem. I'll laught at you! That's what friends are for.

C Match the sentence halves. Do the sentences refer to general or specific situations? Write zero conditional (Z) or first conditional (F) for each sentence.

How to stay friends

Why do friends stop being friends? Here's our top advice to stay friends.

1 If you have things in common
2 You'll find it difficult to be friends
3 People stop being friends
4 If your friend complains a lot
5 Friends stay together
6 If your best friend gets married

a if they laugh a lot together.
b you'll find it difficult to stay friends.
c you have a lot of things to talk about.
d if you have different priorities.
e you won't want to see that friend.
f if they have a big fight.

D 🟢 **Make it personal** Do you agree with 1–6 in **C**? Give your own examples.

I don't agree with 6. My best friend got married and we still talk all the time.

64

❷ Reading

*We've got to hold on to what we've got,
'Cause it doesn't make a difference if we make it or not,
We've got each other and that's a lot for love
We'll give it a shot, We're half way there, Livin' on a prayer.*

5.4

A Read the brochure and match headings a–f to paragraphs 1–6.
a Make work important
b Show interest and appreciation
c Be a good example
d Help careers grow
e Ask questions
f Give people a chance to grow

Are you worried about losing your best employees?

Here are six key ways to keep your most talented people.

1 ☐ Take an interest in each person who works for you. If you show that you are really interested in the people who work with you, they will be less inclined to leave.

2 ☐ People need to understand the connection between what they do and how it affects other people at the company and in the world. Employees will stay if they see that what they do makes a difference.

3 ☐ Ask what people like about the job and ask what they need. If you ask people what they need to stay, they will tell you.

4 ☐ Give people tasks that are not too easy for them to do. Your best people will get bored if you don't challenge them.

5 ☐ Talk to your employees about their aspirations and what skills they will need in their careers. If you are clear about what employees need to do to advance, this will encourage them to stay.

6 ☐ Remember that your employees evaluate you and what you do as the person in charge. Your employees will be comfortable, honest, and open if you are too.

B ▶5.12 Listen, reread, and match the highlighted words in **A** to their meanings.
1 employees   a naturally good at something
2 talented   b judge
3 tasks   c people paid to do a job
4 challenge   d give them a chance to test themselves
5 evaluate   e jobs or activities

C Do 1–6 encourage you to stay (S) at your job or leave (L)? In pairs, say why.
1 "What's your name again? I don't think I know you. Have we met before?"
2 "What you do will really help other people and make their lives easier."
3 "How are you feeling today? Is there anything I can do to make you more comfortable?"
4 "I have something really easy for you to do. You don't have to think at all."
5 "I think there are a lot of opportunities for you in this company."
6 "I'm not going to tell you why I made that decision. You'll have to guess."

I won't stay in my job if the boss can't even remember my name!

D Think about the places where you work, study, or socialize. What are its good and bad points?

A bad point at my school is that classes are really big and it's difficult to ask questions.

That's a shame. At my job, my boss is very friendly and he talks to me every day.

At my gym, the manager is really aggressive and everybody is afraid of her.

🗣 Make it personal Think of two changes you could suggest to your boss, school principal, or the manager of a local business or club. Compare in groups. Who has the best suggestions?

The owner of our local soccer club doesn't invest enough. If he doesn't buy some new players, we'll get relegated.

5.5 How do you usually get in touch?

ID Skills Understanding references

My grandma always calls on the landline. She still doesn't know how to use a smartphone.

A Think about your family and friends. Who prefers communicating …
1 face-to-face?
2 by phone (audio)?
3 by video call?
4 by email?
5 by text or **in**stant **mes**senger?
6 by social media?

B Read Maria's blog and complete the chart. Do you agree with these generalizations?

Generation	Born	Prefer to communicate
Millenials	after 1980	1
2	1965–1980	3
Boomers	4	5

I don't know about you, but I come from a big Greek family and we all get together every weekend for lunch either at my grandparents' house or in a restaurant. But lately I've noticed a bit of **ten**sion between **us** (1). For example, my grandparents can't understand why their grandkids always have to have their phones next to **them** (2) when we eat. Why don't people talk to each other or just do one thing at a time? And when everyone has a phone, why don't people actually call **them** (3) anymore?

At the same time, my mom and dad don't understand why grandma doesn't want to use the smartphone **they**'ve (4) given her and continues to use her old one.

And … **I** (5) don't get why my younger sister and cousins don't reply to texts or emails. Why are **they** (6) so rude to their family, when they're talking to their friends all the time on social media?

Then last week at work, we had online training about communication across gene**ra**tions, and **it** (7) all seems to make a bit more sense now. **It** (8) said that one of the biggest differences is the way "mill**en**ials" (that's anybody born after about 1980, like my sister and cousins) see technology compared with previous generations. For **them** (9), **it** is totally normal and an essential part of their identity. **They** (10) auto**ma**tically use social media like Facebook and Instagram. Even Skype seems old-fashioned to them! That's why my sister won't put down her cell phone. It really seems like **it**'s (11) attached to her body! In the workplace, **they**'re (12) the ma**jor**ity now.

Then there's "Gen X"– the generation born between 1965 and 1980, like my parents. For **them** (13), technology is great for practical things like shopping, banking online, or making arrangements with friends. But **they** (14) don't message their friends just to chat or gossip as much as **we** (15) do. For **them** (16), email is the way to communicate, especially for anything important.

Finally, of course, there are much older people (like my grandparents, the so-called "**boom**ers", born before 1965), who prefer to talk on the phone or even meet in person.

So, now I think I know why we sometimes misunderstand each other. Millenials know how to get things done quickly, but older generations want to fo**cus** more on personal relationships.

What do **you** (17) think? Have you seen this in your family too? I'd love to hear your experiences.

C ▶5.13 Listen, reread, and say who or what the **bold** pronouns 1–17 refer to.

us¹ = all of Maria's family

D ▶5.14 Listen to Zack and Vicky at work. Which of them do you think is older? Why?

E ▶5.14 Listen again and complete Zack's email.

Hi all
Our next staff meeting will be on _____ at _____ a.m. in the conference _____.
Attached is the draft a**gen**da. Please send me any _____ for the agenda by the end of the day tomorrow.
See you there,
Zack

Common mistakes
Please see the documents ~~annexed~~.
attached

F 🗣 **Make it personal** In groups, compare your generation with the ones before and after it. What are the biggest differences?

My parents watch a lot more TV than I do.   *Yeah, we usually watch shows online.*

66

5.5 Do you often take risks?

 But I've got a blank space, baby, And I'll write your name, Boys only want love if it's torture Don't say I didn't say, I didn't warn ya

ID in Action Giving warnings and making promises

A Imagine what these people are saying. Write speech bubbles for each cartoon.

 a
 b
 c
 d

Common mistakes

Whatever
~~Do what~~ you do, don't do that!

B ▶ 5.15 Are 1–8 similar to your answers in **A**? Match two sentences to each picture in **A**. Listen to check. Which are warnings (W) and which are promises (P)?

1 Whatever you do, don't eat that ice cream. If you do, you'll have to go to your room!
2 I won't buy you a new bike if you don't get good grades. You'd better do your homework.
3 Watch out! If you're not careful, you'll fall in.
4 Be careful. If you don't improve your work, you'll be fired.
5 If you stay late, I'll give you the day off tomorrow.
6 If you help me get in, I'll row the boat.
7 If you eat all your dinner, I'll give you some ice cream.
8 If you finish your homework, I'll take you to the movies.

C Complete these expressions. Then make warnings and promises for pictures 1 and 2 using the expressions and your own ideas.

Warnings
Be _____!
Watch / Look _____!
Don't move!
You'd _____ (not) do that!
Whatever you do, don't (forget to) ...

Promises
If you (don't) ..., I'll ...
If you (don't) ..., I won't ...

D **Make it personal** Write captions for photos 1–3. Write a warning and a promise for each and share with the class. Which is the best caption?

The boy in picture 1 is probably saying, "If you sit, you'll get a treat."

67

Writing 5 A personal statement

You know that I could use somebody, Someone like you, and all you know, and how you speak

A Read Matt's statement and number questions a–c in the order he answers them, 1–3.
  a What do you want to study, and why? ☐
  b How would you describe yourself and your interests? ☐
  c What useful experience do you have? ☐

B Are 1–5 relevant (R) or not relevant (NR) to Matt's statement? Which paragraph, a–c, would you put the relevant sentences in?
  1 I worked in a hotel in France for three months.
  2 My parents were both teachers before they bought the hotel.
  3 I'm very good at playing video games.
  4 I like taking courses that are about physical health.
  5 I want to know more about sustainability.

C Read **Write it right!**, then do 1 and 2.
  1 Look at the highlighted expressions in Matt's statement and circle the six verb +-ing forms that follow them.
  2 Underline seven more -ing forms in the text. Which
    • two are adjectives?   • three follow a preposition?
    • two follow a verb?

> ✓ **Write it right!**
>
> To emphasize your abilities in a personal statement, use these expressions to add more information:
>   *along with, apart from, as well as, in addition to, on top of (that).*
> These expressions
>   • can be followed by a noun, a pronoun, or a verb in the *-ing* form.
>   • can come at the start or in the middle of a sentence, but *On top of that* usually comes only at the start.

D Rewrite 1–5 using the expressions in parentheses.
  1 I have a weekend job in a restaurant. I also deliver pizza. (**along with**)
  2 Ramona speaks Arabic and Russian. She is also fluent in Spanish. (**in addition to**)
  3 I enjoy running marathons. I also teach karate. (**apart from**)
  4 Alana works full-time. She also goes to college in the evenings. (**on top of**)
  5 I wrote a paper on ecotourism. I also gave a presentation. (**as well as**)

E 🎤 **Make it personal** Write a personal statement in 150–200 words to apply for a course you'd like to study.

Before	Brainstorm your positive qualities, relevant interests and experience, and the reasons you'd like to take the course.
While	Write your statement in three paragraphs that answer questions 1–3 in **A**. Use a polite, formal tone and include the five expressions from **Write it right!**
After	Exchange statements with two other students. Would you give them both a place on the course?

Personal statement: Matt Harper

a I'm a serious and hardworking person with an inquiring mind. I enjoy reading and learning about other cultures, as well as learning languages – I speak French, German, and Spanish. I'm also extremely sociable and I'm interested in meeting people from other countries.

b My family own a hotel and I have a lot of experience in many different roles. In addition to working in the kitchen and being a server, I have also been a receptionist and night manager. On top of that, I'm fascinated to see how hotels operate in other places. Apart from doing research into the industry, I have learned a lot about running a sustainable business. I'm passionate about conservation in tourism, along with providing top-quality food and accommodation.

c I want to study for a Master's in Sustainable Tourism Management, as well as working part-time in my family's business. I believe in developing my knowledge of the hospitality business and my ambition is to manage my own eco-hotel. This course sounds like the perfect way for me to combine my passion for tourism and travel with a career that I love and have experience in.

5 Man and cyberman!

ID Café

1 Before watching

A Match four of words 1–6 to photos a–d.
1 to blot
2 a crow
3 a deadline
4 napkins
5 a towel
6 a schedule

B Match words 1–6 in **A** to definitions a–f.
a a bird which sings badly
b a plan of events and the times they should happen
c paper items you get with takeaway food
d the end date for something
e what you do after spilling (liquid) on clothes
f you use it to dry yourself after a shower

C Use photo a in **A** to imagine Genevieve and Rory's conversation.

> Maybe she saw his jacket was dirty and offered to clean it?

2 While watching

A Watch up to 1:17 to check your answer in **1C**. Did you imagine correctly? How upset was Rory?

B Complete what Genevieve says to 1) apologize and 2) respond to a compliment. What's the opposite of *coordinated*? Watch again to check.
1 I'm sorry, I d__ __ __ __ __ __ m__ __ __ __ t__.
2 T__ __ __ __ __ s__ __ __ __ __.

C Watch up to 2:37. True (T) or False (F)? Correct the false ones.
1 August's finished his robot project.
2 Genevieve wants a website to get a bigger audience.
3 Genevieve thinks August will be able to help.
4 August doesn't want to involve Rory in the website.
5 Genevieve's not in a hurry and Rory's not busy.
6 August offers to rearrange his schedule to help.

D Imagine how the episode ends. Then order these events logically, 1–7. Watch to check. Were you right?
☐ August tells him not to worry if he can't do it.
☐ August offers to help him build the website.
☐ 1 August apologizes for suggesting Rory can help.
☐ Genevieve loves the website and wants to thank Rory.
☐ Rory's too tired to go to Genevieve's gig after not sleeping all week.
☐ Rory regrets his offer as he's too busy.
☐ Rory says August should invent a "Robot Rory."

3 After watching

A Match *get* expressions 1–6 to meanings a–f.
1 What can I get you?
2 Can I get a coffee?
3 Got any napkins?
4 I can get more people to come.
5 Let me get my ideas.
6 I haven't been getting enough sleep.

a be given
b bring
c Do you have
d find and bring
e persuade
f receiving

B Check 1–6. Zero or first conditional?

	0	1st
1 If I don't sleep enough, I sing like a crow.		
2 If I have a website, I can get more people to come to the café.		
3 If there's someone who's great at building websites, it's you.		
4 If I have a website, I can get more publicity.		
5 If he rearranges his schedule, he'll be able to work on her website.		
6 If I build Genevieve's website too, I'll have to stay up all night.		

C Match expressions 1–6 to their opposites a–f.
1 exhausted
2 let me know
3 I've done enough
4 awake
5 you're only human
6 divide and conquer

a don't tell me
b unite and liberate
c asleep
d fresh and relaxed
e it's the least I can do
f try to do the impossible

D Summarize the episode and explain the title.

E 🎤 **Make it personal** In groups, discuss 1 and 2. Anything in common?
1 Does your behavior change when you
   a) have too many projects?
   b) don't get enough sleep?
2 Have you ever volunteered but then regretted it?

> I don't feel sociable when I'm tired.

> Once, I offered to help a friend move house and ended up in hospital!

69

Grammar Unit 1

1A Review of present tenses and simple past

Simple present

Subject	+	
I / You / We / They	live	in Paris.
She / He	plays	volleyball.

	−	
I / You / We / They	do not / don't live	in Ecuador.
She / He	doesn't play	golf.

A	S	I (O)	Short answers + / −
Do	you	like sports?	Yes, I **do**. / No, I **don't**.
Does	he	live here?	Yes, he **does**. / No, he **doesn't**.

Q	A	S	I (O)
When	do	I / you / we / they	get up on weekdays?
Why	does	Sue	work at night?

Form: infinitive form for I / you / we / they. Add -s for he / she / it except:
- have / has (*She has a dog.*)
- verbs ending C + -y, change -y to -ies (*He often cries!*)
- verbs ending in -ch, -o, -sh, -ss, -x, add -es (*She watches TV then goes to bed.*)

Use:
- routines, habits, repeated actions
- facts
- scheduled events
- time phrases (*every morning, sometimes,* etc.)

Present continuous

Form: present of *be* + verb + *-ing*. See spelling rules for main verb in Grammar 2A p. 140.
- *I'm watching TV right now, so I'm not studying.*

Yes / No

Present of *be*	S	Verb + *-ing*
Am	I	
Are / Aren't	you / we / they	listening to the news?
Is / Isn't	she / he	

Wh-

	Present of *be*	S	Verb + *-ing*
Who	am	I	talking to?
Why	are	they	driving fast?
When	is	it	arriving?

Use:
- an action happening now: *I'm listening to the radio.*
- processes in progress: *I'm studying English (but not today!)*
- future plans / arrangements: *What are you doing after class? I'm going to the dentist.* NOT *I go to the dentist.*

Simple past

Form: the same for all persons. Most verbs are regular, and end *-ed*. Verbs ending *-e*, add *-d*. Verbs ending C + *-y*, change *-y* to *-ied*. (*We studied hard, but didn't pass the test.*)

Yes / No

A	S	I	O	Short answers
Did	they	go	to the concert?	Yes, they **did**. / No, they **didn't**.

Wh-

	A	S	I	O
Where	did	he	go	last weekend?

Subject

	Simple past	O
Who	wrote	the book?

Use: completed past events. *What happened to you last night?* NOT *What did happen to you last night?*

1B Future forms

will / won't

I'll go to the movies tonight. I have a ticket. (definite plan)
OK, I'll have a coffee. (unplanned decision)
It won't rain today. (prediction)

Will you do the dishes? Yes, I will.
Who will they invite to the party? They'll invite their friends.

Form: *will / won't* + infinitive.
Use: definite plans, unplanned decisions, predictions.

Going to

Use *be + going to +* infinitive for predictions and intentions.
I think she's going to win the race. (prediction)
They're going to bring their friend to the party. (intention)

Going to and present continuous as future

Use both *going to* and present continuous for fixed plans or arrangements. There's usually little difference in meaning.
He's going to go shopping. / He's going shopping.

1C should / shouldn't

He should eat healthy food. He shouldn't eat so many fries.
Should we take the train? Yes, you should.
Which one should we take? The first one.
Form: *should / shouldn't* + infinitive for all persons.
Use: advice, opinions, and suggestions.
For **questions**, use the ASI / QASI model.

Unit 1

1A

1 Circle the correct options in 1–5.
1 He's **studying / studies** every night for about two hours.
2 We **paid / pay** our credit card bill last week, so we **don't / didn't** worry about it this week.
3 I always **eat / ate** fast food when I was a teenager. I **loved / was loving** it but now I don't like it at all.
4 My neighbor **wants / is wanting** to take a vacation in the U.S., so **she needs / is needing** to get a visa.
5 At the moment, I**'m working / worked** in a music store. I **help / 'm helping** customers to find the music they **like / are liking**. It's more fun that I **imagine / imagined**.

2 Order the words in 1–6 to make questions.
1 to / did / on your last vacation / go / the beach / you / ?
2 usually / English / study / when / you / do / ?
3 English / why / you / learning / are / speak / to / ?
4 weekend / what / last / do / you / did / ?
5 with / you / now / who / living / are / ?
6 what / next / you / are / Saturday / doing / ?

3 **Make it personal** Write answers to 1–6 in 2 about you.

1B

1 Complete 1–5 with *'ll*, *will*, or *won't*.
1 Buy our new laptop and you _____ be disappointed!
2 That cashmere coat _____ probably still look great in 20 years.
3 Oh, no! I can't believe you _____ be able to come!
4 What _____ you do when you're in NYC next week?
5 I _____ see you when I get back from my trip.

2 Complete 1–5 with *'ll probably*, *'ll definitely*, or *won't*.
1 I _____ do my homework tonight. I'm too tired.
2 She _____ send you a postcard. She always writes to her friends.
3 They _____ join us at the Steak House Restaurant. They're vegetarians.
4 I think they _____ arrive on time. They're usually punctual.
5 He _____ win the Academy Award for Best Actor this year. He's obviously the best.

3 Circle the correct options in 1–5.
1 Your daughter's **going to be / is being** very rich when she's a movie star.
2 A: **Will you / Are you going to** help me with my homework, please?   B: Of course!
3 A: What **will you do / are you doing** this evening?
    B: I **see / 'm seeing** Joe.
4 Do you think we **will win / are winning** the lottery?
5 My sister**'s coming / will come** home tonight. We're very excited! She **has / 's having** a party.

4 **Make it personal** What will happen in these photos? Read the prediction for photo 1, then write predictions for photos 2 and 3.

call friend / be on time   see banana peel / fall   buy girlfriend ring / get married

He's going to call his friend to say he won't be on time.

1C

1 Complete dialogues 1–3 with *should* or *shouldn't* and these verbs.

be   come   go   listen   spend   stay

1 **A:** I need a jacket for this wedding, but everything is too expensive.
   B: You _____ _____ too much. Look for special sales.
2 **A:** My friend loves live music. Where _____ she _____ ?
   B: She _____ _____ to the new club with me tonight!
3 **A:** You sound really sick. Maybe you _____ _____ in class this week.
   B: My doctor said I _____ _____ home, but I don't think I _____.
   A: Maybe you _____ _____ to him!

2 **Make it personal** Give advice to the speakers in pictures 1–3. Use *should* or *need to*.

1 You need to call him on your cell phone.

I don't know where my husband is!
The book is too high.
I'm sorry I'm late for class.

139

Grammar Unit 2

2A Past continuous

S	Past of *be*	Verb + *-ing*
I / He / She	+ was − was not / wasn't	**driving** a truck.
You / We / They	+ were − were not / weren't	**surfing** the Internet.

Form: past of *be* + verb + *-ing*.

Verb + *-ing*	Spelling rules
go + *-ing* = going, see + *-ing* = seeing, study + *-ing* = studying	Most verbs, add *-ing*.
hope + *-ing* = hoping, share + *-ing* = sharing	Verbs ending *-e*, change *-e* to *-ing*.
die → dy + *-ing* = dying lie → ly + *-ing* = lying	Verbs ending *-ie*, change *-ie* to *-y* + *-ing*.
run → running sit → sitting	One-syllable verbs ending consonant-vowel-consonant (CVC), double the final C and add *-ing*.
be**gin** → beginning oc**cur** → occurring **lis**ten → listening **al**low → allowing en**joy** → enjoying **tra**vel → traveling	Verbs with two or more syllables ending CVC, double the final C (except *w*, *x*, or *y*) when the last syllable is **stressed**.

Use: actions in progress at a particular time in the past.

Q	Past of *be*	S	Verb + *-ing*
What	were	you / we / they	**doing** when I called?
Where	was	I / he / she	**going** at 6 p.m?

State verbs

Some verbs that express "state" or "condition" do not appear in continuous forms, for example:

Thoughts: *agree, believe, forget, guess, know, remember, think, understand*
Emotions: *adore, hate, like, love, need, prefer, want*
Senses: *feel, hear, look, see, smell, taste, touch*
Possession: *belong, have, own*

- Our teacher **needs** a new cell phone.
- My grandmother doesn't **understand** English.
- I don't understand the difference. NOT *I'm not understanding the difference.*

Some verbs have both a "state" and an "active" meaning: *be, have, think.*
- He **has** brown eyes. / He **is having** a good time at the party.

It's increasingly common to hear state verbs in the continuous form:
- *I'm loving it!* or *You're looking really good today.*

Be careful with state verbs in the past.
- I didn't know you last year. NOT *I wasn't knowing you last year.*
- When I was young, I wanted to be rich. NOT *When I was young, I was wanting to be rich.*

2B Past continuous vs. simple past

- I was cooking dinner when the phone rang.
- The power went out while I was writing an email to my friend.
- While I was waiting at the bus stop, it began to rain.

Simple past	Spelling rules
We **played** tennis yesterday.	Most verbs, add *-ed*.
He **danced** a lot at the party yesterday.	Verbs ending in *-e*, add *-d*.
The car **stopped** before the accident.	Verbs ending CVC, double the final C and add *-ed*.
They **tried** to talk to you last Monday.	Verbs ending C + *-y*, change *-y* to *-ied*.
She **bought** some new shoes.	Some verbs are **irregular**. See list on p. 158–159.

Use simple past for an action that interrupts an action in progress (past continuous).
Use *when* or *while* to connect the actions. If *When* / *While* is at the beginning of the sentence, use a comma after the main clause.
- When I was shopping, I lost my keys.
- I lost my keys while I was shopping.

Q	Past of *be*	S 1st action	Verb + *-ing*	Linking word	S 2nd action	Past verb
What	were	you	doing	when	the phone	rang?
Where	was	he	going	when	it	happened?

He was playing hockey when he slipped on a banana peel.

140

Unit 2

2A

1 Complete 1–5 with the past continuous of these verbs.

do   go   look   talk   wait

1 What _____ your friends _____ last night?
2 Why _____ you _____ in my bag?
3 _____ he _____ about me?
4 How long _____ she _____ for a taxi?
5 Where _____ you _____ yesterday?

2 Simple past or past continuous? Correct the mistakes in 1–5.

1 What was you trying to do?
2 Did you sleep when I phoned you?
3 My sister was having 19 years when she went to college.
4 While she was at college, she was calling me every week.
5 It was rain at lunchtime yesterday so I ate in the office.

3 Circle the correct options in 1–7.

1 My grandmother **knew** / **was knowing** a lot about cars.
2 I **don't mind** / **'m not minding** doing the dishes.
3 What are you **think** / **thinking** about?
4 I **wasn't understanding** / **didn't understand** what you said.
5 I **agree** / **'m agreeing** with you.
6 My sister **is having** / **has** a new car.
7 I always **liked** / **was liking** swimming.

4 Complete 1–5 by adding the simple or continuous form of the verbs. Present or past?

1 Amy Winehouse a lot of tattoos. (**have**)
2 The milk bad so I threw it away. (**taste**)
3 I couldn't sleep because my neighbors a party. (**have**)
4 you your country will win the next World Cup? (**think**)
5 They pizza with too much pepperoni. (**not like**)

5 🟢 **Make it personal** Write four sentences about yourself using these time phrases.

last night   at 7 a.m. yesterday
this morning   yesterday afternoon

I was eating breakfast and checking Instagram at 7 a.m. yesterday.

2B

1 Complete 1–5 with the correct form of the verbs.

1 We _____ baseball in the park when it _____ raining. (**play, start**)
2 The other car _____ the back of my car when I _____ to work. (**hit, drive**)
3 I _____ you yesterday when you _____ in the mall. (**see, shop**)
4 When Ariana _____ home, we _____ in the kitchen to give her a surprise. (**arrive, hide**)
5 I _____ down the street when I _____ . (**walk, slip and fall**)

2 Order the words in 1–5 and add *was* or *were* to make sentences.

1 he / chicken / cooking / phone / rang / when / the / .
2 an / driving / they / when / earthquake / there / .
3 playing / computer / on / her / she / while / power / games / out / went / the / .
4 cycling / home / Sam / when / he / tire / got / flat / a / .
5 the Internet / funny / found / surfing / video / I / while / I / a / .

3 🟢 **Make it personal** Imagine what the people in photos 1–6 were doing when the power went out. Write six sentences.

1 He was making a date with his new girlfriend.

Grammar Unit 3

3A Present perfect 1: past experiences

S	A	Past participle
I / You / We / They	have / 've have not / haven't	**been** abroad. **done** the dishes.
He / She	has / 's has not / hasn't	**stayed** in a hotel recently. **traveled** a lot. **studied** English before. **worked** hard today.

Form: have / has + past participle. Past participles of regular verbs are the same as the simple past. See list of irregular past participles on p. 158–159.

Use: past experiences without a specific time. Use the simple past for a specific time in the past.

▸ On Monday morning, ask: *How was your weekend?* NOT *How has been your weekend?* (The weekend is finished.)

Yes / No ❓	Short answers ➕ / ➖
Have you (ever) **seen** a panda?	Yes, I **have**. / No, I **haven't**.
Have they (ever) **visited** Thailand?	Yes, they **have**. / No, they **haven't**.
Has he / she (ever) **tried** Peruvian food?	Yes, he / she **has**. / No, he / she **hasn't**.

For short answers, do **not** contract the **subject** with the **auxiliary**.

▸ Have you ever been to New York?
▸ Yes, I have. (NOT *Yes, I've.*) I went there in 2011, just before Christmas. It was great.
▸ No, I haven't, but I'd love to. I've always wanted to see Times Square.

Note: with the present perfect, *ever* means *in your whole life*.

3B Present perfect 2: completed actions

S	A	Participle + O
I / You / We / They	have / 've have not / haven't	**already finished** work. **eaten** lunch **yet**.
He / She	has / 's has not / hasn't	**checked** Facebook **already**. **just woken** up. **read** the news **yet**.

Use with:
▸ *already* for actions completed before now. Note that *already* has two possible positions.
▸ *yet* with sentences for actions that are expected to happen but are incomplete.
▸ *just* for recently completed actions.

Note: Present perfect is more common in British English. In American English, it's more common to use simple past for completed actions with *already, just,* and *recently: I just woke up.*

Yes / No ❓		
A	S	Past participle + O phrase
Have	I / you / we / they	**already finished** your work? **seen** the new Spider-Man movie **yet**?
Has	he / she / it	**eaten** breakfast **already**? **stopped** raining **yet**?

Use:
▸ *already* in questions when you expect a positive answer.
▸ *yet* in a question when you don't know if the answer will be *yes* or *no*.
▸ Have you got 5G yet? NOT *Have you yet got 5G?*

3C Present perfect 3: unfinished past

Use present perfect with *for* or *since* to talk about an action or state that **started in the past and continues now**:
▸ *for* + **time expression** for the duration of an action.
I've had a headache for about two days.
I haven't spoken to him for a long time.

Past — Duration = **for** — Now

▸ *since* + **time expression** for the point in time that an action started.
I've lived here since I was a little girl.
Marion has worked here since 1998.

Past — Point in time = **since** — Now

Duration	Point in time
for a long time	since yesterday
for many years	since 1984
for 10 weeks	since I left college

Wh- ❓

Q	A	S	Past participle
How long	have	I / you / we / they	**studied** here?
	has	he / she / it	**worked** here?

▸ How long have you been here? NOT *Since when are you here?*

142

Unit 3

3A

1 Look at Mark's souvenirs. Complete 1–8 with the past participles of the verbs.

1. Mark's _____ on the Panama Canal. (**sail**)
2. He's _____ to the U.S. several times. (**be**)
3. He's _____ the Statue of Liberty in New York. (**see**)
4. He's _____ in the Andes Mountains once. (**climb**)
5. He's _____ photos of Paris from the top of the Eiffel Tower. (**take**)
6. He's _____ the Iguazú Falls in Argentina and Brazil. (**visit**)
7. He's _____ all the way to China. (**travel**)
8. He's _____ a souvenir of a phone box in London. (**buy**)

2 🟢 **Make it personal** Change 1–8 in **1** so they are true for you. If you haven't had the experience, add *but I've* and include something similar you have done.

I haven't sailed on the Panama Canal, but I've sailed on a yacht.

3 Complete the dialogue with the verbs in the present perfect, ➕ or ➖.

A: _____ you ever _____ Chicago? (**visit**)
B: No, I _____ there. _____ you? (**be**)
A: Yes, I _____. I really enjoyed it.
B: Does Chicago have that big skyscraper ... uh, what's it called?
A: Yes, it does. Its name _____ recently _____. It's now called the Willis Tower. (**change**)
B: Wow, you know a lot about it!
A: Yeah, it's a great place to visit. My brother lives there. I _____ with him and his family several times. (**stay**)

4 🟢 **Make it personal** Write five sentences about places you've been and what you did there.

I've been to Spain with my family. We visited my cousins in Madrid and went sightseeing.

3B

1 Order the words in 1–5 to make sentences.

1. he / abroad / three / has / times / been / .
2. yet / Jenny / learned / hasn't / to / drive / .
3. I / been / to / New York / business / on / several / have / times / .
4. paid / they / already / the / hotel / bill / have / .
5. haven't / spent / money / all / yet / our / we / .

2 Correct two mistakes in each of 1–5.

1. I have ever been to Italy. I've hear it's fantastic.
2. Have you never gone to a musical in a theater?
3. He have yet paid for his trip with his credit card.
4. They hasn't seen the *Mona Lisa* already, so they're going to the Louvre today.
5. Have you ever been in Miami? I've come back just. It's amazing!

3C

1 Complete 1–5 with the verbs in the present perfect, ➕ or ➖. Use contractions. Add *since* or *for* in the correct place in the sentences.

1. He _____ in the UK 10 months and he really loves it. (**live**)
2. They _____ on Baker Street the early 1990s. They moved a long time ago. (**live**)
3. I was a kid, I _____ always _____ staying in hotels. (**like**)
4. She _____ from that seat she sat down! (**move**)
5. Mr. Martin _____ that awful hairstyle the 1990s. (**have**)

2 Read Jackie's profile and correct nine mistakes.

My name is Jackie. I was born in Michigan and moved to California in 2009. I live in L.A. since then. I stay in San Francisco a few times, but I've ever lived there.

Since I was 25, I had the same apartment. I been there 14 years. I lived in San Diego for a few months, but I didn't like it. I never been back. My family lives in Los Angeles too since 2020, but I've only visit them a few times so far.

3 🟢 **Make it personal** Write a similar profile about yourself, saying where you and your family have lived, worked, or studied.

Grammar Unit 4

4A Used to and simple past

- I **used to** play a lot of sports, but I'm too busy now.
- My brother **used to** make fun of me when I was young.
- Did you **use to** watch a lot of cartoons?
- She didn't **use to** like fruit, but she loves it now.
- My family **used to** live in Chicago, but we moved to L.A. in 2019.

Note: *Use to* and *used to* have the same pronunciation: /juːstə/.

S	A	Used to	I	
⊕ I / You / He / She / We / They	–	used to	be	happier.
⊖	didn't	use to	like	swimming.

Q	A	S	Used to	I	
❓ What	did	you / he / she / we / they /	use to	do go feel	in summer?

Form: *used to* + infinitive for all persons. Questions and negatives use the auxiliary *did* (*not*).

Use: past states that have ended and actions that happened regularly in the past but don't happen now.

- My dad **used to** ride a motorbike when he was younger. NOT ~~My dad was riding a motorbike when he was younger.~~
- I usually go to the gym before work. NOT ~~I'm used to go to the gym before work.~~

For short *Yes / No* answers, use:
- ⊕ Yes + subject + *did*.
- ⊖ No + subject + *didn't*.
- Did you use to live in Santiago? Yes, I did, but my boyfriend didn't.

Use **simple past** to talk about past activities and events at specific points in time.
- My uncle arrived a few minutes ago.
- Did you see the news yesterday?
- There was a storm last night.
- We saw a great movie last week.
- My sister was born in 2004.

4B Comparatives and superlatives, as ... as

- Camping is **cheaper than** staying at a hotel.
- It's probably **the ugliest** building in Manhattan.
- That hotel is **the most expensive** in London.
- New York is **as** expensive **as** London.
- She's **as** beautiful **as** her mother.
- The UK is **not as** big **as** the U.S.

One-syllable adjectives

Most one-syllable adjectives, add *-er / -est*.
Adjectives ending **CVC**, double the final consonant and add *-er / -est*.

Adjective	Comparative	Superlative
rich	richer	the richest
big	bigger	the biggest
hot	hotter	the hottest

One- / two-syllable adjectives ending -y

Change *-y* to *-ier / -iest*.

Adjective	Comparative	Superlative
crazy	crazier	the craziest
easy	easier	the easiest
heavy	heavier	the heaviest

Adjectives with two or more syllables

Use *more / the most*.

Adjective	Comparative	Superlative
beautiful	more beautiful	the most beautiful
complicated	more complicated	the most complicated
exciting	more exciting	the most exciting
expensive	more expensive	the most expensive

The opposite of *more ... than* is *less ... than*, and the opposite of *the most* is *the least*.
- The subway is usually less crowded at night.
- Vatican City is the least populated city-state in the world. It has only about 800 residents.

Irregular adjectives

Adjective	Comparative	Superlative
good	better	the best
bad	worse	the worst
far	farther / further	the farthest / furthest

As ... as

Use *as ... as* for two things with similar qualities. It is very common in comparisons that use non-literal images.
- The wind is **as** cold **as** ice.
- It was the scariest movie we've ever seen! My little sister was **as** white **as** a sheet.
- That joke is **as** old **as** a dinosaur.

Use *not as ... as* to criticize and talk about differences.
- His pizzas aren't **as** good **as** Mario's pizzas.
- The U.S. is **not as** populated **as** China.
- Vinyl is **not as** easy to take care of **as** CDs.
- Lionel isn't **as** tall **as** Cristiano. NOT ~~Lionel isn't so tall like Cristiano.~~

Unit 4

4A

1 Order the words in 1–5 and add *used to* or *use to* to make sentences or questions.
   1. father / old / records / collect / my / .
   2. your / you / did / play / friends / with / baseball / ?
   3. a / a / I / horse / beautiful / have / I / child / was / when / .
   4. like / he / math / when / high / was / in / didn't / he / school / .
   5. cleaner / city / your / be / is / now / than / it / did / ?

2 Look at the pairs of pictures and complete 1–4 with the correct form of *used to* and a noun. Then match 1–4 to a–d.

1. They _____ eat a lot of unhealthy _____,
2. She _____ bite her _____,
3. He _____ have much _____.
4. He _____ get good _____,

a but now she's getting a manicure!
b but now he studies a lot more and is top of the class.
c but they are much healthier now.
d He has lots now, but he has no free time.

3 **Make it personal** Write one-sentence answers to 1–5.
   1. Have you changed any bad habits?
   2. What did you use to do for fun when you were a kid?
   3. What kind of music did you use to listen to?
   4. What were your favorite TV programs?
   5. What kind of kids did you use to hang out with?

1 I used to eat too much salt.

4B

1 Complete 1–5 with one comparative / superlative and one *as ... as*.
   1. When I first moved here, the neighborhood was _____ (**quiet**) a mouse. But now it's _____ (**noisy**) than Delhi!
   2. Wow, John's lost a lot of weight. He used to be the _____ (**heavy**) guy at work. Now he looks _____ (**good**) he did 10 years ago!
   3. Tablets are not _____ (**small**) smartphones, but they are _____ (**good**) because you can read them easily.
   4. My mom types _____ (**fast**) than most people, but she's not _____ (**good**) me at sending messages on her phone.
   5. I don't go out _____ (**often**) I used to when I was _____ (**young**).

2 Correct the mistake in each of 1–5.
   1. Instagram isn't popular as Facebook.
   2. My brother is most interested in video games than I am.
   3. We've thought about getting a dog that's not as big like our last one.
   4. That was the most ugly haircut I've ever had in my life.
   5. This new phone is more bad than my last one.

3 **Make it personal** Use 1–5 to make comparisons that are true for you.
   1. soccer / basketball / volleyball
   2. staying in / going out / traveling
   3. Chinese food / Japanese food / Peruvian food
   4. sunny weather / rainy weather / windy weather
   5. playing video games / listening to music / watching YouTube videos

Volleyball isn't as exciting to watch as basketball. Soccer is the best game to play and watch.

Grammar Unit 5

5A Obligation and prohibition: have (got) to / can't

- We've got to take the test tomorrow. / We have to take the test tomorrow.
- You have to bring a pen to the test. / You've got to bring a pen to the test.
- You don't have to write in black, you can use blue. / You haven't got to write in black, you can use blue.
- I can't use a cell phone in the exam room.

Have (got) to

	S	A	Have (got) to	I	
+	I / You / We / They		have to / have got to		work tonight.
	He / She		has to / has got to		
−	I / You / We / They	don't / haven't	have to / got to		
	He / She	doesn't / hasn't	have to / got to		

	A	S	Have to	I	Short answers
?	Do	I / you / we / they	have to	work tonight?	Yes, we do. / No, we don't.
	Does	he / she			Yes, she does. / No, she doesn't.

	A	S	Got to	I	Short answers
?	Have	I / you / we / they	got to	work tonight?	Yes, I have. / No, I haven't.
	Has	he / she			Yes, she has. / No, she hasn't.

Use:
- **have (got) to** to express an obligation. **Have got to** is more common in speaking (*I've got to go now*) and is often pronounced *gotta* (*I've gotta go now / I gotta go now*).
- negative forms to express no obligation: you have a choice.

Note: *got to* is pronounced /ɡɑtə/, *have to* is /hæftə/, and *has to* is /hæztə/.

Can't

S	A	I	
I / You / We / They / He / She	can't		smoke in this building.

Use: to express prohibition.

5B too / enough, too much / too many

- She's **too busy** to study.
- Your bag's going to break. There are **too many** things in it.
- Shhhh! You're making **too much** noise and I can't concentrate.
- Can you get that book for me? I'm **not tall enough**.
- I have 10 cousins. Including me, that's **enough people** for a soccer team.
- I like cooking, but I **don't** have **enough time**.

Too + noun or adjective means excessive.
Use **too many** with countable nouns (*too many cars*) and **too much** with uncountable nouns (*too much time*).
Enough means sufficient, **not enough** means insufficient.
Enough goes **after** adjectives, but **before** nouns.

"Table seven says the fish isn't cooked enough."

5C Zero and first conditional

Zero conditional

Conditional clause			Result clause		
If / When	S	Present verb		S	Present verb
If / When	it	rains	a lot,	the river	floods.
If / When	I	don't sleep	enough,	I	get angry easily.

Use: for facts, generalizations, things that are always true.
If or *when* introduce the conditional clause. When the conditional clause comes first, use a comma to separate the clauses.

- If you don't ask for anything, you don't get anything.
- People sometimes quit when they don't succeed the first time.

First conditional

Conditional clause			Result clause		
If	S	Present verb		S	Will +/−	I
If	I / you / we / they	don't get up	now,	I / you / we / they /	will	miss the bus.
If	he / she	gets up	late tomorrow,	he / she	won't	be on time

Use:
- specific events that are probable or certain and their future results.
- promises and warnings.

Use simple present in the conditional clause. Don't use a comma when the result clause comes first.

- If we see him tomorrow, we'll give him your message.
- I promise I won't tell anyone if you tell me a secret.

146

Unit 5

5A

1 Complete 1–5 with *got to*, *have / has to*, or *can't*.

1. You can leave to use the restroom, but you _____ return in five minutes. You _____ take your phone with you.
2. He's really _____ study harder! If he doesn't improve his grades, he _____ stay on the basketball team.
3. Do you _____ work on Saturday night, or can you come to my party?
4. Mom usually gets home by 6, but tonight she _____ stop at the grocery store first.
5. My brother works in a bar. He doesn't _____ wear a uniform, he can wear his own clothes, but he often ____ work late nights and weekends.

2 Correct the mistake in each of 1–5.

1. You don't got to go to the grocery store later. I've already done all the shopping.
2. I'm allergic to cheese and bread so I don't can eat pizza.
3. I can't come tomorrow. I've to go to the dentist.
4. Lena hasn't to work tomorrow so she can stay in bed.
5. It's important to be punctual. Everybody have to be on time for the test.

5B

1 Complete 1–5 with *too / enough / too much / too many*.

1. My sister has saved 20% of her salary and now she has _____ money to buy a car.
2. That math class is way _____ difficult for me and there is _____ homework. I'm dropping it!
3. Are you strong _____ to carry that bag? Do you want some help?
4. I didn't eat at the party. There were _____ people and there wasn't _____ food.
5. I used to live in the country, but the commute was _____ far and the salary wasn't high _____. So I quit my job and moved!

Match 1–6 to a–f.

1. My son is annoying. He wastes
2. They're going to be late. They haven't got
3. Her eyes hurt. She spends
4. We can't take this course
5. I couldn't study much
6. There wasn't enough time to walk

a. too many hours working on the computer.
b. because it's too advanced.
c. too much time doing nothing.
d. because there were too many people around.
e. so we had to take a taxi.
f. enough time to catch the bus.

3 🟢 **Make it personal** Write your ideas about 1–4 in complete sentences.

1. Name a profession that earns too much money.
2. Name a profession that doesn't earn enough money.
3. Name a car that is too expensive.
4. Name a food that is not tasty enough for you.

I think professional baseball players earn too much money. Some of them get more than 2 million dollars a month!

5C

1 Order the words in 1–5 to make sentences. Notice where there is a comma.

1. Do you love him?
   / know / him, / he / you / don't / won't / tell / if / .
2. His flight leaves very soon.
   / won't / he / if / doesn't / go / he / now, / .
3. Why don't you eat something?
   / you / you / regularly, / angry / get / eat / don't / if / .
4. Are you going on vacation?
   / need / go / you / States / a / the / visa / when / you / to / .
5. Are you doing Internet dating?
   / happy / meet / person, / nice / a / if / you'll / you / be / very / .

2 Correct two mistakes in each of 1–5.

1. We are going to the beach this weekend. If the water be too cold, we don't swim.
2. If is raining tomorrow, they cancel the soccer game.
3. I have a part-time job after school. If I gets home too late, I won't to do my homework.
4. If my roommate get up early, she always make coffee.
5. If I will pass the test next week, I will to get my driver's license.

3 🟢 **Make it personal** What will happen? Write a zero or first conditional sentence for at least five of these situations.

late for work
learn English well
miss the bus
wake up late
win the lottery
get married
feel hungry

When I'm late for work, my boss usually makes me stay later.

Verbs

Irregular verbs

Irregular verbs can be difficult to remember. Try remembering them in groups with similar sounds, conjugation patterns, or spellings.

Simple past and Past participle are the same

Base form	Simple past	Past participle
bring	brought /brɔt/	brought
buy	bought	bought
catch	caught /cɔt/	caught
fight	fought	fought
teach	taught	taught
think	thought	thought
feed	fed	fed
feel	felt	felt
keep	kept	kept
leave	left	left
mean	meant /mɛnt/	meant
meet	met	met
sleep	slept	slept
lay	laid	laid
pay	paid	paid
sell	sold	sold
tell	told	told
send	sent	sent
spend	spent	spent
stand	stood /stʊd/	stood
understand	understood	understood
lose	lost	lost
shoot	shot	shot
can	could	could
will	would	would
build	built /bɪlt/	built
find	found /faʊnd/	found
hang	hung	hung
have	had	had
hear	heard /hɜrd/	heard
hold	held	held
make	made	made
say	said /sɛd/	said
sit	sat	sat
swing	swung /swʌŋ/	swung
win	won /wʌn/	won

Base form and Past participle are the same

Base form	Simple past	Past participle
become	became	become
come	came	come
run	ran	run

No changes across the three forms

Base form	Simple past	Past participle
cost	cost	cost
cut	cut	cut
hit	hit	hit
let	let	let
put	put /pʊt/	put
quit	quit /kwɪt/	quit
set	set	set
split	split	split

Special cases

Base form	Simple past	Past participle
be	was / were	been
draw	drew /dru:/	drawn /drɔn/
fly	flew /flu:/	flown /floʊn/
lie	lay	lain
read	read /rɛd/	read /rɛd/

Simple past + -en

Base form	Simple past	Past participle
beat	beat	beaten
bite	bit	bitten
break	broke	broken
choose	chose	chosen
forget	forgot	forgotten
freeze	froze	frozen
get	got	got / gotten
speak	spoke	spoken
steal	stole	stolen
wake	woke	woken

Verbs

Simple past + -en

Base form	Simple past	Past participle
beat	beat	beaten
bite	bit	bitten
break	broke	broken
choose	chose	chosen
forget	forgot	forgotten
freeze	froze	frozen
get	got	got / gotten
speak	spoke	spoken
steal	stole	stolen
wake	woke	woken

Base form + -en

Base form	Simple past	Past participle
drive	drove	driven /drɪvən/
eat	ate	eaten
fall	fell	fallen
give	gave	given
ride	rode	ridden /rɪdən/
see	saw /sɔ/	seen
shake	shook	shaken
take	took	taken
write	wrote	written /rɪtən/

Base form ending in o + -ne

Base form	Simple past	Past participle
do	did	done /dʌn/
go	went	gone /gɔn/

i - a - u

Base form	Simple past	Past participle
begin	began	begun
drink	drank	drunk
ring	rang	rung
sing	sang	sung
swim	swam	swum

ow - ew - own

Base form	Simple past	Past participle
blow	blew /bluː/	blown
grow	grew	grown
know	knew	known
throw	threw	thrown

ear - ore - orn

Base form	Simple past	Past participle
swear	swore	sworn
tear /tɛr/	tore	torn
wear	wore	worn

Sounds and usual spellings

S Difficult sounds for Spanish speakers
P Difficult sounds for Portuguese speakers

▶ To listen to these words and sounds, and to practice them, go to the pronunciation section on the Richmond Learning Platform.

Vowels

/iː/	three, tree, eat, receive, believe, key, B, C, D, E, G, P, T, V, Z
/ɪ/	six, mix, it, fifty, fish, trip, lip, fix
/ʊ/	book, cook, put, could, cook, woman
/uː/	two, shoe, food, new, soup, true, suit, Q, U, W
/ɛ/	pen, ten, heavy, then, again, men, F, L, M, N, S, X
/ə/	bananas, pajamas, family, photography

/ɜr/	shirt, skirt, work, turn, learn, verb
/ɔr/	four, door, north, fourth
/ɔ/	walk, saw, water, talk, author, law
/æ/	man, fan, bad, apple
/ʌ/	sun, run, cut, umbrella, country, love
/ɑ/	hot, not, on, clock, fall, tall
/ɑr/	car, star, far, start, party, artist, R

Diphthongs

/eɪ/	plane, train, made, stay, they, A, H, J, K
/aɪ/	nine, wine, night, my, pie, buy, eyes, I, Y
/aʊ/	house, mouse, town, cloud

| /ɔɪ/ | toys, boys, oil, coin |
| /oʊ/ | nose, rose, home, know, toe, road, O |

Sounds and usual spellings

▢ Voiced
▢ Unvoiced

Consonants

/p/	pig, pie, open, top, apple	
/b/	bike, bird, describe, able, club, rabbit	
/m/	medal, monster, name, summer	
/w/	web, watch, where, square, one	
/f/	fish, feet, off, phone, enough	
/v/	vet, van, five, have, video	
/θ/	teeth, thief, thank, nothing, mouth	
/ð/	mother, father, the, other	
/t/	truck, taxi, hot, stop, attractive	
/d/	dog, dress, made, adore, sad, middle	
/n/	net, nurse, tennis, one, sign, know	
/l/	lion, lips, long, all, old	

/s/	snake, skate, kiss, city, science
/z/	zoo, zebra, size, jazz, lose
/ʃ/	shark, shorts, action, special, session, chef
/ʒ/	television, treasure, usual
/k/	cat, cake, back, quick
/g/	goal, girl, leg, guess, exist
/ŋ/	king, ring, single, bank
/h/	hand, hat, unhappy, who
/tʃ/	chair, cheese, kitchen, future, question
/dʒ/	jeans, jump, generous, bridge
/r/	red, rock, ride, married, write
/j/	yellow, yacht, university

161

Audioscript

Unit 1

1.2 Notice unstressed *and* = /ən/, *for* = /fə/, *to* = /tə/, but /tu/ before a vowel.

RH = radio host

RH Hi, and welcome to "Life in 10 Seconds"! Last week, we asked you, our listeners, to call in and, in only 10 seconds, tell us your number one priority in life. Listen to what you said:
1 Hi! Uh … well, your health is the most important thing in your life. Definitely. It's my top priority. I'm planning to live to be 100. Or 120 – why not?!
2 I like to feel comfortable about money. I grew up poor, and my parents were always worried about how to pay the bills, but, you know, I went to college and now I have a good job and earn enough money to feel secure.
3 I live for today! I want to enjoy every day of my life. Fun is the most important thing for me. Oh, and baseball of course: Let's go Giants!
4 My job defines who I am. I want a good career and I'm very ambitious. This means that I work hard, but hard work is good for you.
5 I never stop studying. In fact, I'm taking a class in neuroscience at the moment. Continuing to learn is the best thing we can do. It's good for you and it keeps you young.
6 Without love, what else is there? It's the most important thing in the world. I always need to have a partner. Love is all we have in life … and um …
7 What's the point in having work and money if you have no free time? Time to enjoy things is more important than money. Much more. You don't need a lot of money to have a good time.
8 People are more important than things. My friends and family are the most important thing for me. Oh, and my dog too! Hello, baby! Who's a good girl?
9 You know, I don't want to live in a world without art and music. Culture is so important for me – I need to have art, and literature, and movies, and music and …
10 I live for exercise! I need to look good and I want to stay in shape. I'm running at the gym now! And then I'm …

1.3 Notice unstressed *to* = /tə/, *but* = /bət/, *a* /ə/, and *the* /ðə/.

1
C Hi! I'm Casey Murray and I'm 22 years old. I finished high school, but I didn't go to college. I'm a security guard, but my job isn't very interesting. My hobbies are playing video games and I love shopping! I never have the money to do all the things I want to do. I have to work every day in a boring job because I need to pay my bills, but I really want to be a singer. I love to sing and dance and I want to be a professional singer. Singing is my passion, but I'm not singing at the moment because of my job.
2
R My name's Ricardo Sutton, and I'm a 28-year-old attorney from Canada. I finished grad school two years ago, and I have a good job that I really like. I love travel and languages (I speak Spanish, French, and Japanese), but I work really long hours and I don't have much vacation time. I'm also taking a class, so I'm always too tired to go to the gym – I'm exhausted after work, and I work on weekends, too, so, I'm out of shape. Yup, I really need to exercise more because I'm desperate to get in shape.

1.6 Notice /u/, /ʊ/, and /eɪ/ and their different spellings.

A I'm listening to my brother's band. They sound great! They practice every Friday and I come every week. They're going to be famous one day.
B Do you really think so? I can hear them and I think they sound like they need to practice more than once a week!
2
C That's a nice jacket. It looks really cool.
D Thanks, I bought it on sale last week – it wasn't expensive. I looked at it for a long time before I bought it. I don't really like the color – it's not a color I usually wear.
C It looks good on you.
D Thanks.
3
E This chewing gum is delicious. It tastes awesome!
F I don't like chewing gum.
E I do, and I like unusual flavors like this one: bacon!
F Bacon chewing gum! That's weird.
4
G What is on those pizza slices? They smell awful!
H It says here, it's the chef's secret recipe.
G Hmm … I think maybe we should go somewhere else.
H Yeah, I think you're right – let's get out of here.
5
I I don't like this sweater. It feels rough. I don't like wearing it!
J But it's warm, and it's cold outside, so you need to wear it!
I No!!

1.7 Notice the connections.

1
M1 What do you think about those singers?
W1 They sound_awful. Let's get_out of here!
2
W2 How about going to the beach?
M2 That sounds_awesome. Yeah, I really need a vacation.
3
M3 What do you think about these phones?
W3 Hmm … They look_old. What_about those over there?
4
W4 This movie looks good. Shall we go see_it?
W5 It looks_awful. I hate romantic movies.
5
M4 Do you like this perfume?
W6 Uh-huh. It smells_amazing.
6
M5 Dinner's ready – want some meatballs?
B & G Thanks, Dad. Mmm. They smell_ awesome.
7
M6 I really like this sweater. Do you?
M7 Yes! It feels_expensive.
8
W7 What do you think_of these gloves?
W8 Well, They feel extra_soft, but … umm … how much are they?
9
M8 Do you like the sandwich
W9 Mmmm … It tastes_amazing!
10
M9 What do you think_of these cookies?
M10 They taste old. Where did_you get them?

1.9 Notice dark /l/ and normal /l/.

1
W = waiter   C = customer
W I'll take your order now.
C Great, thanks. I'd like the fish.
W Good choice! You'll enjoy it.
C Mmm! This fish is good. It's really tender and juicy.
2
A What time will you be at the party tomorrow?
B About 8. What about you?
A I'll definitely be there by 9. Hey! Listen to this. You'll love it. It's so cool.
B Yeah, wow, this is amazing! It's fantastic! I'll download it now.
3
A Your mother will love this perfume.
B Hmm … really? It smells … um … interesting. Unusual. No, she won't like it. She doesn't like fruity smells. I'll try another one, please.
A OK … what about this one?
4
A I'm looking for a painting as a gift for my wife on our wedding anniversary.
B I suggest this wonderful new painting by Henrietta Jonquil.
A Ah yes. My wife will love this. It's a beautiful painting. Awesome!
B Yes, and it's only 25,000 dollars.
A Hmm … I'll take this postcard of it.
B That's 2 dollars. Will you need a bag?
A Yes, I will.
5
A This blanket feels so soft. It's 100% wool.
B It looks nice and warm. But my kids won't like it. They're allergic to wool.
A Oh, well, the synthetic blankets are over here.

Audioscript

1.11 Notice /k/, /aʊ/, and /ɔ/.

M Where is everyone? Why's nobody at our party?
W Well, Fran called – she has a headache.
M Hmmm ... What about Lenny?
W He texted. He has the flu.
M And Gaby?
W She has a stomachache.
M Really? What about Helen and Marcos?
W Helen has a cold ... and Marcos has a cough.
M They're both sick? And I suppose Jenny is too?
W Yes ... Jenny has a fever ...
M What about Brad? He's really healthy.
W Oh, he just texted. Sorry, guys. I have a really bad toothache. I'm in bed.
M I can't believe it! Are all our friends are sick?
W Hmmm ... This seems strange. Is there another party tonight?
M I think you're right! They're all at another party ... and we're not invited!

1.12 Notice /h/.

1
M = mom   D = daughter
M What's the matter?
D Oooh ... I have a headache.
M You should take a painkiller and you shouldn't go to the party.
D I guess you're right.

2
D = doctor   M = man
D How are you feeling?
M I have a cough and a fever and I ache all over.
D You have the flu. So, you should stay in bed and rest. Drink plenty of water, but you shouldn't eat anything. Don't eat until the fever goes down.
M OK, doctor, thanks. I'm not hungry anyway.

3
W = woman   M = man
W Are you OK?
M Ow ... I have a toothache.
W Aaah! You should see a dentist as soon as possible. You shouldn't eat or drink anything hot or cold.

4
W = woman   M = man
W How are you?
M Ugh ... I feel awful. I have a cold.
W You shouldn't go out. You should drink a lot of warm fluids and you should stay warm. I'll make you some soup.
M Thanks.

1.14 Notice /aɪ/ and /ɪ/.

This is Lori, with my advice for the Unhappy Wife whose father-in-law comes in and out of their house, borrows things, and gives them no privacy.
Dear Unhappy Wife,
This is a very delicate situation, but you should take your father-in-law out to dinner and tell him that you have a problem. You shouldn't be mean, but you should be very clear that what he is doing is making you unhappy.

If he ignores you and continues to come to the house and borrow things, maybe you should change the locks on the doors.
I hope this helps. That's all for now. See you next week.

1.16 Notice the intonation in offers and responses.

1
A That looks heavy. Do you need a hand?
B Thank you. That's very kind of you.

2
A I can't do this problem.
B Do you want me to help you?
A Yes, please! I have a test tomorrow and I don't understand it.
B OK, let's see.

3
A What are you doing?
B I'm painting the kitchen.
A Can I help you? I love painting.
B Umm ... I think I can do it myself, but thanks for the offer.

4
A How's the art project coming along?
B It's OK, but I can't get the colors right.
A Would you like me to help you? I'm good with this software.
B Thanks, Dad, but I have to do it myself.
A OK, no worries.

Unit 2

2.1 Notice the spelling of /iː/ and /ɪ/.

RP = radio presenter
RP So, we asked six listeners the question: How do you usually get your news? Here's what they said.

1 I still read the newspaper every day. I, uh, don't like reading on a computer screen – I like to hold the paper in my hand and turn the pages. Sometimes I just scan the headlines, to, you know, get an idea of big developments.
2 I get all my news on social media, I guess. When there's anything big happening, I hear about it there. I don't need to make a special effort to go and find out – it's right there.
3 Hmm ... I guess I usually watch news on the TV. I always watch in the morning when I'm getting ready for school. I don't have to waste time reading, I can just listen and watch. Also we often watch the news on TV when we're eating at home. We sometimes have some very interesting discussions!
4 On the radio. I listen all day. I wake up to the radio, listen to the news in bed, and then listen in the car. I love radio because you can listen when you drive to work. I even listen when I'm working out.
5 I work from home – I'm a web designer, so I'm online all day and I have my favorite websites that I use for news. I often check the headlines. I never watch TV, but I watch a lot of TV shows online.
6 On a mobile device, so I can check the news on the move. I'm lucky, I have a smart phone and an iPad, and usually check my news apps when I'm commuting to work. And doing it this way, there's no destruction of trees and there's no trash.

2.2 Notice the connections.

1 And today will be sunny with temperatures_up to_25_degrees in some areas. Tonight we can expect_some_rain, and it will start cloudy in the morning and stay that way for most of the day tomorrow, so it will be a little colder.
2 This week's box_office_hit is *Miracle Men* starring Ben Gardner. It's_just_been_announced that Gardner will be in a_new_movie with Michelle Warren coming_out in the fall.
3 The latest news we have is that all the main highways into the city are clear just_now, but there_is heavy congestion in_the_downtown area and you_are_recommended to stay_away, if possible.
4 In baseball_news, the Cardinals have_reached the final of the_World_Series, where they_will_face Texas. The Cardinals beat Arizona 5–2 tonight.
5 The World Summit_on_climate_change has come to_an_end after only_eight_days with no_real_agreement reached between world leaders from over_50_nations.
6 All_over_the_country today there were protests about the rising_price_of_food. The government is considering reducing_the_tax on fruits_and_vegetables.
7 When a local_news_team went to visit_grandmother, Maria Braun, to ask questions_about_her_daughter they got more than they expected. Maria_chased_the_reporters with a baseball_bat and called_the_police. The reporters got_no_answers to their questions about her daughter, who is suspected_of_hacking into local government_computers.

2.3 Notice /wəz/, /wər/, and the spellings of /tʃ/.

D = Dad   A = Allie   M = Mike
D Hello, Allie! It's Dad. What were you doing when I called last night? You didn't pick up.
A Sorry, Dad. Uh, what time was that?
D It was about 8 o'clock.
A Oh, yeah, I was watching a fantastic nature show about the jungle. I really didn't hear the phone. Did you see the show?
D No, I didn't. What about Mike? I called him too.
A He was making dinner at 8. His famous burgers – you know what he's like – they have to be perfect.
D Hmph! And the twins? I called them too.
A They were playing video games – and anyway, they never answer their phones.
D They couldn't stop playing to talk to their grandfather?! Nobody answered the phone. Nobody wanted to talk to me!

A Don't be silly, Dad – we h**on**estly didn't hear our phones – and you have to send a text me**ss**age if you want to talk to the twins.
D OK – I just wanted to **ch**eck …
A But how are you, anyway?
D Fine … well, it w**as** good talking to you. Bye, dear.
A But we haven't even had a **ch**ance to … Bye, Dad.
M What did your dad want?
A I don't know. He just wanted to say hello, I think!

▶ 2.6 Notice the pronunciation of **sh** and **tch**.

1
M1 What did you wa**tch** on TV last night?
W1 Oh, I wa**tch**ed a great **sh**ow about the **an**imals and plants that live in rainforests in southeast Asia.
M1 Sounds interesting! I love **sh**ows about nature.

2
M2 I was wa**tch**ing a cooking competi**ti**on for young people last night.
W2 Oh yeah – what did they have to cook?
M2 They had to use in**gr**edients they hadn't seen before, and cook a di**sh** in 45 mi**n**utes!
W2 Huh! No pressure then!

3
M3 So, was the **sh**ow interesting?
W3 Yeah, lots of s**ci**entists were giving ex**am**ples of how the weather has changed and why this is h**app**ening. And then they pre**d**icted what might happen in the future.
M3 Mmm. That's scary to think about.

4
W4 Did you see that movie last night? It was awesome. A woman turns into a s**u**perhero and rescues people and, um … then **sh**e ….
M4 Hmm. Sounds awful to me. Not my type of movie.

5
W5 I love c**om**edy – I was wa**tch**ing a great new series about an Au**s**tralian f**am**ily last night. It was really funny. A girl wanted to impress her new boyfriend by baking him a cake – but **sh**e couldn't get the se**c**ret recipe and it was a di**s**aster!
M5 I saw that too! It was hil**a**rious! And I loved it when Brendon …

6
A What were you just wa**tch**ing?
B It was a crime **sh**ow. The de**t**ectives started out looking for some missing di**am**onds and ended up di**sc**overing major crime at an off**sh**ore bank.
A Not again! All those **sh**ows are the same.

▶ 2.7 Notice pronunciation of **oo** and **ou** spellings.

P = presenter   R = reporter

P Tonight on *What on Earth is Happening?*, we have stories from di**ff**erent parts of the world about recent extreme we**a**ther events. We'll be v**is**iting nine different c**ou**ntries – here's a taste of what's to come. From Ba**n**gladesh:
R1 It's been raining and raining for h**ou**rs and now there's a terrible fl**oo**d in **ou**r town.
P And from L**o**ndon:
R2 It hasn't rained much this year, so there's going to be a dr**ou**ght. Get ready for a dry summer.
P And the latest from Argen**ti**na:
R3 The m**oo**n passed between the Earth and the sun and there was a total s**o**lar e**cl**ipse. Everything went dark in the middle of the day! It was really weird, but c**oo**l at the same time!
P And in Fl**o**rida today:
R4 Hurricane Minnie hit today: the wind was so strong that it broke windows. It was a huge hurricane with wind speeds of up to 130 mph.
P Meanwhile in S**ou**th Africa:
R5 There was a ma**ss**ive rainbow because the sun was shining when it was raining in the Na**t**ional Park. There was even a d**ou**ble rainbow. So beautiful!
P And in Chile:
R6 There was a m**ag**nitude 5.0 earthquake yes**t**erday. Some buildings were damaged, but luck**i**ly nobody was badly hurt. The earth sh**oo**k for about 15 s**ec**onds.
P While in Indon**e**sia:
R7 There was a tsun**a**mi warning so everyone made it to safety. The waves were 20 feet high, so there was damage along the coas**t**al areas.
P And in Me**x**ico:
R8 There were huge **th**understorms overnight that left many homes with**ou**t power. Lightning struck trees in the area causing power lines to fail.
P And in Greece:
R9 There were strong winds and the fire is still **ou**t of control. Homes are in danger, but fire**f**ighters are battling the flames …
P So there's been extreme weather all ar**ou**nd the world. Now let's hear the stories behind these headlines. Let's turn first to Bangladesh …

▶ 2.8 Notice **sentence stress** and the intonation in questions.

J = Jack   M = Mel

J Hi, Mel, are you **OK**? ↗
M Yes, but we've got **no electri**c**ity**. There's a **pow**er out**age**.
J On **no**, not **again**! What were you **doing** when the **outage happened**? ↘
M I was **cooking dinner** when su**dd**enly the **lights went out**!
J Did you **finish making dinner**? ↗
M Yes, but it **didn't taste very good** because I **couldn't see** very well!
J What was **Jamie doing**? ↘
M The lights went out while he was **watching TV**, but now he's okay, doing his **homework on his laptop**.
J That's good! So **what did you** do when the lights went out? ↘
M I **found a flashlight** and some **candles**, so it's very rom**an**tic here!
J That's nice. I'll be **home soon** … I just **have to** …
M Oh no! I **have to go**. I need to **charge my phone**, it's about to die.
J Umm … **how** are you **going to charge** it? ↗
M **Plug it in**, of course … doh!

▶ 2.10 Notice /dʒ/, /ŋg/, and two spellings of /n/.

N = Narrator   J = Jane   D = Dad

N Jane was cha**tt**ing online when her phone rang. It was her boyfriend, Jake.
J Hi, Jake, how are you?
N He was calling to make pla**n**s for the week**en**d. But Jane's mom came in a**n**d looked at the computer screen while Jane was talking on the phone. She was reading Jane's emails when Jane got off the phone. She was very, very u**n**happy and told her mom that the messages were pr**i**vate.
J Stop that! Never read my messages! Go away!
N Jane's mom we**n**t downstairs. Her parents were talking when Jane went downstairs later.
D Hmm, yes. I agree.
N They were discu**ss**ing Jane and the online messages.

▶ 2.13 Notice the sentence stress.

A So, I was **cycling to school** when suddenly I **got a flat**!
B Oh, **no**!
A Yeah, so I **walked to school**.
B Uh-**huh**?
A So I was late for **class** and everyone was **taking a test** when I **got there**.
B That's **awful**! And then what happened?
A Well, I **started doing the test**, but I didn't have **enough time to finish**.
B That's **terrible**!
A So, of course, I **didn't pass** the test, but the **teacher said** I could do it **again next week**.
B Phew! **That's** good.

Review 1

▶ R1.1 Notice the sentence stress and intonation.

1 What were you **doing** at 6 p.m. **last night**? ↗
2 What did you **do** yesterday **evening**? ↘
3 Who did you **work with** in the **last activit**[y] ↘
4 What were you **doing** when class **started**? ↗

Unit 3

▶ 3.3 Notice the intonation ↗ ↘ of the questions.

P = Paula   H = Harry

P So, how's Cathy, anyway? ↘
H Fine, fine. Have you seen her ph**o**tos? ↗

P Yep, you showed them to me – last week and then again yesterday.
H ... and she's seen photos of me, too.
P And she still liked you after you showed them to her? ↗
H Yeah, she likes me. Anyway, she, uh, she says she wants to meet me.
P Oh, finally! I mean, you've known each other for a year, right? That's a long time. So, when is she coming to the States? ↗↘
H Uh ... she's not. She wants me to go to Australia ... like, next month.
P That's great. I've been to Australia twice.
H Oh yeah? Did you go on business? ↗ ↗
P Uh huh. Zero fun. Just work, work, work. How about you? ↗
H Nope. Never been there.
P So ... Have you started packing? ↗
H Hmm ...
P What? ↘
H Well ...

◉ 3.4 Notice /d/, /t/, and /ɪd/ for -ed endings.

P = Paula   H = Harry

P So ... Have you started packing?
H Hmm ...
P What?
H Well ... The thing is ... I don't know if I'm actually going.
P How come? I mean, you want to meet Cathy, right?
H I do, I really do. It would be amazing to meet in person.
P So ...?
H You see ... The thing is ... I'm, uh ...
P What?
H I'm afraid to fly. There. I've said it.
P Hmm ... Like a phobia or something?
H Yeah.
P But, uh, have you ever traveled by plane?
H Once. Mom took me to Disneyland when I was five ... I cried all the way there. No, seriously, I was terrified. And all the other passengers were shocked, of course. They thought Mom was killing me or something.
P Dude, I had no idea ... So what are you gonna do?

3.5 Notice how the /h/ sound in her most disappears in fast speech.

P = Paula   H = Harry

H ... Dude, I had no idea ... So what are you gonna do?
P I don't know.
H Well, easy ... Tell her to come to New York. Problem solved.
P Nope, can't do that.
H Why not?
P She lost her job and doesn't have much money, you know ... and she really wants me to meet her parents.
H Well, then tell her you're afraid to fly.
P No way! I'm too embarrassed to admit I'm scared to fly.

P Hmm ... Have you ever tried therapy? Maybe it can help you get ...
H Twice. It didn't work. I really don't know what to do.
P Hey, I have an idea. Why don't ...

◉ 3.8 Notice the long pauses // and the short pauses /.

L = Lisa   M = Meg

Day 1

L Wow ... // this place has changed ... // a lot.
M Have you stayed here before?
L Oh yeah. / A few years ago. // But now ... // I mean, / what kind of hotel is this? // Look at these walls / and this carpet ... Oh my God! A mouse!
M Where? Where?
L There! There! / Oh, it's gone, / thank God. // Meg, / listen, / we've got to get out of here.
M But ... // we've only just arrived!
L Yeah, but we haven't checked in yet. And more important – we haven't paid yet. // I tell you what, / let's stay at the hotel near the station.
M Wait a second. // How much money are we talking about?
L Well, / I guess it's a little more expensive, but ...
M Lisa, / I can only spend $50 a night. I've already told you like five times.
L Well, / no, / not really. // You spent a lot of money shopping for clothes yesterday, so I didn't think money was a problem.
M Well, / it is, actually.

Day 2

L I'm going to the National Gallery today. // Julie's been there / and she says it's fantastic. // What are you going to do?
M Well, // I haven't been to the West End yet / and I really want to go. // We could meet up for coffee at around three o'clock. // What do you think?
L Yeah, but / look ... // the weather has changed. // It's really cloudy now, / a perfect day to go to the National Gallery.
M Well, // I really don't want to see old paintings today. // Sorry.
L Well, // if you're sure. // I'll see you at three / and then I can tell you all about the Gallery.

Day 3

L Oh! / That was a loooong day. // I'm exhausted. / Goodnight, Meg.
M Lisa, / I just want to read a little before I go to bed.
L Oh // Meg ...
M I'm reading 101 Things To Do Before You Die. // It's a book with lots of suggestions of cool, / exciting things to do, // things that can change your life! Have you read it?
L Uh ... // No, I haven't. / And I'm really, really tired.
M I started it when we got on the plane / and I've already read the first 20 ideas. // It's fascinating.

L Look, Meg. / We woke up really early this morning, / I'm exhausted / and I can't sleep with the lights on. // Sorry.
M OK, / OK, / sorry, Lisa. // I'll read downstairs in the lobby, then. // Good night.

◉ 3.10 Notice the stress in the auxiliary verbs.

M Hey, Lisa, have a look at this list!
L What is it?
M It's a kind of bucket list at the back of the book I'm reading.
L Oh, yeah, I remember - 101 Things To Do Before You Die. So ... let's see. Oh look! Visit London! We've both done that so, yup, obviously, we've both been abroad too.
M Yeah. And there are lots more cool ideas here too. Look at these ones – see? I've never swum with dolphins, uh, or ridden an animal. I'd love to ride a camel or an elephant.
L Oh, I've already done that. I used to ride horses when I was a girl. But I haven't swum with dolphins yet!
M And look at this one – learn to dance. Ah! I've never learned to dance, because, uh, I have two left feet.
L Oh! I can't dance either, I want to learn tango.
M Me too! Daradaradara ...
L OK, so what else have you done?
M Hmm. Well, I've made lots of birthday cakes ... oh and I've just fallen in love.
L No way! With who?
M With London.
L Ha ha, very funny.
M Sorry! Uh ... I've been a DJ a few times, so that's another one, and, uh ... I've already tried extreme sports.
L Yeah?
M I went snowboarding in Colorado last year.
L Nice!
M Yeah, awesome! But you know what, I've never done volunteer work, or planted a tree, or donated blood. Oh my god, I'm so selfish!
L Look at this one – have a child. Have you had a child yet?
M Lisa! Of course I haven't!

◉ 3.12 Notice /t/, /d/, and /ɪd/ for -ed endings.

I = interviewer   R = Rita   T = Tina

1

I ... really true, isn't it? So, Rita, how long did you live in Barcelona?
R I lived there for, uh, seven months ...
I Did you have a job?
R Yep. I worked as an au pair for four months.
I How was the experience?
R Well, when I first looked at Raul and Ricardo, I thought ...
I Who?
R The twins.
I Oh, OK.
R So, when I first saw them, I said to myself: "I'm going to get on the next plane and get

back home now." But after a while ... well, I fell in love with the boys ... and I realized that I was born to be around kids. Period. So that's how I decided to be a teacher, not a lawyer.
I Oh, so you wanted to study law?
R Well, Mom and Dad insisted for a long time – they really wanted me to be a lawyer. But now they don't talk about it anymore. Thank God. So what I really ...

2
I ... absolutely right. So, Tina, how long have you been in the UK?
T Uh, I've been in the UK since September, so ... yeah, that's six months ... But I arrived in Scotland six weeks ago.
I How do you like it?
T Honestly?
I Uhhuh.
T I hate it. Life sucks here. Yeah, I thought it was going to get better when I got a job, but ...
I Oh, so you're working?
T Yeah, I got a job at Tesco and ...
I What's that?
T Oh, a big grocery store. Or supermarket as they call them here.
I How long have you worked there?
T Three weeks. The longest weeks of my life.
I Have you made any friends?
T No, not yet. But my cousin's just come to visit, I haven't seen her for a long time, so that will be great!

◐ 3.14 Notice the intonation in the questions and expressions of surprise.

B = Barry   L = Linda   M = Miguel

1
B ... exactly, and that's when I wrote my very first song.
L What? ↘ Wait a second. ↘ Did I hear you say that you wrote a song, Barry? ↗
B Uh huh. I called it "The Moon and the Stars." Grandma still cries when she hears it.
L Wow! ↘ Really? ↗ How old were you at the time? ↘
B Uh, about nine, I guess. I learned how to play the piano when I was four, so ...
L You're kidding me! ↘ When you were four? ↘ Wow. ↘ You've never told me that.
B Really? ↗ I thought you knew. Anyway, when I got into college, I had to ...

2
L ... much, much better when I was a child. These days, there's nothing good on – absolutely nothing.
M What? ↘ What do you mean nothing? ↘
L Well, maybe one or two shows, but they're either late at night or on cable.
M Hmm ... I don't agree ... I think the late night news is good and some of the documentaries ... come on ... they're just fantastic.
L Oh, come on, fantastic? ↗ Well, I don't agree, Miguel. I think they're just stupid. That's why I don't let the kids watch TV at home.
M But, uh, then you let them spend hours on the Internet, right? ↗

L Well, not hours, but ... You know, I have no problem with them being on their phones.
M No way! ↘ But that makes no sense, Linda. You see ...

Unit 4

◐ 4.4

1 Notice /z/ and the three spellings of /s/.

M = Michael   G = Gloria (Mom)   D = Dad

M Mom. Can I have these?
G What? Headphones? What's wrong with yours?
M They're really big and uncomfortable. I want wireless ones, Mom! Please!
G No, honey, those are too expensive.
M But, Mom, come on. All my friends have these wireless headphones! It's not fair! You promised, remember? You said that if I helped you with the housework, you'd buy what I wanted.
G Michael, I know, but we're talking about three hundred dollar headphones here, not just a toy! That's a lot of money. Listen, I can get you these wireless earbuds instead. How about that?
M My life is awful! I hate my life ...
D Oh dear ... Gloria, rule number 1: if you make a promise to a kid, you can never, ever break it.
G I know, especially a kid like Michael.
D Look ... It's important to make children do the dishes, make the bed, and help around the house ... I get that ... But promising a gift in return? Bad idea.

2 Notice the intonation ↗ ↘.

F = Freddy   S = Susan   B = Brenda (Mom)
P = Phil (Dad)]

F Hey, Susan. Wanna play? ↗
S I can't leave the house. I have homework to do – a lot of it! ↘
F We can watch a couple TV shows and then we can go to McDonald's. ↘
S No, I have a big test next week and I need to get an A plus this time. ↘
F Well, will you die if you get a B? ↗
S Yeah! Duh! ↘
B Susan, close those books now and go have some fun. ↘
S But, Mom! I haven't finished ... ↘
B Susan, you're a smart kid. You should know that children who do a lot of homework every day don't necessarily do well in exams ... ↘
S But, Mom ... there's nothing healthy to eat at McDonald's! I haven't had any vegetables today! Please, let me stay home. ↘
B Susan, it's not a request – it's an order. Go out and have fun! ↘
P Brenda, I'm a little worried about our daughter.
B Me too. Where did we go wrong, Phil? ↘
P Well, once I read somewhere that young parents usually make more mistakes with

their children. Guess they're right. Are we awful parents, Brenda? ↘ ↗
B No, of course not. But we could do better. How about if we ... ↘

◐ 4.7 Notice /ð/ (voiced) and /θ/ (unvoiced).

J = Julia   D = Dad

J Oh, I miss those days. Life was so much easier.
D What do you mean? Do you miss school? I thought you hated that place!
J Well, yes, but I was just a kid, you know, and that's what kids do, right, Dad? They hate school, they sit at the back of the class, they...
D Hmm ... your brother likes school.
J Well, Danny's a nerd, so of course he does. Uh ... Dad, there's something, uh, there's something I've never told you, you know ...
D Oh yeah? What?
J Remember that time you and Mom thought I was sick?
D You used to be sick all the time, Julia – at least until you were 12. You used to eat everything you found! One day you ate bird food, remember?
J No, I mean that time you took me to the hospital ...
D Oh, your leg. Of course. Your mother and I almost went crazy that day.
J Well, I was sort of ... lying.

◐ 4.8 Notice pronunciation and spelling of the final /l/ and /m/ sounds.

D = Dad   J = Julia

D What do you mean? We saw it! Your left leg was dead.
J No, it wasn't, Dad. I was lying.
D Lying? What do you mean lying?
J Look, I really didn't want to go to school, Dad. We had a big test and, uh..., well, I was afraid to get a bad grade. I'm sorry.
D But ... Julia, we took you to the hospital! Why didn't you tell us?
J Look, I'm sorry. I really am. I didn't use to do it all the time. I never lied about the serious stuff. I swear.
D Wow ... five hours at the hospital ... for nothing! I can't believe you did something like that. We were so worried. Unbelievable ...

◐ 4.9 Notice /iː/ and /ɛ/.

To some people, vinyl records bring back memories of growing up in the 1960s and 70s when rock and roll was king. Back then, music lovers listened to Elvis Presley and The Beatles on black disks spinning on a turntable.
Today's younger generation didn't grow up with records. So for them, vinyl is cool.
Jack Lowenstein came to Crooked Beat Records in Washington, DC. and told us "I prefer to buy vinyl records over CDs." Sarah Griffith is into vi too. "More recently I've started buying more, y know, like old punk records and stuff."
In the early 2000s people turned away from C and started to download music online. Then

Audioscript

vinyl made a comeback. Today, people buy more CDs and vinyl records than they buy music downloads. But the real story is music streaming. Streaming has revolutionized the music industry and more people stream music than download or buy either CDs or vinyl. In our next episode we look at the music streaming revolution.

▶ 4.16 Notice the /d/ sounds and silent d endings.

R = Roy   B = Brenda   A = animal shelter assistant

R Ooooh, they all look so adorable!
B Yeah, right, Roy, adorable ...
A Uh, excuse me, Miss... Hi... We, uh, we have a four year-old daughter and we'd like her to have a pet. She's an only child, so we want a pet that can keep her company ...
A No brothers or sisters? Oh yeah, you should definitely get her a pet.
B Like a bird ... or a goldfish, right?
R Brenda, we've talked about that – goldfish are not as interactive as dogs. End of discussion.
B But goldfish are quieter than dogs.
R You see, we both work all day and, uh, we live in a small apartment. What would you recommend?
A Have you considered getting a cat?
R Well, to be honest, we were kind of thinking of a dog. We, uh ... prefer dogs.
B Roy, YOU like dogs. I'd do anything to stay pet free. They're a lot of work!
R Come on, Brenda, it's not as bad as it looks!

▶ 4.17 Notice the weak forms in comparatives.

– Roy, you like dogs. I'd do anything to stay pet free. They're a lot of work.
– Come on, Brenda, it's not as bad as it looks!
– Well, cats are not as good with kids, I know, but, well, they're independent animals, which is great if you're both busy and...
– Hmm... and they're much quieter than dogs too.
– But you see, we want Lynn to walk the dog, take it to the park, teach it how to sit... stuff like that.
– Well, why don't you get a dog that's easy to train? You know, like a poodle or a Lab.
– Like a what?
– A Labrador – come here, let me show you.
– Oh, he looks adorable! Come here, little doggy! Now who's the cutest dog in the world?
– Does he bark a lot?
– Well, yes, but not as much as a poodle.
– I don't like noisy animals, you know. My life's stressful enough, thank you very much.
– Hmm ... in that case, have you thought about getting a house rabbit? You won't hear a sound, I promise.
– Hey, wait a second ... That's a great idea.
– Yeah ... Why not? Rabbits are cute, small and quiet. Can you show us?

Review 2

▶ R2.1 Notice the connections.

1 I've been_to Australia twice.
2 But ... we've_only just_arrived!
3 Yeah, but look ... the weather_has changed.
4 I lived and worked_as_an au pair in Barcelona for nine months.
5 Digital songs don't sound as_good_as LPs.
6 She used_to follow strangers around the house and make weird noises.

▶ R2.2 Notice the sentence stress.

1 Oh, we used to fight over the remote control every single day. There were three TVs at home, but we all wanted to watch the big one in the living room. Good old days.
2 I swear! It never was. I mean, what was I supposed to do if the dog liked to paint itself purple and daddy's car used to like driving itself? I had nothing to do with any of that!
3 That's what grandpa used to say every night before my sister and I went to bed. Every single night. Oh, how I miss him.
4 Of course not! I was just trying to push him away using my foot. There was no violence, of course! I mean, he was my brother, come on!

Unit 5

▶ 5.1 Notice the connections.

Welcome to Marlbury College! We hope you'll enjoy your visit. My name is Karen Crawford. First of_all, let me present some_of our classes. In picture one, we see a biology class. Slide two shows_a geography class. Number three shows_ some_of our history students and number four shows psychology students. Photo five is_a philosophy class and in six some_of our foreign languages students are doing a role-play. Slide seven is_a sociology class and number eight is_a chemistry class in our new chemistry lab. It's wonderful! Then slide nine shows_some_of our politics students having a very serious debate ...

▶ 5.3 Notice the intonation of the questions ↗ ↘, /g/, and /dʒ/ sounds

Here at Marlbury College we have something for everyone! We offer degree programs at bachelor's and master's level. Call us today for a catalog! Are you interested in a new profession? ↗ We have vocational Certificate and Diploma programs in everything from cooking to banking. Is it difficult for you to come to class? ↗ Don't worry! We offer a lot of our courses online – so you can study any time you want. Do you work all day and want to take classes in the evening? ↗ We can help you there too. We have a large choice of classes in the evenings, including French, Chinese and ESL classes. All this and more is available at our attractive campus with our high-tech modern facilities. Call Marlbury today and find the best class for you. Not sure where to begin? ↗ Come to one of our free classes that are open to the public. You can meet our great teachers, and administrators, and get more information about Marlbury College.

▶ 5.5 Notice intonation in the instructions.

T = teacher   S = student

1
T OK – this is your final examination. You have ONE HOUR. Answer three out of five questions. You should spend about 20 minutes on each question. Remember, this is an exam, so there should be silence and no communication between any of you. You can start now.
2
T OK! Let's do an exercise to practice the words. Look on page 18. Complete these sentences with an appropriate word from the list below. Then listen to check.
3
T So this is a group work activity. In a group of four, discuss the movie extract that we watched and find two things that you liked about it and two things you didn't like. OK?
S1 But what if we didn't like anything about it?
T You need to find two things in your group that you liked, so ask the other people in your group.
4
T Search online for a song line that you like featuring the words "used to." Bring a recording of it to the next class.
5
T In your journal, write or record an audio about how you felt about class today. What were the things you understood? Write a question that you have for next class.
S2 How much do we have to write?
T As much as you want, but at least one paragraph.
6
T We're going to do a pair work activity. In pairs. Talk about your plans for the weekend. Ask your partner what she or he is going to do. Then answer your partner's questions.
S3 I don't have a partner.
T Work with Loni and Michelle.
7
T This is your presentation for next week. Use PowerPoint to present your family to the class. Prepare at least four pages. For Monday morning, please.
S4 Monday! No way! We need more time! That's too soon! There's not enough time.
T That gives you a whole week. That's more than enough!
8
T So for this month's project we look at houses. We'll look at the construction of houses in different parts of the world and we'll consider the materials used and why. Yes, Mike?
S5 Are we working in teams?

T For some parts you'll be in teams and for some parts you'll be on your own.
9
T OK. Take out a piece of paper, we're going to have a quick test. You have two minutes to write the past tense of these verbs. Then hand your answers to me.
10
T All right, then. So, we've finished reading the book now and I want you to write a one-paragraph summary of the last chapter of the book.
S6 For when?
T Next class.

5.6 Notice pronunciation of *have to* and *got to*.

M = Mark   C = Candy

M Wow! This class is going to be hard. Ms. Cosby says we can't miss even one session.
C That's not so bad! So we've got to come to every class – that's good.
M And we have to write a paper for next week.
C It's OK. It's just two pages.
M But I hate writing papers.
C You've got to write papers whenever you take a class.
M I guess so. And the teacher said we can't arrive late!
C Of course not, that's good! That will make you come on time.
M But what if I don't feel like coming?
C Come on, Mark! It's not that bad. And she also said we don't have to take notes, because all the handouts and the slides are available online.
M Hmm, I guess you're right! That should be easy!

5.7 Notice the linking between two vowel sounds.

M = Mark   C = Candy   MM = Mrs. McCormack

M What are you doing tonight?
C I've got to study, because I have a test tomorrow.
M Another one! That's too bad! Do you have to study_on Saturday too?
C Uh, I don't have to study_on Saturday, but I want to, because I really need to get good grades this time. Why?
M Well, I wanted to invite you to_a party on Saturday. Should be_a good one!
C Oh! Well, my mom gets worried, so_I can't stay_out later than 12, but I could go for a while. But you'll have to_ask my mom, and persuade her.
M OK, pass me_over. Hello, Mrs. McCormack. This is Mark.
MM Hello, Mark. Busy studying?
M Yes, you know_me! Er, can Candy come to_a party with me_on Saturday?
MM Sure, but she has to be home by 12, please. I really worry if she stays out too late.
M Not a problem, Mrs. McCormack. I can't drive my dad's car after 11, so_I have to be home by then anyway.

5.9 Notice the sentence stress and weak forms.

1
There were **too** many **exams**. **Awful**. My **grades** were **never** good enough. Or I just **failed too** many **times**. **Waste** of **time**. **Awful**. **Bye, bye!**
2
Well, **basically** I spent **too** much **time**, uh …, having **fun**. You **know**, too **busy** with **friends**, **concerts**, all the **parties**. I just **didn't** have **enough** time to **study**! So, I just **quit**.
3
It was **too** hard to choose a **major**. I did **psychology** – **hated** it – started **again**. **Philosophy**, hated **that**, and, **then**, well, there were **too** many **choices**, so I **quit**. And uh, got a **job**. And then **another** job. I **guess** I'm not **decisive** enough. But **then**, maybe I **am** … Oh, I don't know.
4
It wasn't **interesting** enough and I, uh, just stopped **enjoying** it. **Totally**. **Every** morning, I wanted to do **anything**, **an-y-thing**, except go to school. **Man**, just **thinking** about school was **too** de**pressing**. **Miserable**. **Enough** was **enough**. So, uh, **boom**! Time to say **goodbye** and **fly**.

5.10 Notice the phrases for agreeing.

W = woman   M = man

M I'm reading an article about the top reasons why people quit school or their job.
W Oh yeah? That's interesting. I bet reason number 1 for leaving jobs is money.
M Yep. It says "The number 1 reason why people leave their job is money, money, money."
W Sure, I mean, if employees are unhappy with their pay, they leave – if they can find another job.
M Well, I mean, uh …, we all want more if we can get it.
W And the second reason is …?
M Uh … uh … they'd like better benefits, like health insurance and pensions.
W Sounds right to me. Number 3?
M They feel they don't have a good relationship with their boss.
W Yeah, I hated my last boss – he lied all the time.
M Yuk. And the fourth reason is …?
W The stress of too much work?
M Uh-huh, their workload is too heavy. And …
W And number 5 must be that they don't like the place where they work.
M Yup, good job!
W I guess 'cos it doesn't have good facilities.
M Or it's dirty …
W Yeah, stuff like that. What about dropping out of college? Is that for financial reasons too?
M No, it says the first reason is that they don't have enough self-discipline to go to class every day. And to keep up with assignments and homework.
W Right! So, if students miss a lot of classes, they drop out of school. Well, no surprises there!

M Number 2 is when they feel too isolated or homesick away from their family and friends.
W I can see that – I felt like that in college.
M Money is only number 3! When they don't have enough money to continue studying.
W So that's pretty different from work, then?
M Yeah, interesting, and 4 is … personal reasons. They have too many personal problems like breaking up with a partner or needing to care for a sick relative.
W That's terrible when that happens.
M Really. And the final one is …?
W Wrong choice?
M Yup, when they find they chose the wrong thing to study, and, uh, feel they're not interested in what they're studying.
W Oh, yeah! I know people like that!
M Me too. Remember John …

5.14 Notice intonation in the questions.

Z = Zack   V = Vicky

Z Oh hi, Vicky. How's it going? ↘
V Oh hi, Zack. Everything's fine.
Z Uh … Vicky? Did you see that email I sent out yesterday? ↗
V What about? ↘ You kind of send out a lot of emails!
Z The staff meeting we're having on Friday.
V Oh, yeah, I saw it and programmed it into my calendar, so it will remind me. It's at 11 a.m., right? ↗
Z That's right.
V And it's in the conference room, right? ↗
Z That's right. I also said I wanted ideas for the agenda. I don't have anything from you.
V That's weird. I posted my ideas on the team chat app as soon as I read your email.
Z Oh … you posted them on the team chat app? ↗ – of course you did - uh … OK … I'll check that now. Um … Thanks.
V Sure, Zack.

5.15 Notice the intonation.

a
W = woman   M = man
W1 Watch out! If you're not careful, you'll fall in
M1 If you help me get in, I'll row the boat.
b
D = Dad   M = Mom
D Whatever you do, don't eat that ice cream. you do, you'll have to go to your room!
M If you eat all your dinner, I'll give you some ice cream.
c
D = Dad   M = Mom
D If you finish your homework, I'll take you ou to the movies.
M I won't buy you a new bike if you don't get good grades. You'd better do your homework.
d
W = woman
W4 If you stay late, I'll give you the day off tomorrow. But be careful! If you don't improve your work, you'll be fired.

PAUL SELIGSON
TOM ABRAHAM
CRIS GONTOW

2nd edition

English ID

Workbook 2

1.1 What's really important in life?

1. **1.1** Listen and answer. Follow the model. Write or record your answers.

   Model: *What's your full name?*
   Student: *My name's…*
   Model: *How do you spell your last name?*

2. Complete quotes a–f with one of these life priorities. Check the one you like best.

career	education	family
free time	friends	have fun
		love

   a "If you think _____ is expensive, try ignorance!"
      Andy McIntyre
   b "_____ is when the other person's happiness is more important than your own." H. Jackson Brown Jr.
   c "Communication—the human connection—is the key to personal and _____ success."
      Paul J. Meyer
   d "When you _____ you can do amazing things."
      Joe Namath
   e "Too much _____ on your hands just leads to trouble." K. Jeffrey Miller
   f "You can choose your _____ but you sure can't choose your _____." Harper Lee

3. Match these priorities to the evening course ad titles a–d.
   - [ ] fitness
   - [ ] culture
   - [ ] financial security
   - [ ] health

   a ART HISTORY

   b Do you want to get in shape?

   c Healthy cooking for less money

   d Manage your money

4. Match titles a–d from **3** to these ads.

   [ ] Our exciting evening Zumba class fuses fitness fun with hypnotic Latin rhythms! Any fitness level. Complete beginners welcome.
   One week free for 50+

   [ ] Learn how to prepare dishes that are good for you and don't cost much. Cook 12 dishes over the four-week course, each with a different healthy ingredient. Ingredients are not included.

   [ ] Would you like to know more about European movements of the 19th and 20th centuries? This course introduces art from the Impressionists to Cubism, exploring painting, sculpture and architecture. Please bring a pen and a notepad.

   [ ] Are you frustrated by your finances? We can help. Our four-week free course tells you everything you need to know about saving and spending. Thursdays, 7–9 p.m.

5. Choose the correct option.
   a Yesterday we **cooked** / **cook** a healthy pizza and I **take** / **took** it home for dinner.
   b Last night we **watched** / **watch** a presentation about 19th Century architecture.
   c At the moment we **learn** / **'re learning** how to make risotto.
   d I **'m wanting** / **want** to learn how to save more money. That's why I **chose** / **choose** this course.
   e Don't worry, this course **doesn't cost** / **isn't costing** anything.
   f We **meet** / **'re meeting** every week and it's great fun. I love dancing!
   g I **love** / **'m loving** this type of art so I **really enjoy** / **'m really enjoying** this course.
   h I **'m going** / **went** to the first class last night. It was good but I **'m** / **was** very tired today!

6. Match statements a–h in **5** to the four ads in **4**.

7. **Make it personal** What's important to you? Record your own "Life in 10 seconds" and email it to a friend or your teacher.

1.2 Which sense do you use the most?

1 Complete the conversations with the pairs of adjectives in the box.

> awesome / soft   great / bland   fantastic / awful   sour / spicy

1 A: This food smells _____ .
   B: I agree, but it tastes a little _____ .
2 A: Your sweater looks _____ .
   B: Thank you. The material feels so _____ and lovely.
3 A: What did you think of the band? I thought they sounded _____ .
   B: Really? I thought they sounded _____ ! I have a headache now.
4 A: Is there anything you don't like?
   B: Well, I don't like anything that tastes too _____ or anything too _____ .

2 ▶1.2 Complete ads a–d with the words above the photos. Listen to check.

look at   see   touch   watch

a _____ this awesome offer! This new _____ -screen laptop for only $300. You can use it for work or study, then take off the keyboard and _____ movies and play games when you travel, and use it like a tablet. Come and _____ this and other great prices at Tony's Technology Store. Tony's Tech **store**. Fantastic new laptops and **more**!

eat   smell   smells   taste   tastes

b Breathe through your nose. Can you _____ our fresh bread? If you think it _____ good, wait until you _____ it. It _____ even better! _____ Brenda's bread for **breakfast**! From the best kitchen in **Texas**.

feel   listen to   look   smells

c When you use new UltimaColor laundry detergent, your clothes _____ soft, the colors _____ bright and the fragrance _____ awesome. But don't believe us, _____ this happy customer: "I put UltimaColor in my washing **machine**, and now my clothes are super **clean**!"

hear   listen to   read   sound

d When you _____ loud rock, you don't want the music to stop. You don't have to _____ the neighbors **fight**, because your music will _____ great all **night**! Warning: loud music can cause hearing problems. _____ the safety instructions before use.

3 ▶1.2 Listen again and notice the rhymes in the **bold** words in each text.

4 ▶1.3 Listen and react personally. Follow the model.
Model: *Fresh coffee. Taste.*
You: *It tastes <u>great</u>!*
Model: *Old shoes. Smell.*
You: *They smell <u>terrible</u>.*

5 🎧 Make it personal Think of things you would describe with sentences a–e.
a It tastes awful.
b They smell great.
c It feels soft.
d They sound awesome.
e It looks interesting.

1.3 Do you read, hear, or watch a lot of ads?

1 ▶1.4 **Complete the dialogue with *will* or *won't*. Listen to check.**

Rachel *Iron Man*! I love it! But I can't believe Yinsen is going to die!
Chris I know, but at least Stark _____ escape, and become a super hero when he returns to America. I think they _____ make another *Iron Man* movie soon.
Rachel No, they _____, it's getting too old now. Anyway, what's for dinner?
Chris Well, I don't have much food in the kitchen. How about pizza? I _____ call and order some. I want Meat Feast. What do you want?
Rachel Hmm? I _____ have the vegetarian one, please.

2 **Order the words in a–f to make sentences.**
  a will / of / she / money / take / all / probably / his / .
  b die / Yinsen / will / .
  c call / I / some / order / will / and / pizza / .
  d get / she / married / will / .
  e vegetarian one / will / I / have / the / .
  f will / Stark / become / definitely / a superhero / .

3 **Mark sentences a–f in 2 as either predictions (P) or unplanned decisions (U).**

4 ▶1.5 **Listen to the rest of Chris and Rachel's dialogue. Check the two problems they have.**
  a Chris doesn't get the pizza he wants.
  b Chris can't afford the pizza.
  c The Meat Feast smells bad.
  d Rachel's pizza is too big.
  e Rachel's pizza smells strange.
  f Rachel doesn't want to take it home.

5 ▶1.5 **Listen again and complete a–e. Then mark them predictions (P) or unplanned decisions (U).**
  a Ah, that's the pizza, _____ _____ _____.
  b Oh yes that's right. _____ _____ and get it.
  c Chris, it's enormous. _____ _____ _____ all that!
  d I think _____ _____ _____ home with me.

6 ▶1.6 🔵 **Make it personal** Listen and answer. Write or record your answers.

> 🔊 **Connect**
>
> Think of two predictions for the year 2030. Write them in a short tweet.

7 **Complete the sentences with the words in the box.**

bubbles	countryside	cozy	leather	moist

  a When it's cold I love a nice, hot bath with plenty of _____ .
  b I love my new jacket. It's really _____ and warm, and it looks stylish too.
  c This cake's lovely! So _____ and delicious.
  d That's a nice bag. Is it real _____ ?
  e We used to live in the city but then we moved to the _____ .

6

1.4 What shouldn't you do to stay healthy?

1 Read the introduction to the article. Underline the four suggested reasons for taking a day off.

Everybody needs a little break sometimes.

Maybe you feel stressed, maybe you have to care for your children, maybe you went out late last night or maybe it's a beautiful sunny day and you just don't want to work. Whatever your reason, here is our step-by-step guide to taking a day off work, but don't tell your boss that you read this article!

2 Read the rest of the article and match the headings to each paragraph. There is one extra heading. Then put them in the correct order, 1–4.

| Going back to work | Inform your boss | Party time! | Preparation | Your time off |

a _____
Now you are free to enjoy your time off. But be careful! If your phone rings, be careful how you answer it, it might be your boss. And if you have a lot of fun, NEVER post it on social media! In fact, it's a good idea to stay at home.

b _____
Remember to look ill when you return to the office. Watch a late-night movie so you go to work looking tired. Put a box of painkillers or cough medicine on your desk so that everyone can see it. REMEMBER! Never take medicine if you don't really need it, or you will really get sick. And your boss will get suspicious if you take more time off!

c _____
Call your boss early in the morning. Your voice will sound bad and they will be getting ready for work so they won't have time to ask any difficult questions. Keep the conversation short. Don't give too many details, but be ready to answer any questions.

d _____
Choose your illness carefully and be sure you know the right symptoms. We recommend a stomachache for a short break, and flu or a bad headache if you need more time. Try to choose something contagious so that your boss doesn't want you in the office. A few days before you plan to be "sick", start to show symptoms. A loud cough is easy to do and will get attention. You can also say that you hurt in various places, but you should try not to be too specific.

3 ▶1.7 Based on the article, give advice with **should / shouldn't**. Follow the model.

Model: *Investigate the symptoms.*
You: *You should investigate the symptoms.*

Model: *Give details.*
You: *You shouldn't give details.*

4 Complete the advice with **should** or **shouldn't**.
a You _____ take a day off on Mondays or Fridays. Long weekends are suspicious.
b If you can, you _____ get a letter from a doctor.
c You _____ take time off when your work is very busy—you will be unpopular with your colleagues.
d You _____ play dangerous sports. If you break your arm it will be difficult to explain!
e You _____ go to work when you have a bad cold unless the doctor tells you to.

5 ▶1.8 Read these sentences aloud and listen to check your pronunciation.
a You **shouldn't** wear **shoes** in the house.
b **Put two** painkillers in a glass of water.
c How did you **cook** this **soup**?
d This **book** is a **true** story.

6 Put the **bold** words in **5** in the correct column according to the sound of the underlined letters. Listen again to check.

/ʊ/	/uː/
shouldn't	

7 🅜 Make it personal   What advice would you give to someone to stay healthy? Write five pieces of advice.

7

1.5 When do you ask for help?

1 Read five predictions about the future made in the past. Which came true?

a Gold has even now but a few years to live. The day is near when bars of it will be as common and as cheap as bars of iron or blocks of steel.
(Thomas Edison, 1911)

b We will have high-definition, wide-screen television sets and a push-button dialing system to order the movie you want at the time you want it.
(Roger Ebert, 1988)

c Nuclear-powered vacuum cleaners will probably be a reality in ten years.
(Alex Lewyt, 1955)

d There will be no C, X or Q in our everyday alphabet. They will be abandoned because unnecessary.
(John Elfreth Watkins, 1900)

e It will soon be possible to transmit wireless messages all over the world so simply that any individual can carry and operate his own apparatus.
(Nikola Tesla, 1909)

2 Complete a–e with a reflexive pronoun if necessary.
  a Can you see _____ in this photo?
  b Please wash your hands _____.
  c There's food in the kitchen, so just help _____.
  d Fredo gets up _____ at 7 a.m. every morning.
  e Then he shaves _____ and gets dressed.

3 ▶ 1.9 Listen to three dialogues and select how the person can help.

4 Divide these lines into mini dialogues.
  a Ihavetogototheairportdoyouwantmetodrivethat'sverykindofyou.
  b I'mgoingtowashthedisheswouldyoulikemetodryyesplease.
  c Thesebagsarereallyheavyl'llcarryoneforyouthat'sverykindofyou.
  d Idon'tunderstandthisproblemdoyouwantahandyesplease.
  e It'sreallycoldinheredoyouwantmetoturnoffthea/cthanksfortheofferbutIcandoit.

  I have to go to the airport.
  Do you want me to drive?
  That's very kind of you.

5 Put the words in the correct order to make offers.
  a hand / you / a / need / Do ?
  b to / me / Would / help / like / you ?
  c me / Do / you / want / off / music / the / turn / to ?
  d you / I / Can / help ?

> **Can you remember ...**
> ▶ 10 life priorities? SB ▶ p. 6
> ▶ the 5 senses and verbs to talk about them? SB ▶ p. 8
> ▶ how to make ⊕ and ⊖ predictions? SB ▶ p. 10
> ▶ 7 common illnesses? SB ▶ p. 12
> ▶ how to make ⊕⊖ sentences with *should*? SB ▶ p. 12
> ▶ ways to offer help and how to accept and refuse help? SB ▶ p. 15

2.1 Do you ever read newspapers?

1 Read the article, then label a–e in the graph with:

~~Generally~~   Internet   Newspapers   Today   TV

● **Newspapers Are Dead!** Long Live the Internet!

Newspaper circulation is declining, and now more people get their news on the Internet than ever before. In a recent survey we asked commuters on the morning train two questions: "Where do you generally get your news?" and "If you saw the news today, what format was it in?".

Our results show that generally the Internet is now more popular than newspapers for news, although TV is still the most popular. Interestingly, when we asked where people got their news today, more people said newspapers than the Internet. Maybe this is because people read the news on the Internet on their lunch break at work, but read newspapers in the morning.

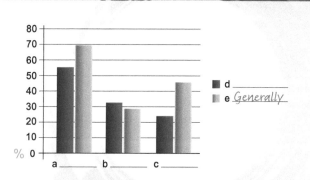

2 According to the article and graph, are a–c True (T) or False (F)?
  a More people got today's news from a newspaper than online.
  b More than half usually get their news from the Internet.
  c The time of day affected the survey.

3 ▶2.1 Match the phrases with the correct preposition. Listen to a monologue to check.

| an article   a magazine   the front page   the sports section   a tablet   TV |

in	on

4 ▶2.1 Listen again and complete a–f with two words.
  a He only gets a newspaper o_____ S_____s.
  b He thinks the editorial articles are v_____ i_____.
  c On weekends, he reads the s_____ s_____.
  d The TV guide is in _____ m_____.
  e He thinks the rest of the magazine is a w_____ of p_____.
  f From Monday to Friday he reads important items on t_____ l_____.

Connect

Find an interesting news article online, then summarize it to a classmate.

5 Circle the correct options in sentences a–f.
  a **Yesterday / Yesterday's** news **was / were** very sad.
  b I only **look at / see** the photos **in / on** newspapers.
  c It's easy to **lose / waste** time **in / on** the Internet.
  d My brother has a lot of books **in / on** his shelves.
  e I sometimes read a novel **in / on** the bath.
  f We have a lot **of / in** common.

6 ▶2.2 **Make it personal** Listen to questions a–e and check your answers.
  a ☐ Every day.   ☐ Once a week.   ☐ Only sometimes.   ☐ Other.
  b ☐ I'm always connected. ☐ Once a day.   ☐ No, never.   ☐ Never.
  c ☐ Yes, always.   ☐ Yes, sometimes.   ☐ Yes, but it depends on
  d ☐ Yes, I love it.   ☐ No, I think it's stupid.   the celebrity.
  e ☐ Yes, I did.   ☐ No, I didn't.

2.2 What were you doing at 8 o'clock last night?

1 Choose the correct verb form.
   a What **were you liking** / **did you like** watching when you were a child?
   b I **watched** / **was watching** TV at 8 p.m. last night.
   c We both **loved** / **were loving** that movie.
   d I **was talking** / **talked** to Anna when you called.
   e Misha **played** / **was playing** video games at 10 p.m. last night.

2 ▶2.3 **Excuses, Excuses!** Order the words to make questions and complete the replies. Listen to check.
   a **Mother:** you / fighting / why / were / ?
      Sons: We _____ (not fight). We _____ (play).
   b **Boss:** Why were you on the Internet? weren't / why / working / you / ?
      Employee: I _____ (send) an e-mail to a client.
   c **Angry girlfriend:** Is this SMS from your ex-girlfriend? was / you / why / texting / she / ?
      Boyfriend: She _____ (ask) for a friend's phone number.
   d **Angry boyfriend:** you / me / didn't / call / why / ?
      Girlfriend: Sorry, but my phone _____ (not work).

3 ▶2.3 These words from **2** have silent letters. Practice saying them, then listen again to check.

   | fight | phone | friend | why |

4 ▶2.4 Listen and respond with a reason from **3** after the beep.

5 **State or Action?** Complete a–f with the verbs in the simple past or past continuous.

a I _____ (not eat) it, I _____ (taste) a little.

b _____ the milk _____ (taste) OK this morning?

c _____ you _____ (have) a headache yesterday?

d Sorry, I _____ (have) breakfast when you called.

e _____ you _____ (like) the video I sent to you?

f I'm sorry, I _____ (not listen). What did you say?

6 🎤 **Make it personal** What were you doing at these times yesterday? Record your answers.

   | 7 a.m. | 11:30 a.m. | 1:15 p.m. | 4 p.m. | 6:30 p.m. | 8 p.m. |

📶 **Connect**

Choose a photo on your phone. Write a short description of what you were doing when you took it.

2.3 What's the world's most serious problem?

1 ▶2.5 **Listen to extracts a–h and match them with the problems below.**

- [ ] animal extinction
- [ ] climate change
- [ ] corruption
- [ ] crime
- [ ] disease
- [ ] pollution
- [ ] poverty
- [ ] unemployment

2 ▶2.5 **Listen again and match the numbers below to extracts a–h. There's one extra number.**

- [ ] 1
- [ ] 13
- [ ] 30
- [ ] 88.2%
- [ ] 2,300
- [ ] 3,200
- [ ] 200,000
- [ ] 2,800,000
- [ ] 200,000,000

3 Match the words to definitions a–i.

a A large curve of different colors which can appear in the sky when there's sun and rain.
b When the moon goes between the Earth and the sun.
c A sudden shaking of the Earth's surface.
d A fire that moves quickly and out of control.
e A huge storm that moves over water.
f A long period of no rain when there isn't enough water for plants and animals to live.
g A very large wave, usually caused by an earthquake at sea.
h When a place becomes covered with water.
i A storm with thunder and lightning.

- [ ] a hurricane
- [ ] a rainbow
- [ ] a flood
- [ ] a thunderstorm
- [ ] an eclipse
- [ ] a tsunami
- [ ] an earthquake
- [ ] a wildfire
- [ ] a drought

Connect

Search online about one of the types of natural phenomena in 3. Read about it, then share what you found out with a classmate.

4 Complete the posts with the words in the box and the past continuous of the verbs in parentheses.

> drought   earthquakes   eclipse   flood
> hurricane   lightning   rainbow   thunderstorm

Weird Weather Website

a Yesterday, there was an _____. It was really strange. When the sun went behind the moon, the temperature dropped for a few minutes. We _____ (watch) it in our yard with a special protective mask. It was amazing. BTW, I read a theory that this causes _____. Did anybody feel the ground move?

b During the first few months of this year there was a _____. There was no water, so the plants _____ (not grow). I work in agriculture, so I really depend on the weather. I won't make much money this year.

c There was a _____ in my town last night. There's a lot of water damage to buildings and possessions. Thankfully, I _____ (stay) with my grandparents, so I didn't have to move, but my neighbors had to leave their houses in the middle of the night.

d I love photography and I _____ (play) with my new camera the other afternoon when suddenly the sky went dark. There were these huge black clouds and a few hours later, a _____ started. I took some photos of the _____ hitting the ground. They're great photos, I'll post some.

e I _____ (watch) TV last night. It was a program about _____ Katrina in New Orleans. It was terrible. We don't get weather like that here, in fact, it _____ (rain) a few moments ago and now the sun is out and there's a beautiful _____.

5 ▶2.6 **Read the three poems and underline the picture word sounds in each one. Listen to check.**

a *I have two y<u>ou</u>ng cousins.
I call them "double trouble."
Everywhere they go they cause
problems for their mother.*   /ʌ/

b *This is a story about a house in the clouds,
Two thousand steps up, three thousand steps down.
The sun was hot in summer,
The wind was loud at night.
The couple couldn't live there,
So they found a place in town.*   /aʊ/

c *It would be good to visit Hollywood.
If you get a chance to go, you should.*   /ʊ/

6 ▶2.7 **Make it personal** Listen and answer. Write or record your answers.

11

2.4 Was your mom living here when you were born?

1 ▶ 2.8 Listen to stories 1–3 and match two of photos a–f to each of them.

2 Use the photos to complete sentences a–c with the simple past or past continuous of the verbs in parentheses.
  a Abby _____ (work) with some kids when suddenly the door _____ (open) and Meghan and Harry _____ (walk) in!
  b Pete _____ (watch) TV when he _____ (hear) a loud BANG.
  c Zoe _____ (talk) to some people on the bus and they _____ (offer) her a job.

3 Choose the correct alternatives.
  a When I was a child I **didn't like / wasn't liking** broccoli.
  b What **were you doing / did you do** when I **phoned / I was phoning** you last night?
  c Paulo **was chatting / chatted** online when the power **went out / was going out**.
  d What **were you talking / did you talk** about when I **came / was coming** in?
  e Chiara **was walking / walked** downstairs when her heel **was breaking / broke**.

4 Correct two mistakes in each sentence.
  a When I was more young I was playing a lot of video games.
  b My phone was ringing when I was in middle of taking a test at school.
  c My friends wasn't smiling when I was taking a photo of them.
  d What you were doing the last night when the outage happened?

5 ▶ 2.9 Listen to sound effect stories a–d. Use the words to tell each one in a single sentence.
  a walk / street / start / rain
  b work / be / power outage
  c jog / park / dog / attack
  d play / piano / cat / jump

6 🙂 Make it personal Mark which events a–e you have experienced, and write a sentence about each.

What were you doing the last time there was…

a a power outage? ( )
The last time there was a power outage, I was watching TV at home.

b a thunderstorm? ( )
_____
_____
_____

c an earthquake? ( )
_____
_____
_____

d a flood? ( )
_____
_____
_____

e an eclipse? ( )
_____
_____
_____

2.5 What do you carry in your pockets?

1 ▶2.10 Order the pieces of paper, 1–12, to make a joke. Can you guess the ending? Listen to check.

- [1] A man and his wife were having some…
- [ ] … he woke up and looked at his alarm clock. It was 10:30 a.m.!
- [ ] … to watch her favorite drama show every evening. One day, the man came…
- [ ] … the next morning. But he didn't want to talk to his wife, so he wrote a…
- [ ] … he went to bed. In the morning…
- [ ] _____

- [ ] … message: Please wake me up at 4:30 a.m. He put the message on the TV and…
- [2] … problems in their marriage and they weren't…
- [ ] … talking to each other. Their house was completely…
- [ ] A piece of paper was lying on the table next to his alarm clock. It said:
- [ ] … home from work. He was tired and he had to catch a plane early…
- [ ] … silent. Only the TV made noise at night because the woman liked…

2 ▶2.11 Listen to some more anecdotes and respond with one of these phrases after the beep.

- No! You're joking!
- Oh dear. That's bad luck.
- Wow! That is lucky.

3 ▶2.12 Listen to a firefighter from the story "Strange Things Happen". At each beep, choose the best question.

a
- [ ] What happened?
- [ ] Where did you go?

b
- [ ] Where was the house?
- [ ] Why was she on fire?

c
- [ ] They were in her pocket?
- [ ] The stones caught fire?

d
- [ ] Is she OK?
- [ ] Can you buy these stones?

4 ▶2.13 **Make it personal** Listen and match answers a–e to the questions.
- [ ] Did you read the news today?
- [ ] Is crime a big problem in your area?
- [ ] What kind of TV shows do you like?
- [ ] Do you remember the 2011 tsunami?
- [ ] Do you know any funny stories?

a No, it's very safe where I live.
b Nah, I can never remember jokes. But my brother knows a lot.
c Yeah, the front page had a story about politics.
d Yeah, I saw it on the news. It was terrible.
e Hmm. I like comedies and dramas.

Connect
Write your own answers to the questions in 4 and send them to a friend or your teacher.

Can you remember …
- 7 news genres? SB→p.19
- Past be + -ing ⊕ ⊖ ❓? SB→p.20
- 8 global problems? SB→p.22
- 9 natural phenomena? SB→p.23
- 2 words to connect past continuous and simple past clauses? SB→p.24
- 3 ways to show you're listening? SB→p.27
- 8 phrases to react to positive or negative things? SB→p.27

3

3.1 How often do you travel?

1 Match the verbs and nouns. Then number them in a logical order.

pack	in line ___
board	your bags ___
be stopped at	a ticket _1_
book	the plane ___
take	customs ___
have	a taxi to the airport ___
stand	to your hotel ___
check in	a snack on the plane ___

2 Read three travel stories, then complete 1–8 with the correct form of these verbs.

arrive   board   book   break down
crowded   hitchhike   miss   pack

3 ▶3.1 Circle the correct words in bold in the stories. Then listen to check.

4 Reread and answer a–e.
a Which person didn't like the other passengers?
b Which two people were scared?
c Who didn't want to hitchhike?
d Who is the youngest traveler?
e Which person was traveling alone?

5 **Make it personal**   Order the words in a–d to make questions. Circle the best answer for you.
a go / do / stressed / get / when / you / wrong / things / ?
_____
Never. / Sometimes. / Often.

b well / last / did / go / your / vacation / ?
_____
It was a disaster. / It was OK. / I had a great time.

c get / when / bus / you / you / miss / do / angry / the / ?
_____
No, I wait for the next one. / Only if I'm going to an important place. / Always. I hate being late.

d impatient / you / kids / on / get / young / do / planes / with / ?
_____
No, I love kids. / Only if they are loud. / Yes, kids shouldn't be permitted on planes.

Person 1   Last weekend I went **in / on** the worst trip ever. It was Saturday and Mom decided that we were all going to the beach for the day. So we _____ ¹ our bags with bathing suits and started **in / on** the two-hour drive. Dad was driving but he doesn't like the GPS. This was fine **in / on** the highway but, after about 30 minutes **in / on** the back roads, Dad started to look worried. We were lost! Mom got the map and soon they were both arguing about which road to take and which direction to go in. And **in / on** the back of the car things weren't much better. My brother can sleep anywhere at any time, too, and that was exactly what he was doing. His head was falling **in / on** my arm, and when I pushed him away, he woke up and started crying. This continued until we finally _____ ² at the beach, four hours after we left home. And guess what? It was raining, and I _____ ³ my friend's party, too! Never again!

Person 2   Around four years ago I was traveling **in / on** India. I took a lot of night buses and they were usually great. _____ ⁴ your ticket, find your seat, fall asleep. It was easy. And this time everything was going well until… SMASH! One of the windows fell from the bus. Suddenly a cold wind was blowing around us, and I mean cold! The driver continued, and I put **in / on** my sweater and shared a blanket with another passenger until… BANG! And the bus slowly stopped. This time it was the engine and the driver couldn't continue. The bus _____ ⁵ **in / on** the middle of the night, **in / on** the middle of the road, **in / on** the middle of nowhere. We were stuck and just had to wait. Some passengers _____ ⁶ in passing trucks, but I was too scared. I can laugh about it now, but at the time it was terrible.

Person 3   OMG, what **a / –** day! I usually drive, but today I took **a / the** train for **a / the** first time on a Saturday—never again! Those soccer fans are crazy! I was going home with Bruna, and **a / the** train was nice and quiet, and then we got to **the / –** stadium. The station was _____ ⁷ with thousands of fans, and they all looked violent and scary and **the / –** police had bulletproof vests and **the / –** dogs and everything. **The / –** fans _____ ⁸ the train, and they were shouting and using **a / –** bad language—it was terrible. But then **– / the** worst thing was they started jumping up and down. I couldn't believe it. **The / A** train actually started moving from side to side. It was **a / –** really dangerous. I was terrified!

14

3.2 Have you ever been to another country?

1 ▶ 3.2 Listen and complete the survey for Tanya.

The Internet has changed many aspects of modern life: the way we communicate, get information, work, etc. Even the way we think and act has changed. And shopping has changed dramatically too. Have you bought any of these things online? Please check ✓ the boxes on the computer screen.

	This month	In the last 6 months	Never
books	✓		
music			
movies			
travel tickets			
hotel rooms			
event tickets			
electronic equipment			
clothes			

2 Use the survey in **1** to write present perfect sentences and questions.

a Tanya / buy / books / this month / .
   Tanya has bought books online this month.

b what / you / buy / online / this month / ?
   _____

c she / watch / a movie online / twice this month / .
   _____

d you / ever / book / a hotel online / ?
   _____

e she / book / travel tickets online / .
   _____

f she / go shopping / today / .
   _____

3 🎤 **Make it personal** Complete the survey with your own answers and sentences.
I've never bought a book online!

4 Use these ideas to make guesses about your class.

eat crocodile	try martial arts
go abroad	give money to charity
see a celebrity	plant a tree

a I think no one in my class has …
b At least three people have …
c Only one person …
d I think my best friend …
e I think my teacher …

5 Order the words in a–i to make questions. Which experiences in **4** do they refer to?

a lake / where / the / was / ?
b you / it / when / wear / did / ?
c often / money / how / give / you / do / ?
d him or her / did / speak / you / to / ?
e did / like / what / taste / it / ?
f you / did / it / where / plant / ?
g you / vacation / go / did / on / ?
h you / me / something / can / teach / ?
i did / long / for / how / you / fly / ?

6 Correct two mistakes in each of a–d.

a Have you ever swimmed in a lake? No, but I have swum in a river when I was on vacation.
b The last time I have worn a tie was when I was at the school.
c You have ever buy clothes online?
d Have you gone abroad ever? Yes, I have been in Canada twice.

7 ▶ 3.3 Match the words to the sound pictures. Listen to check. Notice the different spellings.

a mean / seen / clean
b swum / money / done
c board / orange / before

8 🎤 **Make it personal** Which of the sentences in **6** are true for you? Record your answers.

3.3 Have you sung a song in English yet?

1 ▶3.4 A couple are preparing to go on vacation. Listen and order the photos, 1–4, as they mention them.

2 ▶3.4 Add *just*, *yet* or *already* to extracts a–e. Listen again to check.
   a The dogsitter hasn't arrived.
   b I've told you.
   c Have you fed the dog?
   d I've bought some food for her.
   e I've remembered!

3 Circle the correct meanings for extracts a–e.
   a He's late again. – 's means **is** / **has**.
   b Just a minute. – *just* means **recently** / **only**.
   c I've just finished eating. – *just* means **recently** / **only**.
   d I've already bought some food. – *already* means **all prepared** / **before now**.
   e OK. All ready? Let's go. – *all ready* means **all prepared** / **before now**.

4 **Make it personal** What has happened today? Write sentences with *just*, *already* and *yet*.
   a I / have breakfast
      I've already had breakfast. / I haven't had breakfast yet. / I've just had breakfast.
   b I / go online
   c My friend / call me
   d I / leave home
   e I / eat dinner
   f I / take a shower
   g I / check my email
   h I / do a lot of exercise

5 *Web Hunt!* Read the article. Then go online to research the four projects. Mark them **A**, **B** or **C**.
   A: Construction has not started yet.
   B: Construction has already started.
   C: Construction has finished.

Since the very earliest days of humanity, civilizations have demonstrated their power through architecture. Today we can marvel at structures like the ancient Mayan temples of Central America or the Pyramids of Egypt. But what will we leave for future generations? Today we look at four super-buildings around the world.

1 Basilica and Church of the Sagrada Familia. Barcelona. *Started in 1882.*

2 1,000 Trees. Shanghai. *A tree-covered building.*

3 The Diamond. City of London. *Jewel of the city.*

4 Costanera Center, Santiago. *The tallest building in Latin America.*

16

3.4 How long have you lived here?

1 Match choices a–e to the reasons.

a I'm volunteering in a school
b I decided to travel for a year
c I didn't take a gap year, I went straight to college
d I spent two years working before college
e I decided to try lots of different jobs

☐ as I don't want to waste my time traveling or volunteering.
☐ because I didn't really know what I wanted to do and college is sometimes a waste of time.
☐ to earn money. Studying is expensive!
☐ because I want to be a teacher after college and the experience will help me get a job.
☐ to learn about different cultures and see the world.

2 Read an interview from a student magazine. Which choice from **1**, a–e, best describes him?

Marvin Powers—Self-Made Millionaire

a You are very successful. Tell us, what do you do?
Right now, I am the director of a transportation company. When I started it, we only had three trucks… ☐

b Very impressive. How long have you had the business?
Not very long… ☐

c That is a short time! Did you study logistics at college?
No, I didn't go to college… ☐

d So where did you learn to be a businessman?
I guess I studied at the University of Life!… ☐

e OK. So what has been the most important lesson you've learned?
Ummm. I guess the most important thing is to learn from your mistakes… ☐

f Good advice. Now, apart from your business successes, what are you most proud of in your life?
It has to be my family: my two daughters and my beautiful wife… ☐

g Congratulations. And now our final question. What do you do to relax?
Ummm. I don't really have time to relax. I played soccer and went to the movies a lot when I was younger… ☐

3 Complete with *for* or *since*. Then use these sentences to complete a–g in **2**.

a … I've done a lot of jobs _since_ I left school.
b … I think that studying _____ three or four years is a waste of time.
c … We've been married _____ almost eight years now.
d … And I've made a lot of them _____ I started out in the big, bad world!
e … I guess I've been in this business _____ about six years.
f … But I haven't done that _____ a long time.
g … _____ then, it has grown to over fifty vehicles.

4 ▶ 3.5 Follow the model. Listen and answer with *for* and *since*.

Model: *How long / live in your house?*
You: *How long have you lived in your house?*
Model: *October.*
You: *Since October.*

Model: *How long / live in this city?*
You: *How long have you lived in this city?*
Model: *Five years.*
You: *For five years.*

5 ▶ 3.5 **Make it personal** Listen again but now give your own answers.

Connect

Interview your partner using the questions and record it on your phone.

17

3.5 Are you a logical person?

1 Read and complete the introduction to an article with the correct form of **have** or **be**.

MONSTER MYTH

Humans _____ always _____ a fascination for strange creatures. From the Himalayan yeti to the Chinese dragon, every culture _____ a terrifying monster or mysterious giant to populate their stories, to make children _____ good and, nowadays, to attract tourists. Here _____ one of our favorites.

2 Complete 1–11 in the text with these suffixes.

-ic -ment -al -ion

☐ They have even taken photographs to support their convict___s¹, but they are never clear, and so there is no corroborat___² for the story.

1 Nessie, or the Loch Ness Monster, lives in a deep lake in Scotland and swims to other lakes through underground tunnels. The perfect environ___³ for a monster!

☐ Many people believe that Nessie is not a monster and is, in fact, a dinosaur that has survived since pre-histor___⁴ times in the lake.

☐ In 2003, a team did a scientif___⁵ investigat___⁶ of the lake. They used sonar equip___⁷ and satellite technology capable of extreme precis___⁸ and they found…

☐ However, despite this long existence, the monster myth only started in 1933. And so the argu___⁹ between Nessie believers and non-believers was born.

☐ Believers have come to this remote locat___¹⁰ for almost a century hoping to see the famous monster, and there have been occasion___¹¹ reports of the reptile.

☐ You guessed it. Absolutely nothing.

3 ▶3.6 Reread and order the rest of the article, 1–7. Listen to check.

4 ▶3.7 Listen to four dialogues and complete the reactions 1–4.

5 ▶3.7 Listen again and repeat the reaction after the beep.

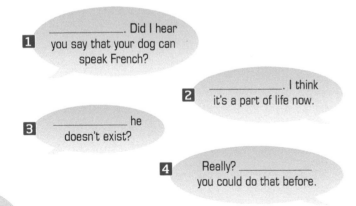

1 _____. Did I hear you say that your dog can speak French?

2 _____. I think it's a part of life now.

3 _____ he doesn't exist?

4 Really? _____ you could do that before.

Connect
Tell your partner about something surprising. Record their reaction on your phone.

Can you remember ...
▸ 7 stages of a trip? SB→p.32
▸ 4 past participle verbs? SB→p.34
▸ how to ask about past experiences and how to ask follow-up questions? SB→p.34
▸ which adverb means a past experience was very recent? SB→p.37
▸ 2 words to use when you talk about the duration of an action? SB→p.39
▸ 4 suffix endings to make nouns or adjectives? SB→p.41

4.1 Were you spoiled as a child?

1 What's the form of the underlined verbs in questions a–b: infinitive or past?
   a How old were you when you went to your first school?
   b When did you go to your first school?

2 Complete a–f with the correct form of the verbs.
   a How old were you when you _____ (buy) your first pair of shoes on your own?
   b How old were you when you _____ (get) your first cell phone?
   c Do you remember when you _____ (take) your first exam?
   d When did you _____ (go) on your first date?
   e How old were you when you _____ (go) to your first party without your parents?
   f When was the last time you _____ (laugh) a lot?

Connect
Interview your partner with the questions and record it on your phone.

3 Read the first part of the article. True (T) or False (F)?
   a Only Japanese people believe that blood type affects personality.
   b People use blood type to predict more than just personality.
   c Many scientists accept the connection between blood type and personality.

It's in the blood

Do you believe that the stars really determine our personalities? Why not something a little closer to home, a little more… biological? Well, in Japan and South Korea that is exactly what they believe. Over there, your blood type predicts your personality… and a whole lot more too. It all sounds very scientific, right? Wrong, there is very little scientific evidence.

4 Read the rest of the article and match adjectives 1–16 to each blood type.

   1 active   7 hardworking   13 sensitive
   2 aggressive   8 honest   14 shy
   3 creative   9 independent   15 sociable
   4 critical   10 responsible   16 spoiled
   5 curious   11 kind
   6 funny   12 obedient

Type A
These people like to help other people and they are good listeners. However, they don't like to share their emotions and sometimes cry when other people are critical of them. This means they sometimes spend time alone, but they don't mind that. They can also be very obsessive about small details.
Career: s_ftw_r_ _ng_n__r,   l_br_r__n.

Type B
These are the artists and the explorers. They love making new things, experimenting and discovering how things work. And they don't like taking orders—they want to do things their way. This means that they often ignore their duties and obligations.
Career: c__k,   h__r styl_st,   j__rn_l_st.

Type AB
These people want to succeed, and they will really work for it. If their boss or teacher asks them to do something, they will do it without any questions. They hate to see bad work or lazy workers and they will share their opinions and their feelings. Sometimes this is good, but not always!
Career: l_wy_r,   t__cher.

Type O
These people love to be the center of attention. They love to make new friends and they are always joking and always doing something exciting. However, if they don't get what they want they can quickly change, and sometimes they try to get what they want physically.
Career: _thl_te,   b_nk m_n_g_r,   p_l_t_c__n.

5 ▶ 4.1 Complete the career words with vowels. Listen to check.

6 **Make it personal** Answer questions a–f in 2 about yourself.

4.2 What did you use to do as a child?

1 ▶4.2 Order pictures a–g to make a story. Listen to check.

2 ▶4.3 Listen and complete an interview for ID with Silvio Roma, an Italian immigrant.

ID   So, Silvio. _____ use to work a lot at school?
Silvio No, I didn't. But I used to _____.
ID   Uh-huh. And _____ did you use to play?
Silvio I used to play soccer every day _____ young.
ID   What _____ before you came here?
Silvio I lived in Milan and I _____ to college. I was a music student.
ID   And do you like this country?
Silvio Well, I _____ like it. It was very strange coming to a new country with a different language. But now I am very happy here.

3 ▶4.4 You are Silvio! Use the answers in 2 and make sentences with **used to**. Follow the model.

Model: *not / like school*
You: *I didn't use to like school.*

Model: *love playing sports*
You: *I used to love playing sports.*

4 Match the two parts of sentences a–d.

a My parents didn't use to let me watch TV after 9 p.m.
b I used to have a lot of CDs
c I used to play sports a lot more
d I didn't use to like English

☐ but I think it's OK now.
☐ than I do now.
☐ when I was young.
☐ before I bought an MP3 player.

5 **Make it personal** Order the words in a–c to make questions. Then answer them.

a you / used / school / who / take / to / to / ?
b did / to / cartoons / use / watch / which / you / ?
c food / hate / what / use / to / did / you / ?

Connect
Record your answers on your phone. Send them to a classmate or your teacher.

6 ▶4.5 Listen and cross out four silent *t*s in these words.

advantage   castle   Christmas   digital   kitchen   listen   often   turntable   watch

4.3 Has your taste in music changed?

1 **Use the clues to complete the crossword.**

ACROSS
1 round, black things which play music
5 popular music
6 playing music over the Internet
7 what records are made from

DOWN
2 transfer something from the Internet to your computer or mobile device
3 digital music files
4 a machine which plays vinyl records
5 an old type of music from the 70s

2 **Read quotes 1–5 about music. Which talk about the past (PA)? Which talk about the present (PR)? Which talk about both (B)?**

1 "I don't really like pop music at all. It all sounds the same to me. I like rock music much more. I actually play guitar in a rock band, and we write all our own music."

2 "My parents used to listen to punk music when they were teenagers. They used to wear really weird clothes and go to concerts and just jump around for hours. I saw a photo of them and it was really embarrassing, they were wearing very strange clothes!"

3 "When I was a teenager I used to listen to heavy metal music. I had long hair and only wore black clothes. I thought I was very cool, but nowadays I just think I was a bit silly."

4 "I love electronic music, and I make my own music alone on my computer. I don't do it to become famous or anything, it's just a hobby and something I do in my free time. If you're interested, you can listen to my music online."

5 "I used to have a huge CD collection. I think I had over 500! Then one day I decided to sell them and buy all the music as MP3s. I miss my collection now though, I still have all the music on MP3s, but it's not the same as having a big collection you can look through and organize."

3 **Read the quotes again and write the number of the person who …**
a thinks their parents were weird.
b thinks a type of music sounds the same.
c regrets something they did with their music collection.
d thinks differently now to how they did when they were a teenager.
e makes music on their own.
f plays a musical instrument.
g talks about the clothes they used to wear.

4 **Make it personal** Answer a–d.
a What music did you use to listen to when you were younger?
b Do you still like this music now? Why (not)?
c What's your favorite way to listen to music?
d What music DON'T you like? Why not?

Connect
Record your answers and email them to a friend or your teacher, or write them as a tweet.

21

4.4 Do you speak English as often as possible?

1 Read the reviews and match the highlighted adjectives to their opposites.

big   easy   expensive   heavy   unclear   unpopular

TECHREVIEW

Star 100
The *Star* is a very popular piece of equipment. It is the biggest and heaviest of the tablets here. One disadvantage of the *Star* is usability. Many people find it difficult to use.

Price: $299
Dimensions: 24 × 18 cm. 660 g
Screen: 146 pixels per cm
Memory: 512GB
Usability: ★★★☆☆

Eye-let Mini
The *Eye-let Mini* is selling very quickly. Most people love its user interface (UI) and we agree. It is very, very easy to use. It is also relatively small and light so it is easy to carry. However, it has quite a small memory, only 128GB.

Price: $299
Dimensions: 20 × 13 cm. 312 g
Screen: 128 pixels per cm
Memory: 128GB
Usability: ★★★★★

Dall P45
The *Dall P45* will be in stores soon. The big advantage of the *P45* is the picture; with 204 ppcm it is really clear. We watched some movies online and they were perfect! And at $250, it is quite cheap.

Price: $250
Dimensions: 22 × 15 cm. 314 g
Screen: 204 pixels per cm
Memory: 512GB
Usability: ★★★★☆

2 Mark all ten adjectives Type A, Type B or Type C using the chart on Student's Book p. 50.

3 Use the information in the reviews to make sentences about the tablets.
   a The Star's picture / clear. *The Star's picture is the clearest.*
   b The Eye-let Mini / expensive / the Star. *The Eye-let Mini is as expensive as the Star.*
   c The Dall P45's memory / big / the Star's. _____
   d The Dall P45's picture / clear / the Eye-let Mini's. _____
   e The Dall P45 / not / easy to use / the Eye-let Mini. _____
   f The Eye-let Mini / about / big / the Dall P45. _____
   g The Dall P45 / cheap. _____

4 ◉ 4.6 Read sentences from 3, one at a time after each beep. Listen to check your pronunciation and then read it again. Follow the model.
   Model: *The Star's picture is the clearest.*
   You: *The Star's picture is the clearest.*

5 **Make it personal** Which tablet would you choose? Complete the sentence below with all the reasons you can think of.
   I would choose the _____ because it _____.

 Connect
Send your answers to 5 to a classmate. Compare. Who has the most and best reasons?

4.5 How many pets have you had?

1 Order this story, 1–4, about an intelligent dog.

AMAZING PETS

☐ Each lesson is five hours but Chaser loves learning, so if her owner doesn't want to teach, Chaser makes him! She is a very enthusiastic student!

[1] Have you ever tried to learn a foreign language? If you have, then you know how difficult it is to remember new words.

☐ How did it start? Well, Chaser's owner read about a dog in Germany that knew about 200 words so he decided to give his dog some lessons.

☐ Well, maybe you should take some advice from Chaser the dog. Chaser learns one or two new words every day and already has a vocabulary list of over 1,000 nouns. And now she is learning verbs too!

2 Match the sentences and join them with *so* or *but*.
a I walk my dog at the same time every day
b I have a dog and two cats
c My dog doesn't like dog biscuits
d I love dogs
e Our dog has a lot of energy
f I don't have time for a dog

☐ I live in an apartment so I can't have one.
☐ we play with her a lot.
☐ I bought a goldfish.
☐ they never fight.
☐ she knows what time to go.
☐ she loves cake.

3 ▶ 4.7 Listen to a woman shopping and check the right answers.
a She is buying a gift for
☐ her husband. ☐ her son. ☐ her nephew.
b He is going to be
☐ 20. ☐ 21. ☐ 22.
c She wants to spend around
☐ $12. ☐ $20. ☐ $200.
d She decides to give him
☐ money. ☐ a book. ☐ a tablet.

4 ▶ 4.8 Match a–d to the correct endings to make suggestions. Listen to check and repeat.
a That is an important birthday. You should definitely
b Have you considered
c Twenty dollars? Have you thought about
d 21-year-olds always need money. Why don't you
☐ buying him some new technology?
☐ just give him some money so he can buy what he wants.
☐ get him something special.
☐ getting him a nice book?

5 ▶ 4.9 Listen and match answers a–e to these questions. Listen again and give your own answers.
☐ What blood type are you?
☐ Do you always do your homework?
☐ Did you use to hate any food?
☐ Do you like buying technology?
☐ Is 21 a special birthday in your country?

a Yeah, I love having the latest technology, but it is very expensive!
b I didn't use to like tomatoes, but I can eat them now.
c Uh, I don't know. I know O is the most common, so maybe I have type O blood.
d Uh, I think 18 is more special, and the 16th birthday is more important for girls.
e I usually do, although I'm sometimes busy doing other things.

Connect

Record your answers on your phone. Send them to a classmate or your teacher.

6 Choose the correct alternatives.
a Why don't you **have** / **having** a rest? You look tired.
b You should definitely **talk** / **talking** to Kate about it.
c Have you thought about **buy** / **buying** a new car?
d Have you considered **ask** / **asking** Janice for help?

Can you remember ...
▶ 16 personality adjectives? SB→p. 44
▶ 11 *make* and *do* phrases? SB→p. 45
▶ *used to* in ⊕, ⊖ and ❓ forms? SB→p. 47
▶ 2 forms of comparatives and superlatives adjectives? SB→p. 50
▶ 1 word to link a consequence? SB→p. 52
▶ 1 word to make a contrast? SB→p. 52
▶ 4 ways to make recommendations? SB→p. 53

5   5.1 What would you like to study?

1 Cross out the school subjects in the word snake to find the hidden statement. How strongly do you agree with it?
   1 completely agree   2 partly agree   3 don't agree

> you~~get~~biologyasmucomputersystemscheeconomicsducageographytioliteraturenoumathematicstsidephysicsschpoliticsoolpsychologyassociologyin

2 Complete the stressed syllables in the following subjects.
   ☐ __ __ __ iness   ☐ __ __ __ mistry   ☐ engi __ __ __ ring
   ☐ __ __ __ guages   ☐ l __ __

3 🎧 **Make it personal** Check the subjects in **1** and **2** that you study / used to study in school. Double check the ones you get / got good grades in. Email your answers to a friend to compare.

4 ▶5.1 Listen and match people 1–5 to their degree subjects in **2**.

5 Circle the correct option in a–d.
   a He has a master's **of** / **in** history.
   b She studies **at** / **in** New York.
   c They study **at** / **in** the State University.
   d She studies **—** / **in** math.

6 ▶5.2 Listen to Helen and Janet, then match them to the information in the chart.

	College	Marlbury ☐	Arleston ☐	Brinton ☐
a Helen b Janet	Why did you choose this college?	it has a great reputation ☐	I can get here easily ☐	it's a long way from home ☐
	What do you like about the college?	an attractive campus ☐	modern facilities ☐	babysitting facilities ☐
	Degree	master's in chemistry ☐	vocational certificate in cooking ☐	bachelor's in business ☐
	Why do you like this subject?	the evening classes ☐	the good teachers ☐	the excellent technology ☐
	Ambition	make a million dollars a month ☐	open a café ☐	develop new medicines ☐

7 ▶5.2 Listen again and use their answers as a model to write four sentences about Leona.

> Hi, I'm…
> _____
> _____
> _____

8 🎧 **Make it personal** Now write four sentences about you, your school and your plans. Use the model in **7**.

> 📶 **Connect**
> Record your sentences on your phone. Send them to a classmate or your teacher.

24

5.2 What do you have to do tonight?

1 Read Carrie's school journal and match two of these activities to each day.

a an exam
b an exercise
c a group work activity
d homework
e a pair work activity
f a paper
g a project
h a quiz
i a summary
j a journal entry

2 Reread the journal and match these subjects to the days. There's one extra subject.

chemistry   economics   ~~foreign languages~~
literature   mathematics   physics

3 Order the words in a–d to make questions. Reread the journal and answer them.

a Carrie / why / pollution / talk / about / didn't / ?
b she / exercise / enjoy / Tuesday / did / what / on / ?
c long / have / paper / write / does / she / to / how / the / ?
d bad / was / Thursday / about / what / ?

4 ▶5.3 Complete the quiz with *can't* / *don't have to* / *have to*. Listen to check.

Monday 21st <u>foreign languages</u>

[b] First we did an activity—matching vocabulary to
[c] pictures and practicing the pronunciation. That was good because my pronunciation is terrible and I learned some new words. Then we had to discuss the effects of pollution on our city. I worked with Sandra, Rafael and Nathalia. It was kind of interesting, but Rafael just dominates every conversation so I didn't speak a lot. It wasn't very useful for me because I didn't practice speaking.

Tuesday 22nd _____

[ ] Great class today. We finished reading a novel last week and today the teacher gave us some fun questions to answer. I got 20/25 correct—not bad! Then we had to write two or three paragraphs about the entire story. That was difficult because the story is a little complicated and I didn't know how to put all the information into a short text.

Wednesday 23rd _____

[ ] The most boring class today—about credit and inflation and a hundred other things I don't understand. And I have to write 2,000 words on the causes of the global recession for Wed. 30th. I hate this class!

Thursday 24th _____

[ ] Cool! We're going to look at different kinds of electricity—static, electro-magnetic, etc. And then we are going to find some practical applications for it. Finally, something useful in school! The only problem is that we have to do it with a partner, and I have to work with Jordan – she talks a lot!.

Friday 25th _____

[ ] Oh great! Fantastic! The perfect way to finish the week—one hour sitting in silence answering stupid algebra questions. Did you know that $2/x = (3 \times y - 2)$? No? I didn't either and I don't think I will ever need to use it. And then we have to write a journal entry about what we've learned! But I guess I didn't learn anything! OMG!

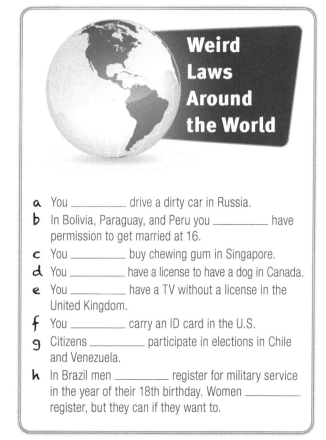

Weird Laws Around the World

a You _____ drive a dirty car in Russia.
b In Bolivia, Paraguay, and Peru you _____ have permission to get married at 16.
c You _____ buy chewing gum in Singapore.
d You _____ have a license to have a dog in Canada.
e You _____ have a TV without a license in the United Kingdom.
f You _____ carry an ID card in the U.S.
g Citizens _____ participate in elections in Chile and Venezuela.
h In Brazil men _____ register for military service in the year of their 18th birthday. Women _____ register, but they can if they want to.

5 ▶5.4 Follow the model.

Model: *Obligation. I / work / on Saturday.*
You: *I have to work on Saturday.*
Model: *No obligation.*
You: *I don't have to work on Saturday.*
Model: *My brother.*
You: *My brother doesn't have to work on Saturday.*

6 🗣 **Make it personal** Which laws in **4** would you find most difficult to live with? Why?

5.3 Are you a good student?

1 ▶5.5 **Make it personal** Match a–e to 1–5 to make advice for students. Listen to check and write two more pieces of advice.

a Be enthusiastic about what you are learning. When you are…
b If you want to optimize your classes, you can download material about the topic in…
c You will have to do a lot of reading, so find a good online dictionary so you can look…
d Don't miss too many classes! You can use the college portal to find…
e If the schoolwork is too much for you, don't drop…

1 out. Of course college can be difficult, but talk to your teacher, we are here to help.
2 out exactly where they are and what time they start and store the info on your phone planner.
3 really into a topic it's a lot easier to learn.
4 advance. You will benefit a lot more if you already understand a little about the topic of each lesson.
5 up new academic words and then use them when you write a paper.

2 Complete song lines a–d with *too* or *enough*.
   a "You've got a fast car. But is it fast _____ so we can fly away? We've got to make a decision. We leave tonight or live and die this way." Tracy Chapman
   b "I called up my congressman and he said, quote: 'I'd like to help you son but you're _____ young to vote." Eddie Cochran
   c "_____ many people going underground. _____ many reaching for a piece of cake." Paul McCartney
   d "Ain't no mountain high _____, ain't no valley low _____, ain't no river wide _____ to keep me from getting to you, baby." Marvin Gaye and Tammi Terrel

3 Order the words in a–h to make sentences and match two of them to each picture 1–4.

   a don't / enough / we / gasoline / have / .
   b been / there's / rain / much / too .
   c big / the / shirt / isn't / enough / .
   d it's / away / far / too / .
   e boats / enough / aren't / there .
   f heavy / is / him / suitcase / the / too / for / .
   g too / to / the / the / man / suitcase / is / lift / weak / .
   h eaten / food / much / he's / too .

4 Complete the captions for pictures a–d.

a I'm tired. This is *too* much exercise for me.
b I don't want to get in line. There ___ ___ many ___.

c Give me the keys. You're ___ old ___ to drive.
d I ___ have ___ ___ to buy a phone.

5 ▶5.6 Listen, then circle the /ʌ/ sounds and underline the /uː/ sounds in the bold letters. Notice the different spellings.
   a D**o** y**ou** have en**ou**gh f**u**n in sch**oo**l?
   b Bl**ue** ch**ew**ing g**u**m isn't good f**oo**d.
   c Do y**ou** know s**o**meone wh**o** has t**oo** m**u**ch m**o**ney?

6 **Make it personal** Write your answers to questions a and c in **5**.

/ʌ/
/uː/

26

5.4 What will you do when you pass this course?

1 ▶5.7 Use the pictures and these phrases to complete the man's excuse. Listen to check.

| divorce | get jealous | ~~get up~~ | go out | ~~go to work~~ | meet my friends |

I'm not getting out of bed today. If I do, you'll divorce me.

If I get up, I'll go to work. And if I go to work...
_____
_____
_____

2 Match the columns to make travel questions.
a If I take cash in our currency with me,
b Will the airline give me a hotel room
c Will my laptop be OK

☐ if I take it with me?
☐ will I be able to change it when I arrive?
☐ if my flight is canceled?

3 Circle the correct option, then match the answers to questions a–c in **2**.
☐ The airline will **to help** / **help** you if there is a problem with the plane.
☐ Don't put it in your suitcase. If you do, you probably **will** / **won't** see it again.
☐ Probably yes. But if you **will take** / **take** some US dollars or Euros, you'll be safe.
☐ If the the flight **is** / **will be** canceled because of the weather, you probably won't get a hotel.
☐ If you **will travel** / **are traveling** by plane, you can carry it with you.

4 Order the words in a–d to make travel tips.
a Put your hotel's phone number in your cell phone. them / you / if / call / lost / get / .
b you / close / bus / the / by / door / travel / if / sit / to / . It's easier to get on and off with your bags.
c shy / someone / don't / talks / if / to / you / be / ! You can learn a lot from a conversation with a local person.
d speak / if / the / don't / don't / worry / you / language / . You can communicate a lot with gestures.

5 Rewrite a–g as zero (0) or first (1st) conditionals.
a (1st) rain / I use / umbrella. _If it rains, I'll use an umbrella._
b (0) you / not have / passport / you / not can / go abroad. _____
c (1st) I take vacation / I / go / beach. _____
d (0) I feel sick / I eat too many cupcakes. _____
e (0) you travel / you learn new things. _____
f (1st) your vacation / be great / it be sunny. _____
g (1st) What / you do / it snow? _____

6 ▶5.8 Listen to check. Repeat the sentences after the beep and copy the intonation.

7 🅐 **Make it personal** Write five pieces of advice to someone traveling to another country for the first time?

27

5.5 How do you usually get in touch?

1 Read the blog post and replace the underlined words with the correct pronoun or possessive adjective.

Paula's blog Mothers and Technology

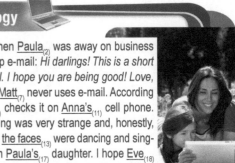

My
Paula's children all have e-mail addresses now, even Paula's₍₁₎ nine-year-old, so when Paula₍₂₎ was away on business last week Paula₍₃₎ decided to embrace technology. Paula₍₄₎ sent the children₍₅₎ a group e-mail: *Hi darlings! This is a short message to say I'll be home on Saturday and I'm really excited about seeing you all. I hope you are being good! Love, Mom.* Matt, 17, didn't reply. Matt₍₆₎ only communicates on Facebook and Twitter and Matt₍₇₎ never uses e-mail. According to Matt₍₈₎, e-mail₍₉₎ is "*last century.*" Anna, 15, occasionally uses e-mail, but Anna₍₁₀₎ checks it on Anna's₍₁₁₎ cell phone. Eve, 9, replied immediately: *hi m! luv u.* There were no capital letters and the spelling was very strange and, honestly, Paula₍₁₂₎ was a little disappointed. The rest of the e-mail was full of small yellow faces – the faces₍₁₃₎ were dancing and singing. Paula₍₁₄₎ had never seen the faces₍₁₅₎ before so Paula₍₁₆₎ learned something from Paula's₍₁₇₎ daughter. I hope Eve₍₁₈₎ will learn spelling from Paula₍₁₉₎! But although technology gives me, Matt, Anna and Eve₍₂₀₎ some problems, Paula, Matt, Anna and Eve₍₂₁₎ can still communicate face-to-face – real communication, so I'm pleased about that.

2 Re-read and answer a–e True (T), False (F), or Not mentioned (N).
 a Paula usually sends group emails to her children.
 b All of her children replied.
 c Paula doesn't mind if her children use cyber English.
 d Animated emoticons are new to Paula.
 e Paula's happy because her children talk to her.

3 ▶5.9 Listen and order the pictures, 1–6.

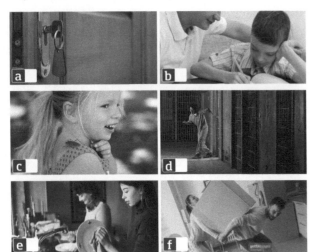

4 ▶5.9 Complete a–f. Listen again to check and repeat after the beep.
 a _____ out! If you _____ _____ they'll hear you!
 b Be careful. If you drop it, _____ _____.
 c Don't _____! _____ _____ something on your back.
 d Whatever you do, _____ _____ lock the door.
 e I'll do the dishes _____ _____ _____ with my homework.
 f If you _____ _____ _____, I'll take you out to eat.

5 🎤 **Make it personal** Make your own promises. Complete a–d and email them to a friend.
 a If you help me with my homework, _____.
 b If you lend me some money, _____.
 c If you buy me a coffee, _____.
 d I'll love you forever if _____.

6 ▶5.10 🎤 **Make it personal** Listen and match questions a–e to the answers. Then write or record your own answers.
 a Why did you choose this school?
 b What did you do at school today?
 c What advice can you give to a new student?
 d Do you ever make terrible excuses?
 e Do you send a lot of emails in English?

 ☐ Uh, I guess "make an effort" is good advice.
 ☐ I can't remember. Oh, yes! We started a project in chemistry class.
 ☐ No, not many. But I send a few texts now and then.
 ☐ I didn't choose it. It's just the closest to my house.
 ☐ No, I'm pretty honest, so I just tell the truth.

📶 **Connect**
Write a short tweet with your advice.

Can you remember ...
▸ 18 school subjects? SB→p.58
▸ 10 class activities? SB→p.60
▸ the difference between *have to*, *don't have to* and *can't*? SB→p.61
▸ which is correct — *miss* or *lose a class*? SB→p.62
▸ how to use *too* and *enough* with adjectives? SB→p.63
▸ 2 sentence structures with *if*? SB→p.64
▸ 6 phrases to use with warnings? SB→p.67

28

Audioscript

Unit 1

▶ 1.5

C = Chris   R = Rachel

C Ah! That's the pizza, I'll get it. Uh, Rachel, I don't have enough money. Can I borrow some?
R I don't have any with me. What about that money Andy gave you?
C Oh, yes, that's right. I'll go and get it.
R OK. Let's eat! Is this the vegetarian? Chris it's enormous. I won't eat all that.
C Don't worry, I can help.
R Well thanks for the offer, but I think I'll take it home with me.

▶ 1.6

1 Will you buy any clothes this weekend?
2 What time will you get up tomorrow?
3 What will you do after you finish your homework?
4 Will you go to the countryside soon?
5 What will you eat for dinner?

▶ 1.9

B = boy   W = woman   M = man

1 B Mom... MOM!
  W What is it?
  B What's going on? It's Saturday morning.
  W Oh, your grandparents just called. They're coming for a surprise visit and, well, you know what grandma's like. She likes everything just perfect...
  B Oh, right. Do you want some help?
  W Oh, yes, please, love. Can you wash the dishes for me? And...
2 M Mmmmmm. What's that smell? It smells delicious.
  W Oh, I'm making seafood lasagna.
  M Ah! My favorite dish. You're fantastic. Do you want me to help?
  W Uhm. You can make me a cup of coffee if you want.
3 M What are you doing?
  W I'm fixing my bike.
  M Can I help you?
  W Ummm. Can you pass me that Allen key, please? No, not that. The Allen key. It looks like a big "L".
  M Sure. Here you are.
  W Thank you.

Unit 2

▶ 2.1

Uh, I only buy one newspaper a week on Sundays. Uh, it's really big and has a lot of supplements, so it takes me an entire week to read it all! Of course, they always put the most important news on the front page, and they, uh, they often give the newspaper's opinion about it in an article, I think that's usually very interesting. Umm, they have all the soccer results in a separate section, in the sports section, and I usually read that on the weekend. Uh, what else? Oh, they also have a TV guide in a magazine, so you know what's on TV. I read that during the week. To be honest, the rest of the magazine is often a waste of paper. If an important piece of news happens during the week, I just read about it on the Internet, uh, you know, on my tablet.

▶ 2.2

A How often do you buy a newspaper?
B How often do you use a social media site?
C Do you listen to the news on the radio?
D Are you interested in celebrity gossip?
E Did you watch the news on TV yesterday?

▶ 2.5

a Scandal in the news today as a powerful businessman is accused of paying over two hundred thousand dollars to politicians as part of a development scheme. Here's our business reporter, Kimberley Chu, with more details.
b Over 200 million gallons of oil entered the Gulf of Mexico. This is possibly the world's worst environmental contamination disaster.
c ... announced today that there will be a new government initiative to end the financial problems of millions across the country. Great news for families that live on less than $5 a day. They will finally receive real government support. That means...
d The police apprehended the leader of a drug-trafficking gang in his home last night. Reports say that they found over $50,000 inside a refrigerator as well as a collection of 13 assault rifles. Francisco Giannini, known as "the pirate," was arrested...
e Scientists claim that there is a major downward tendency in the volume of polar sea ice. They can prove a reduction of 70% over the last 30 years during the summer months.
f The number of young people, aged 16-25, without jobs is rising, says a new government report. Figures show numbers are up from 2.5 million last year to 2.8 million.
g A century ago, there were around 100,000 tigers. Today, after losing almost 93% of their territory, there are only approximately 3,200 animals.
h The number of influenza vaccinations for people over 65 is growing worldwide. In 2011, Mexico had the highest rate of vaccination, at 88.2%, followed by Chile at 87.9%.

▶ 2.7

1 What's your favorite kind of weather?
2 What's the weather like right now?
3 Does it rain a lot in your city?
4 Do you ever have floods or droughts?
5 Do you have earthquakes in your country?

▶ 2.8

1 H = Hannah   A = Abby
  A Hannah, Hannah! Guess what! I saw Meghan Markle today!
  H Abby! You didn't! What happened?
  A Well, I was working with some kids when suddenly the door opened and and she walked into the library with Prince Harry. It was crazy! I didn't know what to do.
  H No! You're joking! I'm sure the kids loved her.
2 M = man   P = Pete
  M Pete, what happened to your car?
  P I don't know. I was watching TV when I heard this loud BANG! So I went outside and found my car like this.
  M Oh dear. That's really bad luck. How much will it cost to repair?
3 M = man   Z = Zoe
  M Hey, Zoe. Congratulations on your new job. How did you get it?
  Z Oh, I was really lucky. I was talking to these people on the bus about my college course and they offered me a job in their laboratory. I couldn't believe it!
  M Wow, that is lucky. Can you ask them to give me a job too?

▶ 2.11

W = woman   M = man

1 W1 I was shopping on Saturday. I had a lot of beautiful clothes, but then, for some reason, my credit card didn't work. The stupid machine couldn't read it!
  W2 Oh dear. That's bad luck.
2 M1 While I was walking in the park I found twenty dollars.
  W3 Wow! That's lucky.

54

Audioscript

3 W4 I decided not to go to school on Tuesday, I went to the city with my friends. We were sitting in a café and my dad saw me.
W5 Oh, dear. That's bad luck.
4 M2 There was a storm when I was walking home yesterday, but suddenly my mom drove past and she picked me up in the car.
W6 Wow! That's lucky.
5 M3 I was visiting the zoo on the weekend and I saw a chimpanzee take a tourist's camera. And then, get this, the chimpanzee took a photo. I couldn't believe it!
W7 No! You're joking.
6 M4 I was with my friends the other day. We were playing soccer in the park and guess what! Some Barcelona players came and joined us. It was unbelievable.
M5 No! You're joking.

▶ 2.12

M = man   W = woman

M This crazy thing happened to me at work the other day.
W Oh, yeah? What happened?
M Well, we got this call to go to a house because a woman was on fire.
W What! Why was she on fire?
M Apparently, she had some stones that caught fire in her pocket.
W Wait a minute? The stones caught fire?
M Yeah, they had some kind of chemical that reacts with oxygen.
W No way! So, is she OK?
M Yeah, the paramedics took her to the hospital but she had some severe burns.

Unit 3

▶ 3.2

J = Jed   T = Tanya

J Hi... excuse me... hi. I'm doing a survey about online shopping. Do you have a minute?
T Uh, yeah, I guess.
J Great! Uh... I'm Jed. What's your name?
T Uh... I'm Tanya.
J Oh, that's great! Now, let's get started Tanya. Uh... could you look at this list of products and tell me: what have you bought this month; what have you bought in the last six months; and what have you never bought online.
T Sure, that sounds easy! Well, let's see. Uh, books, yeah I buy a lot of books online. I'm a student and it's a lot cheaper to get the things I need from a website, and, uh, many bookstores don't sell them—they are kind of specific. Umm, music. Sure, I download a lot of songs from the Internet, uh, legally, of course! And sometimes movies too. I watched a great one last weekend, and the weekend before, so yeah, twice this month.
J OK, and how about vacations? Have you ever booked a vacation online? You know, travel tickets, hotel rooms. That kind of thing.
T Uh, travel tickets and hotel rooms. Well, I don't have much money and, uh, vacations are kind of expensive. I've never booked a vacation online, I, uh, I usually go and stay with some friends near the ocean and they drive so I don't need to book anything! Event tickets, well, I went to see a concert a couple of months ago and I booked that online, it was really easy. Uh, next is "electronic equipment". You mean like cameras and MP3 players and things like that, right?
J Uh-huh.
T Well, no, I've never bought any of that kind of stuff online. I don't trust the delivery service with expensive equipment, and, well, what if they drop it or something? No, I don't think so. And finally, clothes. Well this T-shirt came from an online store, but my boyfriend bought it for me. I've never actually bought clothes online, I want to try them on first, you know? In fact, I went shopping for shoes today.
J Yeah, a lot of people say that. Well thank you very much and have a nice day.
T You too.

▶ 3.4

M = man   W = woman   B = boy

M Honey, it's almost 7:30. Are you ready to go?
W We can't go now. The dogsitter hasn't arrived yet.
M The what?
W You know, that boy from down the road. He's going to look after the dog while we're away.
M Oh right. I forgot about the dog! He's late again. OK. I'll give him a call.
W I can't find my glasses. Hon, have you seen my glasses?
M I've already told you. They're in the living room, on the laptop.
W Ah! Honey, the dogsitter's here.
B Hi Mr. Adams, how are you?
M Hi. Good, thanks. Come in, come in.
W Have you fed the dog yet, George?
M No, I haven't. Just a minute.
B Hi Mrs. Adams. You look nice.
W Oh, thanks dear. Now I've put her food and toys and everything in this bag.
B Oh, I've already bought some food for her.
W Oh, really? That was very nice of you. All ready? Let's go.
B Bye, see you next week.
M/W See you.
M Oh no! I've just remembered!
W What is it hon?
M I've left our passports at home. I'm such an idiot!
W Oh, George! Not again! You...

▶ 3.7

M = man   W = woman
B = boy   G = girl

1 M1 My dog can speak French.
  W1 Wait a minute. Did I hear you say that your dog can speak French?
2 W2 The Internet is a complete waste of time.
  M2 I'm sorry, I don't agree. I think it's a part of life now.
3 M3 I'm sorry to have to tell you that Santa Claus doesn't exist.
  B1 What do you mean he doesn't exist?
4 B2 I can play the guitar with my teeth.
  G1 Really, you never told me you could do that before.

Unit 4

▶ 4.1

Typical blood type A jobs are software engineer or librarian, jobs that suit their quiet personality. Type B people are creative so they are often cooks, hairstylists or journalists. Type ABs are a strange group, they could be anything, but they are often lawyers or teachers. They are also very romantic and can match any other blood type. Finally the type Os. These people are often top athletes, bank managers or politicians.

▶ 4.2

When I was young I used to love being in the kitchen with my mom.
One day I was helping her to make a cake. We put it in the oven and then... we heard these really strange noises. Something was making a small "beep... beep... beep". We looked in the kitchen but we couldn't find it, so we emptied all the cupboards. Nothing.
So we went into the living room and looked under the sofa, behind the TV, everywhere. Still nothing.

Audioscript

So we went into the garage and looked in all the boxes and all the cupboards. And then we found it.

It was an old smoke alarm and the battery was dying: "beep...beep...beep".

We went back into the kitchen and guess what! It was full of smoke! The cake was burning!

▶ 4.7

S = salesperson   C = customer

S Hello, can I help you?
C Yes, I'm looking for a gift for my nephew's birthday.
S OK, well, how old is your nephew?
C He's going to be 21.
S Oh, well, that is an important birthday. You should definitely get him something special.
C Yes, but I really don't know what to get him. Could you give me some ideas?
S Sure, uhmm well, have you considered buying him some new technology? This is the new *Eye-let Mini* tablet, it's really popular with young people and...
C Hmm, I think he already has a tablet. And I was hoping to buy something a little cheaper than two hundred and ninety-nine dollars. Maybe around twenty dollars.
S Twenty dollars? Have you thought about getting him a nice book? We have a very big selection of...
C Oh, no, no. He doesn't like reading. Well, not books anyway! And I want to get him something more... uh, more appealing for his age.
S Hmmm, well I shouldn't say this madam, but 21-year-olds always need money. Why don't you give him some money so he can buy what he wants?
C Yes, that's a good idea. Thank you.

Unit 5

▶ 5.1

1 Hi, I'm Vicki. Um, uh, I always wanted to defend clients in court, like in the movies, but now I work for a business in the city. I check all the legal documents—contracts, that kind of thing.
2 Hello, I'm Ben and I work in a pharmaceutical laboratory outside the city. I couldn't do this job without my degree.
3 Hi, my name's Kathy and I run a small company right here in California. My degree helped me to understand marketing, management and economics.
4 Hi, I'm Ross. Uh... well I work for the government planning bridges and roads, all the major construction that happens around here.
5 My name's Rose and I work with business people from the U.S. or Canada, and even China sometimes. I help them with conferences and meetings. And I translate documents too.

▶ 5.2

1 Hi, my name is Helen and I study at Brinton College. I chose this college because it's a long way from home and it's good because it has an attractive campus. I'm studying for a bachelor's in business and I really like it because of the good teachers. One day, I want to make a million dollars—a month!
2 Hi, my name is Janet and I study at Arleston College. I chose this college because I can get here easily and it's good because it has babysitting facilities. I'm studying for a vocational certificate in cooking and I really like it because of the evening classes. One day, I want to open a café.

▶ 5.3

OK, so here are the answers. Officially you can't drive a dirty car in Russia, although many people do of course. In most countries you can only get married without permission from your parents at 18. However, in other countries, including Bolivia, Paraguay and Peru, you don't have to have permission to get married at 16. In some countries it is even younger. Chewing gum and bubble gum are both illegal in Singapore, you can't buy it anywhere. Strange, huh? There are some strange licenses around the world. For example, you have to have a license to own a dog in Canada and you can't have a TV without a license in the UK. On the other hand, you don't have to carry any personal ID in the UK or in the U.S. In many countries around the world it is compulsory to participate in elections. Until recently, this was true in Chile and Venezuela but now voting is voluntary. There citizens do not have to vote. Brazil still has military service for its citizens. All men have to register when they are 18, and women can choose to register as well, if they want to.

▶ 5.5

Hello and welcome to Streetwise College. I hope you are going to enjoy your time here and, before we give you a tour of the facilities, I would like to offer you some advice to help you make the most of your time here. First, your education is your responsibility, so be enthusiastic about what you are learning. When you are really into a topic it's a lot easier to learn. If you want to optimize your classes, you can download material about the topic in advance. You will benefit a lot more if you already understand a little about the topic of each lesson. Now this next piece of advice depends on your course, but, in most cases, you will have to do a lot of reading, so find a good online dictionary so you can look up new academic words and then use them when you write a paper. The next point is very important: don't miss too many classes! If you are absent from too many classes, we will ask you to leave the college. Now, as you will see, this is a big campus but you can use the college portal to find out exactly where your classes are and what time they start, and you can store the info on your phone planner. And finally, I know that at times you will be under a lot of pressure. If you find that the school work is too much for you, don't drop out. Of course, college can be difficult, but talk to your teacher, we are here to help. Any questions? OK, and now we will show you around the campus...

▶ 5.7

M = man   W = woman

M Uhm... honey. I'm not getting out of bed today.
W What?
M If I do, you'll divorce me.
W Oh no, not again! Get up Dan.
M Look. If I get up, I'll go to work.
W And?
M Well, when I go to work, I'll meet my friends.
W Yeah?
M And, see, if I meet my friends, we'll go out.
W Hmmm.
M And if we go out, you'll get jealous.
W But...
M And if you get jealous, you'll divorce me. So, I'm staying in bed.
W And I... am leaving. Goodbye!

Answer Key

Unit 1

1.1
2 a education b Love c career d have fun
   e free time f friends / family
3 b fitness a culture
   d financial security c health
4 b, c, a, d
5 a cooked / took b watched c 're learning
   d want / chose e doesn't cost f meet
   g love / 'm really enjoying h went / 'm
6 Ad 1: f, h   Ad 2: a, c   Ad 3: b, g   Ad 4: d, e
7 Personal answers.

1.2
1 1 great / bland 2 awesome / soft
   3 fantastic / awful 4 sour / spicy, spicy / sour
2 a Look at / touch / watch / see
   b smell / smells / taste / tastes / Eat
   c feel / look / smells / listen to
   d listen to / hear / sound / Read
3 The rhymes are:
   1 store / more 2 breakfast / Texas ("Brenda," "bread," "breakfast" all have the same "br" consonant sound) 3 machine / clean
   4 fight / night ("rock" and "stop" have the same vowel sound)
5 Personal answers.

1.3
1 will / will / won't / 'll / 'll
2 a She will probably take all of his money.
   b Yinsen will die. c I will call and order some pizza. d She will get married. e I will have the vegetarian one. f Stark will definitely become a superhero.
3 a P b P c U d P e U f P
4 Chris can't afford the pizza (b) and Rachel's pizza is too big (d).
5 a I'll get it. (U)
   b I'll go. (U)
   c I won't eat. (P)
   d I'll take it. (U)
6 Personal answers.
7 a bubbles b cozy c moist d leather
   e countryside

1.4
1 Four reasons: feel stressed / have to care for your children / went out really late last night / it's a beautiful sunny day and you just don't want to work.
2 a 3 Your time off c 2 Inform your boss
   b 4 Going back to work d 1 Preparation
3 Personal answers.
4 a shouldn't b should c shouldn't
   d shouldn't e shouldn't
6 /ʊ/ put, book, cook
   /uː/ shoes, soup, two, true
7 Personal answers.

1.5
1 b (Netflix, etc.) e (Text messaging)
2 a yourself b – c yourself d – e –
3 1 a 2 b 3 c

4 b I'm going to wash the dishes. / Would you like me to dry? / Yes, please. c These bags are really heavy. / I'll carry one for you. / That's very kind of you. d I don't understand this problem. / Do you want a hand? / Yes, please. e It's really cold in here. / Do you want me to turn off the A/C? / Thanks for the offer but I can do it.
5 a Do you need a hand?
   b Would you like me to help you?
   c Do you want me turn off the music?
   d Can I help you?

Unit 2

2.1
1 a TV b Newspapers c Internet d Today
2 a T b F c T
3 **in** the sports section, an article, a magazine
   on the front page, a tablet, TV
4 a on Sundays b very interesting c sports section d a magazine e waste of paper
   f the Internet
5 a Yesterday's / was b look at / in
   c waste / on d on e in f in
6 Personal answers.

2.2
1 a did you like b was watching c loved
   d was talking e was playing
2 a Mother: Why were you fighting?
     Sons: We **weren't fighting**. We **were playing**.
   b Boss: Why weren't you working?
     Employee: I **was sending** an email to a client.
   c Angry girlfriend: Why was she texting you?
     Boyfriend: She **was asking** for a friend's phone number.
   d Angry boyfriend: Why didn't you call me?
     Girlfriend: Sorry, but my phone **wasn't working**.
4 1 She was asking for a friend's phone number.
   2 We weren't fighting. We were playing.
   3 Sorry, but my phone wasn't working.
   4 I was sending an email to a client.
5 a wasn't eating / tasted b Did / taste
   c Did / have d was having e Did / like
   f wasn't listening
6 Personal answers.

2.3
1 a corruption b pollution c poverty
   d crime e climate change f unemployment
   g animal extinction h disease
2 a 200,000 b 200,000,000 c 1 d 13
   e 30 f 2,800,000 g 3,200 h 88.2%
   The extra number is 2,300.
3 a rainbow b eclipse c earthquake
   d wildfire e hurricane f drought
   g tsunami h flood i thunderstorm
4 a eclipse / were watching / earthquakes
   b drought / weren't growing c flood / was staying d was playing / thunderstorm / lightning e was watching / hurricane / was raining / rainbow
5 a cousins, double, trouble, mother
   b about, house, clouds, thousand, down, loud, found, town c would, good, Hollywood, should

6 Personal answers.

2.4
1 Story 1: a, b   Story 2: c, f   Story 3: d, e
2 a was working with / opened / walked
   b was watching / heard
   c was talking / offered
3 a didn't like
   b were you doing / phoned
   c was chatting / went out
   d were you talking / came
   e was walking / broke
4 a When I **was young** / **younger** I **played** a lot of video games.
   b My phone **rang** when I was in **the** middle of taking a test at school.
   c My friends **weren't** smiling when I **took** a photo of them.
   d What **were you** doing **last** night when the outage happened?
5 a I was walking on the street when it started to rain.
   b I was working when there was a power outage.
   c I was jogging in the park when a dog attacked me.
   d I was playing the piano when my cat jumped on it.
6 Personal answers.

2.5
1   1   8
    10   2
    5   3
    7   11
    9   6
    12   4
2 Personal answers.
3 a What happened? b Why was she on fire?
   c The stones caught fire? d Is she OK?
4 c, a, e, d, b

Unit 3

3.1
1 2 pack your bags 3 take a taxi to the airport
   4 board the plane 5 have a snack on the plane
   6 stand in line 7 be stopped at customs
   8 check in to your hotel
2 1 packed
   2 arrived
   3 missed
   4 Book
   5 broke down
   6 hitchhiked
   7 crowded
   8 boarded
3 Person 1 on / on / on / on / in / on
   Person 2 in / on / in / in / in
   Person 3 a / the / the / the / the / – / The / – / the / The / –
4 a 3 b 2 and 3 c 2 d 1 e 2
5 a Do you get stressed when things go wrong?
   b Did your last vacation go well?
   c Do you get angry when you miss the bus?
   d Do you get impatient with young kids on planes?

60

Answer Key

3.2

1

	This month	In the last 6 months	Never
books	✓		
music	✓		
movies	✓		
travel tickets			✓
hotel rooms			✓
event tickets		✓	
electronic equipment			✓
clothes			✓

2 b What have you bought online this month?
c She has watched a movie online twice this month.
d Have you ever booked a hotel online?
e She has never booked travel tickets online.
f She has gone shopping today.

3 Personal answers.

4 Personal answers.

5 a Where was the lake?
b When did you wear it?
c How often do you give money?
d Did you speak to him or her?
e What did it taste like?
f Where did you plant it?
g Did you go on vacation?
h Can you teach me something?
i How long did you fly for?

6 a Have you ever **swum** in a lake? No, but I **swam** in a river when I was on vacation.
b The last time I **wore** a tie was when I was at **school**.
c **Have** you ever **bought** clothes online?
d Have you **ever been** abroad? Yes, I have been **to** Canada twice.

7 three, tree – a mean, seen, clean
run, sun – b swum, money, done
four, door – c board, orange, before

8 Personal answers.

3.3

1 a 3 b 1 c 2 d 4

2 a The dogsitter hasn't arrived **yet**.
b I've **already** told you.
c Have you fed the dog **yet**?
d I've **already** bought some food for her.
e I've **just** remembered!

3 a is b only c recently d before now
e all prepared

4 b I've already / just gone online.
I haven't gone online yet.
c My friend has already / just called me.
My friend hasn't called me yet.
d I have already / just left home.
I haven't left home yet.
e I have already / just eaten dinner.
I haven't eaten dinner yet.
f I have already / just taken a shower.
I haven't taken a shower yet.
g I have already / just checked my e-mail.
I haven't checked my e-mail yet.
h I have already / just done a lot of exercise.
I haven't done a lot of exercise yet.

5 1 **Basilica** – B (planned completion 2026-2028).
2 **1,000 Trees** – B (planned completion 2020).
3 **The Diamond** – A (planned but building won't start till 2023).
4 **Costanera Center** – C.

3.4

1 c, e, d, a, b

2 e

3 a d b for / c c for / f d since / e
e for / b f for / g g since / a

4 Personal answers.

3.5

1 have / had / has / be / is

2 1 convict**ions** 2 corrobor**ation** 3 environ**ment**
4 pre-histor**ic** 5 scientif**ic** 6 investig**ation**
7 equip**ment** 8 precis**ion** 9 argu**ment**
10 locat**ion** 11 occasion**al**

3 3, 5, 6, 1, 4, 7

4 1 Wait a minute. 2 I'm sorry, I don't agree.
3 What do you mean 4 You never told me

Unit 4

4.1

1 a Past b Infinitive

2 a bought b got c took d go e went f laughed

3 a F b T c F

4 Type A kind (11), sensitive (13), shy (14)
Type B creative (3), curious (5), independent (9)
Type AB critical (4), hardworking (7), honest (8), responsible (10), obedient (12)
Type O active (1), aggressive (2), funny (6), sociable (15), spoiled (16)

5 Type A software engineer, librarian
Type B cook, hair stylist, journalist
Type AB lawyer, teacher
Type O athlete, bank manager, politician

6 Personal answers.

4.2

1 a 4 b 6 c 1 d 3 e 7 f 2 g 5

2 Did you / love playing sports / what sport / when I was / did you do / used to go / didn't use to

4 d, c, a, b

5 a Who used to take you to school?
b Which cartoons did you use to watch?
c What food did you use to hate?

6 ca**s**tle, Chri**s**tmas, li**s**ten, of**t**en

4.3

1 Across
1 records 5 pop 6 streaming 7 vinyl
Down
2 download 3 MP3s 4 turntable 5 punk

2 a PR b PA c PA d PR e B

3 1 b,f 2 a 3 d,g 4 e 5 c

4 Personal answers.

4.4

1 big / small   easy / difficult
expensive / cheap   heavy / light
unclear / clear   unpopular / popular

2 Type A big, clear, small, light, cheap
Type B heavy, easy
Type C popular, difficult, expensive, unclear, unpopular

3 c The Dall P45's memory is as big as the Star's.
d The Dall P45's picture is clearer than the Eye-let Mini's.
e The Dall P45 is not as easy to use as the Eye-let Mini.
f The Eye-let Mini is about as big as the Dall P45.
g The Dall P45 is the cheapest.

5 Personal answers.

4.5

1 4, 1, 3, 2

2 d – but e – so f – so b – but a – so c – but

3 a her nephew b 21 c $20 d money

4 b, d, a, c

5 c, e, b, a, d

6 a have b talk c buying d asking

Unit 5

5.1

1 biology, computer systems, economics, geography, literature, mathematics, physics, politics, psychology, sociology.
The hidden phrase is: "You get as much education outside school as in."

2 business, chemistry, engineering, languages, law

4 1 law 2 chemistry 3 business
4 engineering 5 languages

5 a in b in c at d –

6 a Helen: Brinton, it's a long way from home, an attractive campus, bachelor's in business, the good teachers, make a million dollars a month.
b Janet: Arleston, I can get here easily, babysitting facilities, vocational certificate in cooking, the evening classes, open a café.

7 Possible answer: Hi, I'm Leona and I study at Marlbury College. I chose this college because it has a great reputation and it's good because it has modern facilities. I'm doing a master's in chemistry and I really like it because of the excellent technology. One day, I want to develop new medicines.

8 Personal answers.

5.2

1 Tuesday: h, i Wednesday: d, f
Thursday: e, g Friday: a, j

2 Tuesday: literature Wednesday: economics
Thursday: physics Friday: mathematics
Extra subject: chemistry

3 a Why didn't Carrie talk about pollution? / Another student dominated the conversation.
b What exercise did she enjoy on Tuesday? / The quiz.
c How long does she have to write the paper? / One week.
d What was bad about Thursday? / The pair work partner was a bit weird.

4 a can't b don't have to c can't d have to
e can't f don't have to g don't have to
h have to / don't have to

6 Personal answers.

5.3

1 a 3 b 4 c 5 d 2 e 1

2 a enough b too c Too / Too d enough / enough / enough

61

Answer Key

3 a We don't have enough gasoline.   b There's been too much rain.   c The shirt isn't big enough.   d It's too far away.   e There aren't enough boats.   f The suitcase is too heavy for him.   g The man is too weak to lift the suitcase.   h He's eaten too much food.
   1 c, h   2 f, g   3 b, e   4 a, d

4 b are / too / people   c not / enough
   d don't / enough / money

5 /ʌ/   enough, fun, gum, someone, much, money
   /uː/ do, you, school, blue, chewing, food, you, who, too

6 Personal answers.

5.4

1 If I go to work, I'll meet my friends.
   If I meet my friends, we'll go out.
   If we go out, you'll get jealous.
   If you get jealous, you'll divorce me.

2 c, a, b

3 b help   c won't   a take   b is   c are traveling

4 a Call them if you get lost / If you get lost, call them.
   b If you travel by bus, sit close to the door. / Sit close to the door if you travel by bus.
   c Don't be shy if someone talks to you! / If someone talks to you, don't be shy!
   d Don't worry if you don't speak the language. / If you don't speak the language, don't worry.

5 b If you don't have a passport, you can't go abroad.
   c If I take a vacation, I'll go to the beach.
   d I feel sick if I eat too many cup cakes.
   e If / When you travel, you learn new things.
   f Your vacation will be great if it is sunny.
   g What will you do if it snows?

7 Personal answers.

5.5

1 1 my   2 I   3 I   4 I   5 them   6 He   7 he
   8 him   9 it   10 she   11 her   12 I   13 they
   14 I   15 them   16 I   17 my   18 she
   19 we   20 us   21 we

2 a F   b N (We don't know if Anna replied or not.)
   c F   d T   e T

3 a 4   b 6   c 3   d 1   e 5   f 2

4 a Watch / make / a / noise   b it'll / break
   c move / You / have   d don't / forget / to
   e if / you / help / me   f pass / your / exam

5 Personal answers.

6 c, b, e, a, d

Phrase Bank

This Phrase Bank is organized by topics.
▶ The audio is on the ID Richmond Learning Platform.

Offering help
Unit 1
Do you want me to drive?
Don't worry. This course doesn't cost anything.
Can I help you?
Do you need a hand?
Would you like me to help you?
Yes, please! That's very kind of you!
Thanks for the offer.

About you
Unit 1
My name's Arturo Hernandez and I'm a web designer.
What do you do to stay in shape?
I'm careful about my diet and do a lot of exercise.
I always need a partner.
I never stop studying.
I'd love to work in the movie industry.
I'm planning to live to be 100.

Unit 3
You have no idea how shy I am.

Expressing opinions, agreeing and disagreeing
Unit 3
I think it's very important to compromise.
No way!

Unit 4
I disagree.
In my opinion, CDs are the highest quality music.
I think it's better to study from home, because you can save a lot of money. But you don't have friends to talk to.
I'm not sure I agree with you.

Unit 5
For me, it's important to have great teachers.
Evening classes aren't important for me.

Making comparisons
Unit 1
People are more important than things.
Time to enjoy things is more important than money.

Unit 4
Cats are not as good with kids as dogs are.
He looks funnier than the other guy.
A tablet is as useful as a laptop.
LPs are better than CDs.

Making guesses
Unit 1
I think she's going to be late.

Making suggestions
Unit 1
You should take a painkiller.

Unit 4
Have you considered getting a fish?
Have you thought about getting a cat?
Why don't you get a small dog?
You should definitely get her a pet.

Memories
Unit 1
It reminds me of a band my brother was in.

Unit 3
That reminds me of my grandma's birthday party.

Unit 4
Did you use to make fun of other kids?
I think I was four or five.
I had a cat. It used to sleep in the sink.
I learned how to drive when I was 18 years old.
When did you get your first pet?
When I was young I had to wash the car every week.

Money
Unit 1
Can you lend me some money?
Can I borrow some money?

Talking about preferences
Unit 1
I enjoy working out.
I enjoy having fun.

Unit 2
I prefer real life so I'd watch the show about the jungle.
I'd like to watch that movie because I love horror.

Talking about problems
Unit 1
Are you OK?
How are you feeling?
What's the matter?
I have a cold.
I missed a class and I have a test and I'm really worried.
If you have a cold, you shouldn't go to class.
My head hurts.
When you take an aspirin, you'll feel better.

Unit 2
I think pollution affects oceans, lakes, rivers, and cities.
I think crime is the most serious problem here.

Defining language
Unit 1
Bland means "without taste".

Unit 2
It's the opposite of easy.
It's like the world, but bigger.

Phrase Bank

Describing events
Unit 2
I was cooking dinner when the lights went out.
Jane was chatting online and her phone rang.
What were you doing when the outage happened?

Reacting to something negative
Unit 2
That's awful!
No way!
Oh no!
That's terrible!

Reacting to something positive
Unit 2
How interesting!
That's good.
That's great!
Wow! Really?

Showing you are listening
Unit 2
And then what happened?
Uh-huh?
Yes?

Talking about news
Unit 2
That's an important piece of news.
Last night's news was shocking.

Talking about TV
Unit 2
Did you see the show last night?
What was it about?
I was watching a show about climate change.

Showing desire
Unit 3
All I want to do is get some sleep.
All I wanted was to get some cash.
I really want to go to Europe.

Showing surprise
Unit 3
But that makes no sense!
Oh, come on!
Wait a second. Did I hear you say that you wrote a song?
What do you mean, nothing?
You're kidding me!
You've never told me that!

Talking about completion
Unit 3
Have you done your homework yet?
I haven't done it yet.
I've already had breakfast.
I've just finished it.

Talking about duration
Unit 3
How long have you been in the UK?
Since last September.

Traveling
Unit 3
Did you go on business?
Have you ever seen the Statue of Liberty?
Yeah, twice.
Really? When did you go to New York?
I don't mind traveling long distances by car. I find it relaxing.
I haven't been abroad yet, but I'm going to Miami next year.
I'd love to take a year off and travel around India.
I've been abroad, but only once.
Oh really? Where did you go?
Oh yeah? Did you go on business?

Promises
Unit 5
If you eat all your dinner, I'll give you some ice cream.
If you finish your homework, I'll take you to the movies.
If you stay late, I'll give you the day off tomorrow.

School and education
Unit 5
A bad point about my school is that classes are really big.
I can't come to class tomorrow.
I chose English because I've always loved reading.
I have a vocational certificate in accounting.
I want to learn a language so I can get a better job.
I was interested in math because I was really good at it.
Why did you choose to study at this school?

Warning
Unit 5
Be careful!
Don't move!
I won't buy you a new bike if you don't get good grades.
Look out!
Watch out!
Whatever you do, don't eat that ice cream. If you do, you'll have to go to your room!
You'd better (not) do that!

Other useful expressions
Unit 1
I can't hear you.
I don't want to live in a world without culture.
I'll take your order now.
He will never amount to anything.
There's no chance that people will stop using the Internet.
Unit 3
I'm not going to waste my time taking a gap year.
In this situation, I shout until I get what I want.
It depends on how much.

Word List

Unit 1

Life priorities
career
culture
education
family
financial security
fitness
free time
friends
having fun
health
love

The senses
to eat
to hear
hearing
to listen
to look
to see
sight
smell
to smell
to stink
taste
to taste
touch
to touch
to watch

Adjectives
amazing
awesome
awful
bland
cool
cozy
delicious
fresh
loud
moist
quiet
rotten
rough
salty
smoky
soft
sour
spicy
spongy
stylish
sweet
terrible

Common illnesses
backache
a cold
a cough
earache
a fever
the flu
a headache
stomachache
toothache

Other words
bathtime
bubbles
collar
countryside
leather
pocket

Unit 2

News
business news
celebrity gossip
entertainment
local / national news
in a newspaper
in the headlines
on a mobile device
on a news website or app
on a screen
on a smartphone
on social media
on the radio
on TV
world news

Global problems
animal extinction
climate change
corruption
crime
disease
global warming
pollution
poverty
unemployment

Geography
cities
deserts
jungles
lakes
oceans
rainforests
rivers
wildlife

Natural phenomena
drought
earthquake
eclipse
flood
high waves
hurricane
lightning
rainbow
thunderstorm
tsunami

Other words
fraud
habitat
huge
to investigate
overated
power outage
rocks
shocking
to survive
totality
uneasy
universe

Unit 3

Traveling
to board a plane
to book a hotel
crowded station
customs
day trip
to hitchhike
to miss a train
to pack your bags
to stand in line

Ambitions
to be a DJ
to do volunteer work
to donate blood
to fall in love
to go abroad
to have a child
to learn to dance
to make a cake
to plant a tree
to ride an animal
to swim with dolphins
to try an extreme sport
to visit London
to write a story

Other words
amenities
basic
cleanliness
disappointment
dramatic
emotionally
equipment
information
intellectual
mental
moon
musical
renovation
resort
romantic
typical

Unit 4

Adjectives
active
aggressive
creative
critical
curious
funny
hardworking
honest
independent
kind
lazy
obedient
responsible
sensitive
shy
sociable
spoiled

Do / Make
to do a favor
to do a project
to do activities
to do chores
to do homework
to do the dishes
to do the laundry
to do well
to make a decision
to make a mistake
to make a noise
to make a promise
to make an effort
to make contact
to make friends
to make fun of someone
to make money
to make the bed

Other words
to bark
to bite
kitten
to laugh
puppy
to scratch
sink

Unit 5

School subjects
art
biology
business
chemistry
computer systems
economics
engineering
geography
history
languages
law
literature
mathematics
physics
politics
psychology
sociology

In college
administrator
bachelor's degree
campus
evening class
facilities
lecture
master's degree
teacher
vocational education

Class activities
exam
group work activity
homework
journal entry
online practice
pair work activity
project
research
summary
test

70

Richmond

58 St Aldates
Oxford
OX1 1ST
United Kingdom

Fourth reprint: 2022
ISBN: 978-84-668-3246-5
CP: 105599

© Richmond / Santillana Global S.L. 2020

All rights reserved. No part of this book may be reproduced, stored in a retrieval system or transmitted in any form by any means, electronic, mechanical, photocopying, recording or otherwise, without the prior permission in writing of the Publisher.

Publishing Director: Deborah Tricker
Publisher: Luke Baxter
Media Publisher: Luke Baxter
Content Developers: Paul Seligson, Neil Wood
Managing Editor: Laura Miranda
Editor: Hilary McGlynn
Proofreaders: Angela Castro, Nicola Gooch, Diyan Leake
Design Manager: Lorna Heaslip
Cover Design: Lorna Heaslip
Design & Layout: John Fletcher Design
Photo Researchers: Victoria Gaunt, Emily Taylor (Bobtail Media)
Audio Production: John Marshall Media Inc.
ID Café Production: Mannic Media

We would like to thank all those who have given their kind permission to reproduce material for this book:

SB Illustrators: Leo Teixeira, Amanda Savoini, Fabiane Eugenio, Odair Faléco, Talita Guedes

WB Illustrators: Alexandre Matos, Rico, Leo Teixeira

SB Photos: ALAMY STOCK PHOTO/AF archive, Aflo Co Ltd, Andrea Spinelli, CJG – Technology, Art Directors & TRIP, Caia image, Chris Howes/Wild Places Photography, Cultura RM, David Moody, Everett Collection Inc, Hero Images Inc, Jit Lim, Justin Kase zfivez, LJSphotography, Mircea Costina, Myron Standret, Nikolaj Kondratenko, Noriko Cooper, Panther Media GmbH, Peregrine, PhotoAlto, RooM the Agency, Science Photo Library, SIRIOH Co LTD, Sueddeutsche Zeitung Photo, Tetra Images, World History Archive, Zoonar GmbH; CARTOONSTOCK/Alexei Talimonov, Mark Lynch; DESIGN GRAPHIC; DIAMEDIA/Martin Poole/Moodboard; DINNERINTHESKY.COM; GETTY IMAGES SALES SPAIN/Abel Mitjà Varela, Adam Burn, Adam Taylor, adamkaz, AFP, akinshin, apomares, alenkadr, alexey_boldin, Andrea Spinelli, andresr, Antonio_Diaz, Archive Photos Creative, Ayumi Mason, Bambu Productions, Bertrand Rindoff Petroff, Betsie Van der Meer, Bettmann Archive, BSIP/UIG, Burak Karademir, Burke/Triolo Productions, Caiaimage, Cavan Images, CEF/Tim Pannell, Chris Ryan, Creatas, CSA Images, DingaLT, doble-d, d3sign, Daniel MacDonald, Darryl Leniuk, David Sacks, Deagreez, DEA/A. DAGLI ORTI, deepblue4you, Digital Vision, Dimitrios Kambouris, DreamPictures, edurivero, E+, Elva Etienne, Elizabeth Barnes, Elisabeth Schmitt, Ekaterina Romanova, erikreis , Eugenio Marongiu, EyeEm, Ezra Bailey, FilmMagic, Fly-Jet, gaspr13, Geber86, George Clerk, Geir Pettersen, Georgette Douwma, Gerhard Egger, grinvalds, Gray Mortimore/Staff, GregorBister, Hans Ferreira, hatman12, Hero Images, Hill Street Studios, Hoxton/Sam Edwards, Highwaystarz-Photography, Holger Leue, Inmagineasia, icarmen13, imageBROKER RF, iStock, iStockphoto, Jasmin Merdan, JGI/Jamie Grill, Jim Hughes, lechatnoir, Maskot, PhotoAlto/Eric Audras, Jackal Pan, JGI/Jamie Grill , Jochem D Wijnands, John Lamb, John M Lund Photography Inc, John Parra, Johner Bildbyra AB, JohnnyGreig, John Rowley, Jon Lovette, Joseph Johnson, Joshua Rainey, Judith Collins, Julian Ward, Juice Images, Katrina Wittkamp, Katsumi Murouchi, Kevin Mazur, killerb10, Kirill_Liv, Ljupco, Klaus Vedfelt, Kryssia Campos, Lawrence Manning, Lilly Dong, lisafx, Ljupco, Luciano Lozano, Luis Alvarez, Lumina Images, Maglara, mapodile, Marc Dozier, Mark Stahl, Maskot, maxkabakov, Media photos, Melvyn Longhurst, Milkos, Mikael Vaisanen, M.M Sweet, Morsa Images, Michael Dunning, Mikael Vaisanen, m-imagephotography, Moelyn Photos, Morsa Images, MStudioImages, mustafagull, mystockicons, nadia_bormotova, natrot, nd3000, Netfalls Remy Musser, Neustockimages, nicemonkey, Nick David, Nora Sahinun, Obradovic, OJO Images RF, Onoky, Owen Franken, ozgurcankaya, PATRICK LUX, pattonmania, penguiiin, PeopleImages, Peter Carlson, Pgiam, photodisc, picturegarden, Pixalfit, pixhook, poba, Presley Ann/Stringer, Prykhodov, RapidEye, Rasulovs, Ray Kachatorian, Roc Canals, REB Images, Religious Images/UIG, RG-vc, RichLegg, Robert Decelis Ltd, Roberto Machado Noa, Roc Canals, Roman Märzinger, rusm, Russ Rohde, RyanJLane, RyanKing999, Samir Hussein, Scott Olson, SDI Productions, Shaul Schwarz, shironosov, SimplyCreativePhotography, Sidekick, Simon Ritzmann, Siri Stafford, Smederevac, solarseven, SSPL/Science Museum, South_agency, Stephen Simpson Inc, Stone Sub, Stuart Westmorland, sturti, Sylvain Grandadam/robertharding, Steven Puetzer, stock_colors, Sylvain Sonnet, Tanya Constantine, Tara Moore, Tatiana Gerus, Tegra Stone Nuess, TheCrimsonRibbon, thongseedary, Tony Garcia, Tom Werner, The Image Bank, The Washington Post, Tom Merton, Thomas Tolstrup, Thinkstock, Tomas Rodriguez, Tim Clayton – Corbis, Tim Hall, Tinpixels, Tisk, Turgay Malikli, Ty Allison, Ukususha, Uwe Krejci, valentinrussanov, VeranikaSmirnaya, View Pictures Ltd, vm, Wavebreakmedia, Westend61, Westend62, WireImage, wonry, wuttichaijangrab, Yamada Taro, Yuri_Arcurs; SHUTTERSTOCK/ A24/Moviestore, Africa Studio, AJR_photo, Alexander Prokopenko, Allmy, Aliaksei Tarasau, Andrey_Popov, Anatoly Maslennikov, Anatoly Tiplyashin, Anna Peisl, Anttoniart, Antonio Guillem, Apple's Eyes Studio, Artur Didyk, Artur Synenko, Bakai, BoJack, baranq, bbernard, Billion Photos, Branislav Nenin, Cbenjasuwan, Constantine Pankin, Chris Ratcliffe, Color Force/Lionsgate/Kobal, Damir Khabirov, Dave Clark Digital Photo, Dean Drobot, Djomas, Elnur, flower travellin' man, Fizkes, Frantic00, Freebulclicstar, Hekla, hlphoto, Igor Marusichenko, Jonas Petrovas, Jorg Hackenmann, Julia Savchenko, Juri Pozzi, Kalamurzing, karelnoppe, Kldy, Kotin, KPG_Payless, Krilerg saragorn, Kzenon, Ifc Prods/Detour Filmproduction/Kobal, LoopAll, lukas_zb, LusiG, Macrovector, Marvel/Disney/Kobal, Maximumvector, Mega Pixel, Mindscape studio, modus_vivendi, Monkey Business Images, nicemonkey, OlegDoroshin, Pattanapol Soodto, pavila, Peter Komka/EPA-EFE, Phil Hill, PPstudio, PONG HANDSOME, PrinceOfLove, RexRover, Roxana Gonzalez, sebra, Serge Gorenko, Serg Zastavkin, shoot66, siamionau pavel, sirtravelalot, Smith1979, Stock-Asso, stockfour, Syda Productions, Tatiana Chekryzhova, Techa Boribalburipun, TeddyandMia, Terekhob Igor, TheRocky41, Thurman James/CSM, Universal/Kobal, Val lawless, Victor Kochetkov, Vitalinka, vovidzha, VStocker, Warner Bros/Kobal, Wavebreakmedia, Yakov Oskanov, Yevgenij_D, 9nong, Zimmytws; ZUMAPRESS/Whitehotpix/Chris Murphy. ARCHIVO SANTILLANA

WB Photos: ALAMY STOCK PHOTO/AGB Photo Library, CHROMORANGE/Herwig Cziek, Diego Grandi, imageBROKER, JN, Mile Atanasov, MNStudio, Montgomery Martin, Minden Pictures; CARTOONSTOCK/Carroll Zahn; GETTY IMAGES SALES SPAIN/aedkais, Ariel Skelley, Beyond foto, Brand X, BrianAJackson, Busà Photography, Caiaimage/Martin Barraud, Carol Grant, Chesky_W, Colin Anderson Productions pty ltd, Copyright Rhinoneal, Corbis, CreativeDJ, Cultura RF, Digital Vision, dmbaker, Drazen_, E+, Erik Isakson/Blend Images LLC, Erikreis, EyeEm, FotoSpeedy, FilmMagic, franckreporter, Fuse, Getty Images AsiaPac, Getty Images North America, George Pimentel, Geri Lavrov, gionnixxx, GlobalP, Hero Images, Huronphoto, Image Source, iStock Editorial, istockphoto, jcrosemann, Jeff Kravitz, Jerod Harris, Jekaterina Nikitina, Juanmonino, Jupiterimages, Jurgenfr, Karl-Friedrich Hohl, Kent Weakley, Kinemero, Michael J Cohen, Mipan, Mint Images RF, Obak, Klaus Vedfelt, oneword, ppa5, Peter Parks, Photo by Brook Rieman, Picture Press RM, Predrag Vuckovic, Roy Hsu, Sergeyryzhov, shapecharge, SolisImages, sturti, Taxi, The Image Bank, Timothy Norris, www.peopleimages.com; LUNCHEAZE; PLAINPICTURE/Jasmin Sander; SHUTTERSTOCK/Anitasstudio, Chiang Ying-Ying/AP, Dmitry Rukhlenko, egd, Gladskikh Tatiana, Hugo Felix, Inxti, Jenny Goodall/Daily Mail, kwanchai.c, Lineicons freebird, Marvel/Paramount/Kobal, Monkey Business Images, Nomad_Soul, Nina Anna, Radu Bercan, Ted Shaffrey/AP, Topseller, Zkruger; ARCHIVO SANTILLANA

Videos: Lori Herfenist

The Publisher has made every effort to trace the owner of copyright material; however, the Publisher will correct any involuntary omission at the earliest opportunity.

Printed in Brazil